Dynamics in Action

Dynamics in Action

Intentional Behavior as a Complex System

Alicia Juarrero

A Bradford Book
The MIT Press
Cambridge, Massachusetts
London, England

This book was set in Palatino by Asco Typesetters, Hong Kong.

Printed and bound in the United States of America.

Library of Congress Cataloging-in-Publication Data

Juarrero, Alicia.
  Dynamics in action : intentional behavior as a complex system / Alicia Juarrero.
    p. cm.
  Includes bibliographical references and index.
  ISBN 0-262-10081-9 (hardcover : alk. paper)
  1. Act (Philosophy) 2. Action theory. I. Title.
B105.A35J83   1999
128'.4–DC21   99-23910
                                                            CIP

For my mother, Alicia Valiente, and in memory of my father, Francisco Juarrero

Contents

Acknowledgments

For those of us who try to write at the same time as we teach—full time and well—at a community college (and there are many of us), the encouragement and support of friends and colleagues who take one's scholarly work seriously are a blessing without which life would be greatly diminished. Both my personal and professional lives have been enriched by countless such persons, many of whom began as colleagues but in time became friends. For their incisive and helpful comments on my work, as well as for their friendship, I will be forever grateful. I wish I could name and thank you all.

For more than twenty-four years it has been a joy to teach at Prince George's Community College, thanks in large part to the presence of my fellow philosophers, Marlene Carpenter and Clyde Ebenreck. Their dedication and devotion both to their students and their friends are unmatched.

Portions of this manuscript were written while Visiting Research Associate Professor at Georgetown University. I want to thank their chemistry department chairman, Joseph Earley, for that opportunity. Isa Engleberg and John McCann provided valuable comments on early sections of the book, and Edward Pols, Carl Rubino, and Robert Ulanowicz trudged through the entire first and oh-so-rough draft of the manuscript. Not only did none of them suggest that I pack it in; they actually encouraged me, as did Isabel Padró. Thanks. I am very appreciative, also, of Stanley Salthe's insightful and thoughtful criticisms over the years. His questions and comments have always helped me think and write more clearly. A special thanks goes to Robert Artigiani. Many of the ideas presented in this book were first articulated during what has become a twelve-year-long conversation. For patiently correcting my many egregious errors—and not complaining when I no longer could tell which idea or phrase was first his and which mine—thanks.

I am endebted more than I can say to David Depew for his supererogatory assistance. Anonymous to me until the very end, David not only served as reviewer of several earlier drafts; he also provided valuable suggestions on the book's content. I am embarrassed at his having been importuned so. Elizabeth Stanton of the MIT Press deserves special mention for believing in this project from the very beginning, and for taking a flier on an unknown. Had she not championed my cause, this book would not have been published. To Melissa Vaughn, my editor at MIT Press, for her efficient and gracious guidance of both book and author, and to Shirley Kessel, for her thorough and elegant index, my sincerest thanks go as well. For the persistent and good-humored help of all of these people, I will always be grateful.

Inevitable errors no doubt still remain in the manuscript. These are, of course, solely my own.

How do I thank my family, not only for instilling in me a love of books and learning, but primarily for the sacrifice of leaving behind their possessions and comfortable lifestyle so that my sister and I could live in freedom? And for making what must have been a very difficult transition for them an adventure for us? Tatu, Lydia, and of course Nana—sine qua non. This one's for you, too.

Finally, to José Díaz-Asper: *De todo corazón, gracias.*

Portions of the following papers I authored have found their way into this book and are reprinted with permission.

Dispositions, teleology and reductionism. *Philosophical Topics* 12 (1983): 153–65.

Does level-generation always generate act-tokens? *Philosophy Research Archives* 9 (1983): 177–92.

Kant's concept of teleology and modern chemistry. *Review of Metaphysics* 39 (1985): 107–35.

Does action theory rest on a mistake? *Philosophy Research Archives* 13 (1987–88): 587–612.

Non-linear phenomena, explanation and action. *International Philosophical Quarterly* 28 (1988): 247–55.

What did the agent know? *Manuscrito* 11 (1988): 108–13.

Fail-safe versus safe-fail: suggestions toward an evolutionary model of justice. *Texas Law Review* 69 (1991): 1745–77.

Language competence and tradition-constituted rationality. *Philosophy and Phenomenological Research* 51 (1991): 611–17.

Causality as constraint. In *Evolutionary Systems: Biological and Epistemological Perspectives on Self-Organization*, ed. G. Van de Vijver, S. N. Salthe, and M. Delpos. 1998. Dordrecht: Kluwer.

Abbreviations

Works cited in this volume are abbreviated as listed here. Full references to these works and to other texts cited appear in the bibliography.

Aristotle
De anima   *De an.*
Nicomachean Ethics   *EN*
Metaphysics   *Meta.*

The pagination of the Bekker edition of the Greek text, published in the first two of the five volumes of the Berlin Academy's 1831–1870 edition of Aristotle's work has become the customary means to locate a passage in Aristotle.

Unless otherwise noted, references to Kant indicate "The Critique of Teleological Judgement," in *The Critique of Judgement*, tr. J. C. Meredith (Oxford: Clarendon Press, 1980). These references also cite, after "Ak.", volume and page number in Kant's *Gesammelte Schriften*, prepared under the supervision of the Berlin Academy of Sciences.

Introduction

What is the difference between a wink and a blink? Knowing one from the other is important—and not only for philosophers of mind. Significant moral and legal consequences rest on the distinction between voluntary and involuntary behavior. Jurors, for example, report that deciding whether the accused caused someone's death is relatively easy. They find it much more difficult, on the other hand, to determine "what class of offense—if any—had been committed" (Hacker 1995, 44). At Supreme Court hearings on the subject of physician-assisted suicide, the discussion turned on the same issue. Suppose a doctor administers a large dose of barbiturates to a patient in pain. The patient slips into a coma and dies. Was it first- or second-degree murder, or accidental homicide? Walter Dellinger, acting Solicitor General, testified at those hearings that "so long as the physician's intent was to relieve pain and not cause death," the behavior was not unlawful. As Anthony Lewis, writing in the *New York Times* (January 1997), noted of the debate, "Everything turned on the shadowy question of intent."

Our judgments concerning moral responsibility and legal liability will be very different, therefore, depending on how we answer the question, "Was it a wink or a blink?" And yet that is precisely the problem: gauging intent in order to establish what the accused did so that jurors as well as the rest of us can then discriminate among degrees of responsibility. We are not responsible and cannot be held accountable for blinking. And rightly so. We think of blinks, unlike winks, as behavior that we do not intend and cannot control—something that "happens to us," a reflex reaction in which we are passive. Winking, on the other hand, is something we "do" (in some unclear sense of "we" that identifies us as agents). Only intentional behavior qualifies as moral or immoral; reflexes are amoral. But what marks off intentional actions from unintentional, accidental or reflex behavior? How do agents (as opposed to their bodies?) *do* things? And how do we tell?

The branch of philosophy called "action theory" has traditionally been charged with articulating necessary and sufficient conditions marking the boundary between action and nonaction, as well as between voluntary and involuntary behavior. The philosophical issues with which action theory is concerned include such topics as the concepts of agency and free will, the relationship between awareness and behavior, and the role that reasons play in causing and explaining actions. Understanding these has required weaving together topics culled from such disparate disciplines as epistemology, metaphysics, philosophy of mind and, more recently, neurology and even genetics.

Although not labeled as such until after World War II, the concerns of action theory go as far back as the ancient Greeks. In Plato's dialogue *Phaedo*, which takes place while Socrates is awaiting execution, Socrates worries that earlier philosophers made air, ether, and water the only causes. What about Socrates's reasons for not escaping from prison? Are they not the true cause of his behavior? Later, and more systematically, Aristotle examined the difference between intentional and involuntary behavior. An adequate explanation of anything, he claimed, must identify those causes responsible for the phenomenon being explained. Aristotle's four causes are final cause (the goal or purpose toward which something aims), formal cause (that which makes anything that sort of thing and no other[1]), material cause (the stuff out of which it is made), and efficient cause (the force that brings the thing into being). Explaining anything, including behavior, requires identifying the role that each cause plays in bringing about the phenomenon. Implicit in Aristotle's account of cause and crucially influential in the history of action theory, however, is another of Aristotle's claims: that nothing, strictly speaking, can move, cause, or act on itself in the same respect. This principle has remained unchallenged throughout the history of philosophy and, as we shall see, has caused many problems for the theory of action.

Because he had more than one type of cause to draw on, Aristotle was able to explain voluntary self-motion in terms of a peculiar combination of causes. By the end of the seventeenth century, however, modern philosophy had discarded two of those causes, final and formal. As a result, purposive, goal-seeking and formal, structuring causes no longer even qualified as causal; philosophy restricted its understanding of causality to efficient cause. And then, taking its cue from Newtonian science, modern philosophy conceptualized efficient causality as the push-pull impact of external forces on inert matter. This mechanistic understanding of cause, too, has had serious consequences for action theory, particularly when combined with the principle philosophy did retain: Aristotle's thesis that nothing moves itself.

Aristotle had insisted that formal deduction from universal premises is the logic of reasoning proper to science (*episteme*). Because human behavior is temporally and contextually embedded, on the other hand, it is the central concern of practical wisdom (*phronesis*). Because of its subject matter and unlike deduction, therefore, wisdom varies "as the occasion requires." In contrast, modern philosophy also brought with it a particular understanding of the logic of explanation: the principle that (ideally) all explanation is fundamentally deductive in form. Following Hume and in opposition to Aristotle, as Stephen Toulmin (1990) has pointed out, philosophers concluded that deduction from timeless and contextless laws is the ideal, not only of science, but of any legitimate form of reasoning. A law of nature—at worst statistical, but ideally strictly deterministic—combined with statements specifying initial conditions must allow that which is being explained (the *explanandum*) to be inferred. Even human actions must be explained in that manner. By the middle of the twentieth century, the principle that the logic of any serious explanation must adhere to such a "covering-law model" was the received view.

Understanding all cause as collision-like, and the explanatory ideal as deduction from deterministic laws, are two examples of a trend that has characterized the history of philosophy for over two thousand years: the progressive elimination of time and context from metaphysics and epistemology. Since time and context play a central role in all living things, including human beings and their behavior, action theory is thus an excellent prism that refracts and separates two key problems in the history of Western philosophy—cause and explanation—and lays bare the role that time and context play in each. The first claim of this book is that an inadequate, 350-year-old model of cause and explanation underlies contemporary theories of action.

In addition to a brief history of the concepts of cause and explanation, Part I consists of a detailed analysis of the major warhorses of contemporary action theory with a view to demonstrating that action theory rests on these two mistaken views of cause and explanation. Chapters 1 and 2 examine the modern understanding of cause and the problems it has occasioned for action theory. In those chapters I survey major contemporary causal theories of action, all of which have consistently adhered to Aristotle's principle that nothing moves or changes itself; intentions, volitions, and other alleged causes of action are supposed to be other than the behavior they cause. In addition, by subscribing to a Newtonian understanding of efficient cause as well, these theories have also uncritically assumed that intentions, volitions, or agents cause action in the collision-like way that cue sticks cause cue balls to move. As a result of these two unexamined presuppositions, causal theories have been plagued by characteristic and recurrent objections. Most of the action theory literature of the past four decades has consisted of repeated attempts to mitigate or circumvent these objections, not recognizing that they will persist until action theory abandons this mechanistic view of cause.

Next, I examine the problems that the received view of explanation has created for action theory. Chapter 3 surveys the history of the covering-law approach to rationality and explanation. Chapter 4 examines how this explanatory framework, in the guise of logical behaviorism, makes an appearance in the theory of action. Behaviorist analyses have tried to reduce the flexibility and appropriateness characteristic of human action to stimulus-response patterns. Motivating such attempted reductions has been the desire to make human behavior explicable by rendering it scientific, that is, tractable by the received view of explanation as deduction. Given modern philosophy's elimination of final cause from its metaphysical framework, even those theorists who recognized the obvious goal-directedness of action tried to do the same. Teleology, too, therefore, was analyzed away as nothing but the lawful regularity of stimulus-response patterns. Chapter 5 chronicles the attempted reduction of purposiveness to behaviorist patterns of stimulus-response.

Modern philosophy's understanding of cause and explanation has failed as a general theory. Today there is no reason to continue to subscribe to this atemporal and acontextual approach. By the nineteenth century, two major challenges to the modern conceptual framework had already appeared. First, the inexorable increase in entropy postulated by the second law of thermodynamics seemed to return temporal direction to physics by identifying a universal and irreversible arrow of time: everything moves from order to disorder. On the face of it, however, biology contradicts the second law. Whence the increasing complexity so much in evidence in biological development and evolution? What went largely unrecognized until recently was the fact that the classical thermodynamics of the nineteenth century treats all systems as if they are closed, isolated, and near equilibrium—which living things are not. Second, in opposition to the inexorable winding down predicted by classical thermodynamics, Darwin's theory of evolution, particularly its concept of selection, appeared to account for the increasing complexity and order that characterizes both ontogeny and phylogeny. More important for our purposes, by giving the environment in which an organism is located a central role as the agent of selection, Darwin's writings returned context to science for the first time in centuries. Darwinism, however, still considers the environment wholly external to the organism. If so, how is the "cause" responsible for speciation to be understood? Certainly not as pushing.

Is the universe winding down or ratcheting up? Fortunately, there is a way out of this impasse. Over the last few decades a new branch of thermodynamics has been developed, variously called the theory of complex adaptive systems, complexity theory, and similar names, that deals with systems far from equilibrium and open in the sense that they exchange matter and energy with their environment. Pioneered by Ilya Prigogine,

1977 Chemistry Nobel laureate for his discovery of so-called dissipative structures, its conceptual framework offers significant implications for the philosophy of science, particularly when combined with dynamical systems theory. Part II of the book explores the potential that far-from-equilibrium thermodynamics has for understanding action.

Before doing that, however, I take a look at information theory. One of the drawbacks of conceptualizing cause as the instantaneous impact of external forces on inert matter is that such causes cannot monitor a process and guide it toward completion. In contrast, because of its concern with making sure that transmitted messages arrive at their intended destination, information theory is fundamentally interested in the way information flows. Through its concepts of equivocation and noise, information theory can track such flow by determining whether information available at the receiver's end is dependent on information generated at the source. Thinking of actions as unbroken trajectories—calculated in terms of information flow, noise, and equivocation—allows us to avoid many of the traditional objections to which causal theories of action are vulnerable. Chapter 6 examines the applicability of information-theoretic concepts to action.

Standard information theory, however, brings along its own weaknesses, in particular the problem of meaning. Communications engineers speak of "bits" of information, a contentless quantity with no relationship to the robust sense of "meaning" that is so much a part of human communication and behavior. Action theory needs, in contrast, an account of how the content of an intention, as meaningful, can inform and flow into behavior such that the action actualizes the content of that intention. The second main claim of this book is that the conceptual framework of the theory of complex adaptive systems can serve as what Richard Boyd (1979) calls a "theory-constitutive metaphor" that permits a reconceptualization of just such a cause, and in consequence a rethinking of action. A different logic of explanation—one more suitable to all historical, contextually embedded processes, including action—arises from of this radical revision.

Several key concepts of the new scientific framework are especially suited to this task. First, complex adaptive systems are typically characterized by positive feedback processes in which the product of the process is necessary for the process itself. Contrary to Aristotle, this circular type of causality *is* a form of self-cause. Second, when parts interact to produce wholes, and the resulting distributed wholes in turn affect the behavior of their parts, interlevel causality is at work. Interactions among certain dynamical processes can create a systems-level organization with new properties that are not the simple sum of the components that constitute the higher level. In turn, the overall dynamics of the emergent distributed system not only determine which parts will be allowed into the system: the global dynamics also regulate and constrain the behavior of the lower-level components. The theory of complex adaptive systems can therefore be used as a metaphor for this form of causal relations, which had puzzled Kant as a form of causality "unknown to us."

In other words, far from being the inert epiphenomenon modern science claims all wholes are, complex dynamical wholes clearly—and in a distributed manner—exert active power on their parts such that the overall system is maintained and enhanced. Understanding dynamical systems can therefore revive Aristotle's concepts of formal and final cause by offering a scientifically respectable model of how such causes cause. Chapter 7 introduces the reader to systems theory in general; chapter 8 provides an overview of nonlinear dynamical systems theory.

Since the active power that wholes exert on their components is clearly not the go-cart-like collisions of a mechanical universe, how are we to explicate these interlevel causal relationships previously "unknown to us"? The third main claim of this book is that the causal mechanism at work between levels of hierarchical organization can best be understood as the operations of constraint. Chapters 9 and 10 analyze interlevel causes in terms of constraints.

Lila Gatlin (1972) distinguishes between two types of constraints: *context-free* constraints, which take a system's components far from equi-probability, and *context-sensitive* constraints, which synchronize and corre-late previously independent parts into a systemic whole. When organized into a complex, integral whole, parts become correlated as a function of context-dependent constraints imposed on them by the newly organized system in which they are now embedded. Catalysts, feedback loops, and biological resonance and entrainment embody context-sensitive constraints.

From the bottom up, the establishment of context-sensitive constraints is the phase change that self-organizes the global level. Or to say it differently, the self-organization of the global level is the appearance of context-sensitive constraints on the system's components. Parts heretofore separate and independent are suddenly correlated, thereby becoming interdependent components or nodes of a system. But even as they regulate alternatives, context-dependent constraints simultaneously open up new possibilities. The more complex a system, the more states and properties it can manifest: novel characteristics and laws emerge with the organization of the higher level. For example, when amino acids self-organize (bottom-up) into a protein, the protein can carry out enzymatic functions that the amino acids on their own cannot. From the top down and serving as a contextual constraint, the dynamics of the global dynamical system in turn close off some of the behavioral alternatives that would be open to the components were they not captured in the overall system. Once folded up into a protein, for example, the amino acids find their activity regulated (top-down); they behave differently as part of the protein than they would have on their own.

Constraints work, then, by modifying either a system's phase space or the probability distribution of events and movements within that space. Since actions are lower, motor-level implementations of higher-level intentional causes, reconceptualizing mental causation in terms of top-down, context-sensitive dynamical constraints can radically recast our thinking about action.

There is ample evidence that the human brain is a self-organized, complex adaptive system that encodes stimuli with context-sensitive constraints. Studies showing that "each cortical pattern is a dissipative structure emergent from a microscopic fluctuation" suggest that this is a plausible hypothesis (Freeman 1995, 51). Not only does the brain have reentrant pathways (Edelman 1987) that function as positive feedback channels; it is also known to determine for itself what counts as a meaningful stimulus and what constitutes meaningless noise. Research increasingly supports the hypothesis that nonlinear feedback and resonance and entrainment among neurons—as well as between the overall nervous system and the environment—are responsible for the self-organization of coherent behavior in neuronal populations.

In Chapters 11 through 13 I examine the implications of such a view for a dynamical account of action. As is true of all self-organized structures, the emergent dynamics of coherent neurological activity can be expected to show novel and surprising properties: as a consequence of the neurological self-organization resulting from context-sensitive constraints, I suppose, conscious—and particularly self-conscious—beings emerge, beings that can believe, intend, mean, and so forth. Since the global level of all complex adaptive systems contextually constrains the behavior of the components that make it up, I postulate that behavior constitutes action (a wink, as opposed to a blink) when the brain's self-organized dynamics, as characterized by consciousness and meaning, originate, regulate, and constrain skeleto-muscular processes such that the resulting behavior "satisfies the meaningful content" embodied in the complex dynamics from which it issued.

Thinking of agents and their actions in this manner provides a previously unavailable way of conceptualizing the difference in the etiology and trajectory of winks and blinks. Bottom-up, formulating a prior intention to wink would be the felt counterpart of a neurological phase change, the dynamical self-organization of a more complex level of coherent brain activity that integrates neuronal patterns embodying wants, desires, meaning, and the like. Unlike Newtonian causes, however, this higher level of neurological organization would not be simply a triggering device. The global dynamics of self-organizing complex adaptive processes constrain top-down their components (motor processes in the case of behavior). As contextual constraints, however, a system's dynamics are not occurrent events like Newtonian forces. An intention's constraints would be embodied in the meta-stable dynamics that characterize the intention's neurophysiological organization, and as such would not immediately dis-engage. Rather, by serving as the brain's operator or order parameter, those contextual constraints that embody an intention (acting top-down) would provide the behavior with continuous, ongoing control and direc-tion by modifying in real time the probability distribution of lower-level neurological processes and, as a consequence, the behavioral alternatives available to and implemented by the agent.

Far from representing messy, noisy complications that can be safely ignored, time and context are as central to the identity and behavior of these dynamic processes as they are to human beings. Unlike the pro-cesses described by classical thermodynamics, which in their relentless march toward equilibrium forget their past, complex adaptive systems are essentially historical. They embody in their very structure the conditions under which they were created (including the chance events around which each self-organized stage reorganizes). The unrepeatable, random fluctua-tion or perturbation around which each phase of a sequence of adapta-tions nucleates leaves its mark on the specific configuration that emerges. The structure of a snowflake, for example, carries information about the conditions under which it was created. Each level is uniquely and pro-gressively individuated, as is the developmental and behavioral trajectory of each organism (Salthe 1993a).

The unpredictability that confounded those theories of action attempt-ing to reduce purposiveness to regular stimulus-response patterns is therefore an ineradicable feature of complex adaptive systems and a con-sequence of their embeddedness in time and space. If human beings and their behavior are complex adaptive phenomena, the precise pathway that their actions will take is simply unpredictable. Covering-law models are therefore clearly inadequate to explain these processes.

How, then, must human action be explained? In chapter 14 I propose an interpretive, narrative model of explanation. In hermeneutical interpreta-tion, the meaning of a complete text is constructed from the relationships among the individual passages. In turn, the meaning of the story's indi-vidual passages is derived from the meaning of the entire text in which those passages are embedded. This continual, interpretive "tacking" from parts to whole and back to parts reproduces the way dynamical systems self-organize out of the interrelationships among the parts—and then loop back to constrain those parts. The similarity in the dynamics of self-organization and hermeneutics makes the latter uniquely suited as the logic of explanation for stable states of the former.

Far enough from equilibrium, however, dynamical systems can abruptly and irreversibly undergo a radical transformation. On the other side of this "bifurcation" (see chapter 8), a system either reorganizes into a higher level of complexity characterized by renewed potential and possibilities, or falls apart. Across phase changes, that is, there are no established dynamics that can serve as the context from which the parts derive their meaning; the change itself in the dynamics governing the system's stable states needs explaining. Since these phase changes are unpredictable, the only way to explain them is with a retrospective narrative that retraces the actual leap. Explaining these individual dramatic transformations, as well as the detailed trajectory that even everyday behavior takes, requires a genealogical narrative that makes ample references to temporal and contextual events. This historical interpretation must provide detailed descriptions of the singular incidents that the agent experienced and that both precipitated the transformation and served as the nucleus around which the bifurcation reorganized.

Narrative, interpretive, and historical explanations of action thus require an expanded appreciation of what counts as "reason" and "explanation," for they explain, not by subsuming an *explanandum* under a generalization and thereby predicting it, as modern philosophy would require, but rather by providing insight into and understanding of what actually happened. They do so by supplying a rich description of the precise, detailed path that the agent took, including the temporal and spatial dynamics (both physical and cultural) in which the agent was embedded and in which the action occurred. Who could have predicted that Ibsen's Nora (*A Doll's House*) would leave her husband and child? And yet, at the play's end, we understand why Nora slams the door, even if no one could have predicted it. We understand her behavior by coming to appreciate all the complicated and messy factors that became entangled in her life; the drama shows how they interacted to produce a break. Moreover, if we learn anything from watching the play, we also learn something about the quirks and idiosyncracies of human psychology, of the circumstances in which humans function, and how these contribute to the unpredictability of our actions. Historical, interpretive stories might not allow us to predict future behavior, but they do allow us to understand why it is unpredictable.

The flaws of contemporary philosophical action theory cannot be understood, therefore, in isolation from the larger context of the history of Western philosophy. In turn, the failure of that history to formulate a satisfactory account of cause and explanation is better understood by viewing those two concepts through the prism of action theory. Doing so refracts the deficiencies of modern philosophy's understanding of cause and explanation. Of necessity, therefore, this book is not only about action theory; it weaves through metaphysics and philosophy of science as well.

Western philosophy's understanding of cause and explanation, too, cannot be understood without showing how these two concepts have been used in modern science. Even after the advent of the theories of evolution and thermodynamics, modern science continued to restrict itself to closed linear systems abstracted from their historical and spatial context.[2] Only with the recent development of complexity theory have openness, nonlinearity, time, and context come to the forefront. Although centrally concerned with the conceptual problems of action, therefore, this book threads not only through other branches of philosophy, but through the history of Western science as well. Like the hermeneutical model for explaining action, an interdisciplinary approach such as the one I am attempting must also, of necessity, tack back and forth between the history of philosophy and science on the one hand, and action theory on the other, in order to bring their relationship into view.

Interdisciplinary books are notoriously problematic: sections that appear overly simplistic and old hat to one audience strike another as brand new and difficult. In this book in particular, the history and science sections (chapters 1, 3, 7, and 8) are unavoidably sweeping and impressionistic, whereas those that present a sort of lawyer's brief against contemporary action theory (chapters 2, 4, and 5) are detailed and technical. Readers familiar with the literature of action theory might do well to bracket these chapters. Readers who know general systems theory and nonlinear dynamics can bracket chapters 7 and 8.

Chapters 9 through 13 make up the theoretical heart of the book. Using the dynamics of complex adaptive systems as a theory-constitutive metaphor, chapter 9 develops a new way of thinking of causality as constraint. In chapters 10 and 11 I show how thinking of self-organized neurological systems as dynamical landscapes makes the heretofore recalcitrant problem of meaning tractable. In those chapters I claim that meaningful intentions are embodied in self-organized neurological dynamics, and that act types are attractors through those brain dynamics. Evidence from biological and developmental research shows that this is a plausible scenario. Chapters 12 and 13 apply these ideas specifically to the problem of action. Doing so either solves or circumvents each of the problems on which traditional theories of action have floundered. Chapter 12 shows that complex adaptive systems theory allows us to conceptualize how the meaningful content of intentions, as embodied in dynamical organization, can cascade across coordinates and terminate in behavior that semantically satisfies the intention from which it issued. Chapter 13 shows how the emphasis that dynamical systems theory places on contextual em-beddedness can resolve many of the problems with which action theory has traditionally grappled.

In part III I leave the metaphysics of action and turn to the subject of explanation. Chapter 14 sketches the narrative and historical model of explaining action mentioned earlier. The chapter with which I end, "Agency and Freedom," addresses some of the implications that a dynamical systems and narrative approach to action and its explana-tion might have for such disparate subject areas as law, psychology, and education.

Part I

Why Action Theory Rests on a Mistake

Chapter 1

How the Modern Understanding of Cause Came to Be

Years ago, while performing surgery to remove the affected parietal cortex of epileptic patients, Wilder Penfield was surprised to find that when he poked a particular location in the brain (patients are awake during brain surgery), the patient might suddenly recall childhood memories in vivid detail. When probing a different site in the brain, the patient might blurt out something and then immediately protest, "*I* didn't say that! *You* pulled it out of me!" In other words, it may have come out of my mouth; but it wasn't *my* action. *I* didn't do it.

If asked the difference between a wink and a blink, we too might reply: *I* wink; blinks just happen. In that general vein, Roderick Chisholm (1964) claimed that unless we suppose that some events are caused by non-events, that is, by persons, personal responsibility is impossible.[3] If a certain ancestry—being caused by an agent or person—is what makes some behavior action, that criterion would explain why we hold people responsible for winks but not blinks. Don't blame me; *I* didn't wink; it was a *blink*! Philosophical problems arise, however, because the same body and the same neurological system are involved whether I wink or blink.

Cynics may notice that this issue is just one of many examples of a more generalized problem: the notorious failure of both philosophy and science to explain and predict human behavior. Rarely noticed, however, is that one reason for the paralysis is that philosophers lack a satisfactory theory of how causes cause and how explanations explain. Considering this egregious lacuna, it is not surprising that philosophers are unable to conceptualize and explain either voluntary self-motion or an agent's purposive actions.

As is often the case in philosophy, it all goes back to Aristotle. In *De Anima* and *De Motu Animalium*, Aristotle carefully examined the subject of self-motion. In the work he dedicated to his son, the *Nicomachean Ethics*, he explored the distinction between action proper and "mere behavior." A passage in book III of this work anticipates many of the problems that twentieth-century philosophy would later gather into the subdiscipline called "action theory."

Suppose a boat is threatened by an oncoming storm, Aristotle writes. To lighten the load and prevent capsizing, the captain throws the cargo overboard. Is his behavior voluntary, involuntary, or compulsory? The difference between voluntary, involuntary, and compulsory behavior, Aristotle insists, depends on whether or not the "origin" or "principle of movement" (*archê*) is within the agent. Behavior is compulsory when the "cause is in the external circumstances and the agent contributes nothing" (*EN* 1110b). Moving because I was pushed, that is, is "compulsory." Easy enough, and in contemporary action theory such reactions are classified alongside blinks and do not qualify as action. What about involuntary behavior? Can you wink involuntarily? As jurors soon discover to their dismay, many subtle gradations exist between the extremes of voluntary intentional action and compulsory behavior—between a wink and a blink.

Throwing the cargo overboard, for example, is "mixed," Aristotle states. On the one hand it is like involuntary behavior —behavior whose principle of movement is within the agent, and so qualifies as action—but with a qualification. It is "painful." Under ordinary circumstances no one would choose to throw valuable goods overboard. "I didn't want to do it, but I did. I had to." On the other hand, throwing the cargo overboard is "more like [a voluntary act], for the behavior was worthy of choice at the time when [it was] done and the end of the action [was] relative to the occasion" (*EN* 1110a11–13). It was the desire not to capsize that caused the captain to throw the cargo overboard; nobody physically pushed him. Voluntary actions are thus both purposive and appropriate to the situation. Appropriate behavior whose principle of movement or cause is within the agent, who is aware of what he or she is doing, is paradigmatically "action."

Aristotle distinguishes those situations in which the cause of a person's behavior is ignorance, which he calls *acting by reason of ignorance*, from those in which someone who is drunk or in a rage acts in ignorance (the cause here is the liquor or the anger, not the ignorance). The former are not voluntary, because the agent did not know what he was doing, but also not involuntary, because he did not regret his behavior. Perhaps the latter should have a name of its own, Aristotle muses. In any case, when the cause is ignorance, the behavior cannot be classified as voluntary. And yet when compared to the role of either the hammer in the patella reflex, or of the lightbulb's flash that makes us blink, ignorance is internal. But how can a lack of something (awareness, in this case) be causally efficacious? What kind of causality would be at work? Aristotle does not address that issue, but it is possible to infer from what he does say that, despite lack of regret, ignorance of "the circumstances of the action and the objects with which it is concerned" makes the behavior that issues from that ignorance nonaction. Thereby absolved of responsibility, the person deserves instead our "pity and pardon." Actions for which we can be held accountable thus require that agents be minimally aware of what they are doing.[4] Not all voluntary behavior, however, is explicitly "chosen." Only those acts brought about by a person's own efforts as a result of deliberation should be described as "chosen." The crucially difficult and to this day unresolved questions are, How do desire and deliberation, choice and intention "cause" voluntary behavior? What, exactly, is involved in claiming that "the principle of movement is within" the agent?

To explain Aristotle's analysis of organisms' actual behavior, it is first necessary to understand his views on change. All becoming, he maintained, involves the transformation of something that is so only "potentially" into something that is "actually" so. Burning wood changes something that was merely potentially hot into something that is actually hot.[5] All such transitions, including those changes that bring about human behavior, must be explained by identifying the role that each of the four causes (formal, final, efficient, and material) plays in making the potential actual.

If wood lacked the potential to be hot, it could never become hot. According to Aristotle, potencies are "originative sources of change in another thing or in the thing itself *qua* other" (*Meta* IX.1, 1046a11–12). There are two kinds of potencies: one the passive potency to be acted upon (a potency to receive change that is "contained" in matter), the other the active potency to act on (a potency found in agents to impart change). Inanimate objects and the elements possess only the first kind; organisms, on the other hand, have both. However, "*in so far as a thing is an organic unity, it cannot be acted on by itself; for it is one and not two different things*" (*Meta.* IX.1, 1046a28–30, emphasis mine). For organisms to act on themselves they would have to possess simultaneously both the passive potency to be acted on as well as the active potency to act upon (something else). Since nothing can simultaneously possess both potencies with respect to the same property, nothing can act on itself. Is nature exempt from this prohibition? A few chapters later Aristotle adds that by "potency" he means "not only that definite kind which is said to be a principle of change in another thing or in the thing itself regarded as other, but in general every principle of movement or of rest. For nature also is in the same genus as potency; for it is a principle of movement—*not, however, in something else but in the thing itself qua thing*" (*Meta.* IX.8, 1049b6–11, emphasis mine).

Is the principle of change of a tree, which produces itself by producing leaves, a principle of movement that acts on itself "regarded as other," or is it a principle of movement that acts on "itself *qua* thing"? If nature is "in the same genus as potency" and not an "organic unity," then nature can act on itself as such. Are trees "nature"? In one sense, of course. But because an individual tree is a substance (an organic unity), Aristotle holds that a tree as such cannot "be acted on by itself."

Earlier, in *Physics* VIII.5, Aristotle had reached the general conclusion that "[t]he whole moves itself not by virtue of having some part such as to move itself; it moves itself as a whole, moving and being moved by virtue of part of it moving and part of it being moved. *It does not move as a whole, and it is not moved as a whole*; A moves and only B is moved" (258a22–27, emphasis mine). What of animal and human self-motion? Suppose a lion pursues a gazelle. This last citation suggests that the lion as a whole (as a substance) cannot trigger its leg movements; that would amount to self-cause. So how does the animal move? Since Aristotle is unwilling to deny the reality of self-motion, how does he account for this obvious fact if he insists that, as a whole, organisms cannot act on themselves, that is, they cannot move their own bodies? A combination of the four different causes is needed to do the job.

Animal and human self-motion is explained as follows: *orexis*—the psyche or soul's one-way reaching out toward an object in the external world perceived by the animal or human as significant—is the active principle that moves by actualizing the (passive) potency to be acted upon that exists in the organism's material body. One aspect of the lion as active (its soul) efficiently causes another aspect as passive (its body) to move. But the soul cannot efficiently cause itself, so in reaching out for the gazelle as food, the lion's psyche is the unmoved mover of its body. The lion's soul thus requires an external object (the gazelle), as intentionally represented, to actualize the soul's desire by serving as final cause (Freeland 1994) or object of desire (Furley 1978, 1994). Aristotle therefore explains animal self-motion by splitting the organism in two: soul (the unmoved mover) and body (the moved). Strictly speaking, the prohibition against self-cause is thereby upheld: nothing moves itself. And so things remain to this day (see Tooley 1987).

The lion's pursuit of the gazelle constitutes voluntary self-motion because the activation of the lion's body is routed through its animal soul. In contrast, blinks can be fully explained in terms of material and efficient causes because they do not route through an agent's soul; blinks are just the bodily effects of the impact of external forces, the sort of process to which pre-Socratic philosophers tried to reduce all human behavior and which the imprisoned Socrates worried about. Blinks are efficiently caused by something external to the agent's soul, which contributes nothing to the behavior; they are, therefore, examples of compulsory behavior. In contrast, the *orexis*'s representation of an external object as desirable locates the active principle that effectively causes the behavior within the agent. The resulting behavior is, accordingly, voluntary action.

As mentioned in connection with the shipwreck example, Aristotle maintains that behavior is an agent's, and thus his or her action (whether voluntary or involuntary), if its principle of movement is internal. But we now appreciate that "internal" does not mean internal to the agent's body; the twitch of a nervous tic is not action even though it originates entirely within the body. Perceiving *x as y* is necessary for voluntary behavior to route through the agent's psyche and thus be purposive and appropriate to the situation. The reaching out of *orexis* plays that role. But *orexis*, that internal principle of movement, as we saw, does not efficiently cause itself; it is not activated by any efficient cause, in fact. The psyche's desire is an unmoved mover elicited by something in the environment, the gazelle, that serves as its final cause or object of desire. However, the gazelle by itself cannot function as final cause; the lion must perceive the gazelle *as food* for it to be the object of the lion's desire. Awareness (intentionally characterized) and the goal-directedness it supports are the hinges connecting the inside and the outside. Because the lion's soul is other than its body, the former, once activated, can trigger the latter as efficient cause. Always, however, one aspect (soul) causes or moves another (body). The animal as a whole does not efficiently move its parts.

Nevertheless, Aristotle pulls off a neat trick. By positing something outside the organism as final cause or object of desire of voluntary behavior, he effectively embeds the organism in the environment. An organism's internal state is dependent on something outside it. As that toward which the soul reaches out, the environment is implicated even in voluntary behavior. Aristotle's concept of "voluntary" therefore suggests a sense of "free" that means in part "routed through the agent's soul." When opposed to "compulsory" in this way, "free" does not mean "nothing outside the agent is involved." This understanding of free will has since been lost.

At least, that is the way the Aristotelian thesis about self-motion has come down to us and has influenced action theory. The catch is that Aristotle confesses (*De an.* II.1, 413a8) that he himself is unclear as to whether the psyche or soul—the formative, active principle that the body realizes—is a thing or object distinct either spatially or in its very nature from the animal. In the case of self-motion, it might be argued, the lion's appetitive soul is the formal cause of the animal's motion, but not in the sense that one thing or aspect of the lion moves a different thing or aspect *as other*. The lion doesn't cause itself to move in that way, the way efficient cause operates. The lion just moves, realizing from the inside, so to speak, the form of the action "pursuit" (and not, for example, "crouching"). What would "realizing from the inside" mean, however? The lion isn't always pursuing the gazelle; the lion does things other than chase gazelles. The formal cause "to pursue" is not always in effect. So why it is in effect at some times but not others requires explanation. Do formal causes require activation, for example, by the gazelle as final cause? Despite being "within" the lion, do formal causes require something external to kick in?

The overall confusion is understandable. In *Physics* VIII, as we saw, Aristotle wanted to make sure the universe is not understood as bringing itself into existence. In *De Motu Animalium*, on the other hand, in apparent contradiction to *Physics* VIII, he wants to allow animal self-motion. How do final and formal causes cause? Certainly not the way efficient causes cause: by injecting an external force into a causal chain (Furley 1978). In the case of nutrition and growth, formal cause operates by *regulating* the motion of the components (Furley 1978). In modern terminology, formal causes cause by modulating, for example, gene expression, that is, by limiting when each component can do what. Viewed in that light, a laser beam, which as a whole "slaves" (Haken 1983, 1987) or entrains its component atomic waves to its frequency, also exercises a type of formal cause.

The problem of self-cause is one example of the puzzles of reflexivity that have fascinated philosophers since the Cretan liar paradox. "Reflexivity," as Hilary Lawson (1985, 9) points out, "as a turning back on oneself, a form of self-awareness, has been part of philosophy since its inception." Champlin (1988) identifies several forms of reflexive paradoxes: self-deception (Can you deceive yourself by telling yourself a lie?); self-contradiction ("p and not-p"); self-evidence and self-explanatoriness (vs. *petitio principii*); self-killing and self-generation of life; self-membership of classes (Russell's paradox); and self-knowledge and self-reference (the Cretan liar). For two thousand years of Western philosophy, arriving at a reflexive paradox was considered unmistakable evidence that something had gone very wrong with one's reasoning. The thinker was counseled to go back and start from the beginning. Self-reflexive paradoxes indicated a fundamental error in one's assumptions. [They] must be avoided, or in some way contained (Lawson).

The ploys to avoid or contain them were similar: if you deceive yourself, one part of you does the deceiving and another is deceived; if a proposition is self-contradictory, one part of the proposition contradicts another part. And so the problem is circumvented by maintaining that nothing, strictly speaking, deceives, contradicts, or efficiently causes— much less explains—itself. If something moves itself, then, one part does the moving while another is moved (Aristotle's tactic). In the case of organisms, which obviously change location on their own accord, self-motion must accordingly be explained as above: one part of the organism (*orexis*, or, later on, free will, intention, volition, the frontal cortex, corpus striatum, anterior cingulate sulcus, etc.) as an active principle efficiently causes another part as passive or potential (the skeleton and muscles) to move or change. When combined with a rejection of the concepts of formal and final cause, this belief—from Aristotle, through Newton, to today—has had serious consequences for biology. More to our purposes, it has had serious consequences for understanding human action.

The Mechanistic Causes of Newtonian Science

In any case, whatever Aristotle himself held, by the early seventeenth century modern science had discarded the concept of formal cause altogether, insisting that organic wholes, no less than aggregates, reduce to their component parts. Only efficient causes are properly causal. Wholes are therefore epiphenomenal, that is, causally impotent by-products. Aristotle's principle that nothing causes or moves itself, however, was retained.

Once gravity was captured in an equation, the seventeenth and eighteenth centuries subscribed to a deterministic universe of universal laws and fully specifiable initial conditions from which the precise location of planets a million years hence could be exactly predicted. Newton's physics take place in an absolute, three-dimensional Euclidean space. Inhabiting this universe are material particles: tiny, discrete objects sometimes pictured as minuscule marbles. These atoms constitute the building blocks of all matter and are acted upon according to fixed laws by external forces such as gravity. According to the clockwork mechanism this view describes, things are related to each other only externally. One atom activates a second by colliding with it and thereby impressing an external force on the latter. Aristotle's ban on self-cause thus became firmly entrenched after Newton.

The basic particles populating this mechanistic world of modern physics are independent of each other and do not interact to achieve a goal or purpose as they would were Aristotle's final cause still in place. Once Aristotle's final causes were disallowed, Newtonian mechanics left no room for either objects in the external world or anticipated end-states to serve as intentional objects of desire and goals of action. Once wholes came to be thought of as reducible to the sum of their component particles, the concept of formal cause likewise became otiose. The principle that makes an integral substance a whole was also, and for that very reason, discarded. Wholes were no different from aggregates, agglomerations whose properties remained the same whether or not they were components of a larger unity. This principle further reinforced Aristotle's prohibition against self-cause: since wholes were seen as mere by-products, they were, as wholes, causally impotent, "epiphenomenal." All causal work was done by the atoms as they bumped into each other.

In a universe where only point masses and forces are considered real, qualities that are a function of the relation between atoms, or between organisms and the world, were also dismissed as subjective. By the end of the seventeenth century, all relational properties, such as temperature and color, that did not to fit into this scheme were relegated to the inferior status of "secondary" qualities. Galileo's ability to set aside the interference of friction from the equations governing the motion of bodies also suggested that context contributes nothing to reality. Once atomism became the ruling conceptual framework, context and environment were thus left without a role to play in either science or philosophy. Indexicals such as here and there, this and that, now and then, lost their claim on reality as situatedness and point of view became unimportant. An object's only real properties were its so-called primary properties, characteristics like mass that, because they are internal to the object, it would exhibit anywhere, anytime. Since only primary properties were essential properties, it was therefore no longer acceptable to explain action as Aristotle had: by embedding the organism in its environment. The consequences of this view for practical reasoning in general and the justification of behavior in particular would find their complete statement in Kant's ethical theory.

Although time constitutes a separate and absolute dimension in Newton's theory, it is a counterintuitive understanding of time. Newtonian atomism reduced the universe to the relationships between single material points whose movements from one position to another are time-reversible. In the notations of Newton's dynamic equations, the equation's sign represents time. Since that sign can be either positive or negative, one should think of time as being able, in principle, to flow backward as well as forward. "Causes" can follow "effects" as well as precede them. And so with this principle of time-reversibility, Newton's heirs dealt the final blow to Aristotle's concept of final cause by dismissing as illusory the apparent unidirectionality displayed both in the development of organic forms and by the aimed-for goal-directedness of voluntary, intentional behavior. In doing so, the one-way reaching out of *orexis* (from soul to world), which accounted for the purposiveness of action, became a problem in need of an explanation, as did the vector-like quality of action itself. If real things (atomic particles), were unaffected by time and context, an object's interactions with its environment and the unique trajectory it traced through time and space also became secondary, "accidental" properties of no account to what really makes a thing the kind of thing it is and no other ("anthropological considerations," Kant would call them).

What was left? Material causes were for the most part ignored until the twentieth century, so with formal and final causes eliminated from the conceptual framework by Newton's heirs, for more than 300 years efficient causes were thought to operate like collisions of lined-up dominoes or billiard balls, one careening into the next, on which it impressed an external force. Each causal process, furthermore, was viewed as an occurrent event that was in principle reversible.

Modern philosophy thus reconceptualized self-motion as follows. In Descartes's dualism, a nonphysical mind, substantially distinct from the body, activates it as efficient cause. The mind does not require anything external to activate it, not even a final cause: that is what it means to say that it possesses free will. Descartes thus upheld Aristotle's ban on self-cause. However, when combined with the billiard ball understanding of efficient cause, this account of the mind-body relationship brought with it its own well-known problems. How does something nonphysical efficiently cause something else to happen in the physical world (or vice versa) without thereby violating the law of conservation of mass and energy? How can the mind insert itself into the chain of physical forces? How does this unique sort of efficient cause operate? What kind of force could that be?

In opposition to the dualists, materialists chose to analyze voluntary motion as one part of the body (in the brain) that, separate and distinct from the rest, activates the latter. One part triggers another, which pushes a third, and so on until something shoves the skeletomuscular system into action. And so the race was on to find the control neuron or set of neurons (the frontal cortex? the left parietal cortex? the corpus striatum?) that serves as the mechanical trigger of intentional action. All the while, behind these conundrums lurked both the Aristotelian understanding of cause that prohibited self-cause, and the modern view of cause as only collision.

The problems that this view of cause and explanation occasioned for explaining action, not to mention biological development and evolution, went unnoticed in the wake of the tremendous payoff promised by a world of aimless atomic particles whose only characteristic is mass in motion and which crash purposelessly into each other: certainty and predictability. Given a particular position in time and space, the exact determinism of Newtonian laws allowed precise retrodiction from the current state of the system to any particular moment in the past. More importantly, strict determinism offered the possibility of predicting exactly the state of the system at any future instant. Pierre Simon de Laplace claimed that once the laws of nature and the initial conditions of the universe were fully specified, complete and accurate knowledge of both past and future would be possible. That promise extended even to human actions.

The philosophical literature of action has remained trapped in this peculiar combination of Aristotelian and Newtonian views of causality. On the one hand Newton's heirs repudiated Aristotle on formal and final causes. On the other, they followed Aristotle in claiming that causes must be "external" to their effects. Nothing can cause or move itself; no environmental embeddedness is allowed. Once modern philosophy discarded the notion of final cause, there was no way to conceive of an internal relation between the outside world and the content of an intention as attractor and guide of voluntary behavior. Once modern philosophy discarded the notion of formal cause, all causes were assumed to be occurrent events operating only as efficient cause, analyzed as the forceful momentum of an external particle activating another in bumper car fashion. No standing causes were allowed. As a result, advocates of agent causality were left with no way of explaining what agents and intentions are, much less how they cause (and even less direct and guide) action. Combined with a continuing belief in the impossibility of self-cause, this conceptual apparatus has framed the theoretical accounts of action of the last forty years.

After a torrent of articles and books published between 1950 and the 1980s, the output on action theory by and large dried up. In articles compiled in Heil and Mele's 1995 anthology on *Mental Causation* (one of the rare exceptions to this general drought), several authors bemoan the sorry state of philosophy's understanding of cause but offer no alternative. The next chapter describes the impact that this understanding of cause has had on contemporary theories of action.

Chapter 2
Causal Theories of Action

Agent Causation

Roderick Chisholm was quoted earlier to the effect that agent causation must be different from event causation if moral attributions are to be possible. What do I claim when I declare (in some sense of the pronoun *I* that implies responsibility) that "I winked"? To qualify as action, agent causation theorists claim, I—not just some event in me—must have caused the behavior. This notion of agent causation presents serious difficulties. Who are these agents? How do they exercise causal power? How, that is, do "agents," as opposed to events in them, cause behavior or anything else? The issue is problematic because, whether or not agents cause their arms to rise, events in their central nervous system make the arm's muscles contract such that the arms rise. What is the relationship between agents and those neurological processes? Do the agents cause *them* too? If agents are not identical to those neurological events, the specter of dualism reappears, along with all its attendant difficulties pertaining to how a nonphysical cause can produce a physical effect. If, on the other hand, as materialists claim, the agent *is* those neurological processes, since self-cause is assumed to be impossible and wholes, as such, cannot act on their parts, there is no way to explain how the central nervous system as a whole can activate its own components.

True self-cause would involve localized parts interacting so as to produce wholes that in turn, as distributed wholes, could influence their components: interlevel causality between parts and wholes. But by following Aristotle in rejecting this possibility, philosophy closed off any avenue for explaining action in that fashion. Having discarded the notions of formal and final cause, moreover, philosophy was left without a way of understanding nonevent causation.

As a result, philosophers who champion agent causation as the distinguishing mark of action have never satisfactorily explained either the identity of agents or their manner of causation. J. J. Thomson (1977, 150) claimed that an action belongs to (is owned by) an agent if that agent is responsible "in some strong sense" for the neurological event, which in turn causes the behavior. The agent is "responsible" in this special sense for an event if he or she causes everything that causes the behavior. But precisely how does "he" or "she" cause? Even as an early advocate of agent causation, Chisholm (1964, 616) nevertheless agreed with the standard view that "in any true causal relationship one can always, in case he knows what both events are, describe them independently of each other." Also adhering to causal orthodoxy, Richard Taylor (1970b), too, subscribed to the principle that causation is always a relation between two things: agents and the behavior they cause. So despite claiming that one of the items in the causal relation is not an event but an agent, Taylor therefore agreed with Chisholm regarding the required externality between cause and effect. Even concerning agent causation, that is, both Taylor and Chisholm ruled out the possibility of self-cause. For a relationship to be properly causal, agents must be other than the behavior they (powerfully) cause. Nothing can cause itself.

Since unlike occurrent events such as intentions, agents are by definition nonevents, there remains, in addition to the recurring question of how agent causation operates, the problem of determining who the agent is. And since according to the received view, causes must be other than their effects and therefore separate and distinct, it should be possible to tell the difference between the agent responsible for a certain instance of behavior and the behavior itself. The agent must be either a nonphysical mind or one part of the central nervous system that causes behavior by efficiently activating another part. What, then, is this agent? A portion of the nervous system?[6] We can turn the tables on Richard Taylor and demand as he did of volitional theorists (as we will see below) that he find those agents independently of the acts they cause. Show us this elusive entity, independent of and separate from the neurological events, that efficiently triggers behavior. The burden of proof then becomes Taylor's —or any philosopher's who advocates agent causation while simultaneously retaining the standard view of cause: find the mysterious agent. Taylor's comments that the agent is not identical with his body, volitions, intentions, or any other events, processes, or states "within" him are of no help. Nor are his statements that "I am a man and ... this man ... is the cause of those acts that are mine"; such language does not, as he claims, "avoid any reference to self or egos" (R. Taylor 1966, 137). A man is not identical with his body, fears, emotions, volitions, acts of will, self, or ego, Taylor insists. Just what, then, is this "agent"? Because he, too, has no way of conceptualizing wholes as integral and causally effective entities, Peter Strawson's (1959) claims about "persons" as the locus of moral responsibility also flounder for the same reason. In light of these difficulties with the concept of agent causation, Chisholm (1995) recently opted for event causation over agent causation. Once again, Aristotle's principle that nothing can cause, change, or move itself is upheld.

In short, agent causation theorists have been unable to break either with the requirement attributed to Aristotle that causes be other than their effects, or with the modern view that all causes are efficient causes. Instead of rethinking the concept of cause so that it can handle agent causation, Taylor, Chisholm, and others (see Heil and Mele 1995) have held on to the requirement that there be must two items in any causal relationship: in the case of actions, agents and their behavior. Lately, philosophers such as Carl Ginet (1995) have claimed that agent causation should not be envisioned as a situation in which agents first cause some intervening event or set of events that in turn causes the behavior. The agent just acts, Ginet holds. However, he offers no philosophical account of cause that explains how the agent "just acts."

Let us examine in more detail the ways in which this understanding of cause has been applied in contemporary theories of action. Consider this representative quote from Harry Frankfurt (1978, 157): "[C]ausal theories imply that actions and mere happenings do not differ essentially in themselves at all ... [they are] differentiated by nothing that exists or that is going on at the time those events occur, but by something quite extrinsic to them—a difference at an earlier time among another set of events entirely." Like Chisholm and Taylor, Frankfurt assumes that causes, even causes of action, and their effects must be discrete and separate phenomena. The former, collision-like, bump into and thereby activate the latter. The only issue to be decided is the identity of that efficient cause. Causal theories also individuate act-tokens, that is, particular actions, according to the type of event that causes the behavior. Whether in dualist or materialist guise, and suitably identified as an intention, volition, want-and-belief complex, and the like, causes of action, following Aristotle, have been assumed to be events entirely inside the agent but other than the behavior itself. In hit-and-run fashion, these intentions, volitions, and so forth, activate another part (the skeleton and muscles) to produce behavior that, as a result, qualifies as action. Nothing in the environment acting as final cause is supposed to influence the mental event. What triggers the mental event? The deus ex machina reply has often been: nothing. Intentions are instances of free will in action.[7]

Causal Theories of Action

Arthur Danto is responsible for the commonplace distinction between basic and nonbasic actions. When S performs a basic action, b, he does so "directly", that is, "there is nothing which is itself an action of his and a component in the doing by him of b" (1973, 31). When I move my hand I perform a basic action; I do nothing else to move my hand, I just do so directly. Flipping the light switch and turning on the light, however, are nonbasic actions; I cannot do either directly. I turn on the light *by* flipping the switch; and I flip the switch *by* moving my hand. Nonbasic actions are therefore those we perform *by* performing other (basic) actions.

When, by (1) moving my hand, I (2) flip a switch, (3) causing the light to go on, which (4) inadvertently startles Smith, does what I do as an action include not only moving my hand but also turning on the light, startling Smith, and so forth? Since the ways in which I do each of these things differ, can I properly be said to do all the things in this "act-tree" as actions at all? If as a result, Smith has a heart attack and dies, did I "murder by startling"? Does each description—moving my hand, flipping a switch, causing the light to go on, startling Smith—identify a distinct action of mine? Which of these events, whether voluntary or involuntary, are my actions?

To characterize a certain behavior as a basic action b, Danto (1973, 31) maintains, is consistent with the claim that an agent performs an action because of the agent's intention to do so, "for the basic action is then an effect, and the intention, since a cause, is not a component of the effect, nor hence a component of the basic action itself." Danto's words are revealing in their statement of the need for a real, spatiotemporal separation between the intention (an occurrent event independent of the behavior it causes) and the action itself.

By adopting this view of cause, however, causal theories of action became vulnerable to a recurrent type of objection. Chisholm's (1964, 616) example is among the earliest and best known of these so-called wayward causal chain objections to which causal theories of action are vulnerable: "A man wants to inherit a fortune and believes that he will do so if he kills his uncle. This decision throws him into such a state of agitation that, while driving, he begins speeding and accidentally hits another car, killing a passenger who turns out to be his very uncle." Did the nephew kill the uncle as an act? After all, he did intend to do so and the uncle's death is in some sense a consequence of that intention. But if causes are occurrent events that cause in bump-and-run fashion, it is always possible for a cause to deactivate in midstream before the behavior has been completed. It is also possible for extraneous, accidental factors to compromise the causal chain and make the resulting behavior nonaction. Contemporary thinkers have resorted to epicyclic contortions to circumvent the deficiencies this uncritically accepted understanding of cause occasions. Like their astronomical ancestors, however, they all fail, as no amount of Band-Aid repair will resolve such a fundamental problem demanding radical revision.

Alvin Goldman

Consider Alvin Goldman, one of the warhorses of contemporary causal theories of action. He holds that for behavior to qualify as a basic action, it must be caused by a complex of wants and beliefs. On pain of infinite regress, the wants and beliefs themselves cannot be actions. The "particular wants and beliefs themselves, however, since they are not generated by any other basic-act tokens, are [themselves] not act-tokens at all" (Goldman 1970, 70). Conforming to philosophical orthodoxy, the role of the want-and-belief complex is to serve as occurrent cause, separate and distinct from the behavioral effect that its impact brings about.

Goldman claims that the last three events in the earlier example, flipping the switch, turning on the light, and startling Smith, are, in fact, actions because they are "level-generated" from the basic action (moving my hand). Roughly, act A level-generates act A' when the agent does A' by or in doing act A (Woodfield 1976). Generation should not be confused with the means-end relationship. Although flipping the switch may be the means I use to turn on the light, I might not have turned on the light in order to startle Smith, yet the light was turned on and Smith was startled. The means-end relationship is a species of the broader category of generation.

Action theorists generally agree that to qualify as a basic act-token, a behavior must be intended. If my hand moved as a result of a muscle spasm, not because I intended it to, I did not move my hand as an action. Aristotle would call that behavior "compulsory." The contemporary consensus regarding nonbasic, generated acts, on the other hand, is that they need not be explicitly intended to qualify as act-tokens. As long as nonbasic actions are generated from basic, intended actions, the generated acts constitute act-tokens. For example, if, by moving my hand intentionally (a basic act), I thereby accidentally flip the light switch, turning on the light is my act, albeit unintentional. Nonbasic events not explicitly intended may be unintentional, that is, but they are still act-tokens, as long as they originate in a basic act. Although some philosophers such as Richard Taylor (1970b) have disagreed with this position, it represents the consensus.

The important points to note are as follows:

1. Philosophers agree that a basic act-token is always at the beginning of an act-tree like the one mentioned above (moving hand—flipping switch—causing light to go on—startling Smith).
2. Since nonbasic acts are generated from basic ones, "all act-tokens, whether basic or not, are at least partly causally related to the agent's [original] wants and beliefs" (Goldman 1970, 71) that produced the basic act-token.

3. According to Goldman, it is precisely that causal background that permits the nonbasic events to qualify as act-tokens at all. Although well aware that "it may not be apparent that acts generated by this basic act-token are caused by [the wants and beliefs that caused the basic act-token]" (Goldman, 72), Goldman assumes that if the downstream event can be causally traced back to those wants and beliefs that originated the basic act, the generated event ipso facto constitutes an act-token. What makes generated events act-tokens at all—even when unintentional—is their causal ancestry.

Are the wants and beliefs that cause action (whether basic or nonbasic) occurrent events or standing dispositions? In the first place, I have already noted that contemporary philosophy has no room for standing causes. In the second place, if Goldman claimed that standing want-and-belief complexes cause actions, he would be vulnerable to objectors quick to point out that someone with a standing want to do x might nevertheless do x because, say, he was pushed—as a reaction, that is, to some external stimulus totally unrelated to the want and belief. Chisholm's nervous-nephew objection is formulated specifically against a position like Goldman's. In such cases, our intuitions would insist that despite the standing want, no act-token was performed because the behavior did not issue from that want, nor was it guided and controlled by it.

As we saw, Aristotle faced a similar problem: the formal cause that identifies a particular instance of behavior as a token of the act-type "pursuit" is not always in effect. Its activation must be explained. Nevertheless, by thinking of formal cause as a standing principle, Aristotle could claim that while (and for as long as) the lion runs after a gazelle the description "pursuit" applies: formal causes remain in effect throughout the behavior, which they structure. That avenue, however, is closed to Goldman. Once causes are considered occurrent events that take place prior to and separate from the behavior they trigger, problems arise pertaining to the continuing control and direction of the behavior throughout its performance.

Goldman is not unaware of this potentially devastating objection against anyone holding that standing wants cause action. But following the only (mechanistic) understanding of cause available, Goldman insists that basic actions are caused by an occurrent want-and-belief complex. He claims that basic act-tokens must be preceded by an occurrent want-and-belief complex that causes the behavior "in the characteristic way." When the agent intends a full series of acts and thus has an action-plan, each nonbasic behavior will itself be preceded by an appropriate want-and-belief complex that causes the nonbasic behavior in the characteristic way, thus replicating and actualizing the overall action-plan. In these cases the nonbasic acts themselves will be as intentional as the basic act-token. In those other cases in which no long-term action-plan is intended, however, the nonbasic acts nevertheless qualify as "action" because they are causally traceable to the generating, basic act.

This "solution" is inadequate because in the end it, too, rests on the principle that causes must be external to the effects that they trigger in a collision-like way, and to its corollary, philosophy's historical aversion to the possibility of self-cause. Ex hypothesi, the occurrent want-and-belief complex that causes a basic act-token is a discrete event that precedes and is not itself a component of the basic act itself. Suppose the agent has no action-plan and performs only the basic act intentionally. If the want-and-belief complex causing the basic act-token is an occurrent event and not a standing disposition, the trigger need not continue in effect throughout the performance of even the basic action, much less the generated ones. Goldman has this objection in mind, I believe, when he warns that basic acts must be caused "in the characteristic way." But precisely what is this way? Although he suggests it is connected with certain neurological patterns "appropriate" to action (1970, 165ff), Goldman confesses that he does not have a fully detailed answer. But the type of cause at work in action is precisely the problem that needs addressing; yet it is the problem everyone avoids.

The deactivation-in-midstream objection cannot be easily dismissed. Events are not instantaneous, as the modern snapshot view of cause requires. Suppose that a basic act spans the albeit small interval t_1 through t_4. It is always possible in principle for the causal want and belief (and appropriate neurological pattern) to become deactivated at t_2 and for another want-and-belief complex, realized in a different neurological pattern, to take over at t_3. The latter phase of the behavior at t_4 could be traced back to the earlier neurological pattern, and therefore to the initiating causal complex. But since modern philosophy's causes are only efficient causes, the latter phase of the behavior would no longer qualify as an act-token since it would not at that point be sustained by the initial neurological pattern "appropriate" to action.

In short, suppose the agent has no action-plan and intentionally performs only the basic act, and the want-and-belief complex causing the basic act-token is an occurrent and not a standing event. Since that complex is not itself an action (it is what brings about the behavior that as a result qualifies as action), there is no reason to suppose that it remains activated throughout the performance of even the basic action it triggers. Supposing that a given basic act spans the minuscule interval $t_{1.1}$ through $t_{1.4}$, it is in principle still possible for the occurrent causal want-and-belief complex (or intention)—and appropriate neurological pattern—to become deactivated at $t_{1.2}$, and another want-and-belief complex instantiated in a different neurological pattern to take over at $t_{1.3}$. The latter phase of the behavior that takes place after $t_{1.2}$ is also causally traceable to the earlier neurological pattern and therefore to the original causal want, but once again, the latter phase of the behavior would no longer be an action, since the first intention and appropriate neurological pattern would not at that point be sustaining the behavior. Goldman's causal theory fails because it should not allow for a possible midstream interruption or disengagement of the cause. But this is precisely what occurrent, Newtonian, efficient causes cannot help but do.

The objection is particularly telling, for Goldman (1970, 88) places "no temporal restrictions on the length of basic acts." Although he insists that both the basic act (A) and the nonbasic act (A') must occur at the "same time," Goldman recognizes that even in the case of nonbasic acts, this description must mean an "interval," not just an "instant" of time. Numerous important articles (Davis 1970; Thomson 1971) have examined the difficulty in determining when an act occurs. Of concern here, however, is the related issue of the deactivation of a causal want-and-belief complex either during the performance of a basic act, or during the interval that spans the basic act and generated events. Even phrasing the problem as "deactivation" highlights the inadequacy of this mechanistic understanding of cause. Unfortunately, except for vaguely mentioning that two events do not occur during the same interval of time if it would be accurate to say, "S did *a and then* did *b*," Goldman is silent regarding this problem.

He has no choice. A worldview with a strobelike understanding of time (as well as a gunshot view of cause) has no way of determining when "now" ends and "then" begins. Goldman (1970, 91) recognizes that his approach runs into problems when trying to account for habitual behavior. Suppose I try to dislodge a piece of food between my teeth. "Fifteen minutes later I find my tongue still going, though I had meanwhile forgotten about it." If the latter tongue movements were not intentional, "perhaps we should say that the tongue was moving rather than that I was moving my tongue." The fifteen minutes of elapsed time are irrelevant, however, since, as mentioned earlier, Goldman places no temporal restrictions on basic acts. He does caution that some projects are just "too lengthy and complicated to be governed by a single occurrent want [and] must be subdivided into smaller, manageable parts, each of which must be preceded by an occurrent want" (90). Without criteria for excessive length and complication, however, it is unclear when "now" ends and "then" begins. The point Goldman wants to make in this example, of course, is that at some point the agent stopped moving his tongue intentionally. At that point ("and then") the behavior ceased to be, by definition, a basic action. But the latter, nonact phase of the tongue activity is traceable through a sequence of efficient causes to the initial wants and beliefs that triggered the first (basic act-token) phase of tongue movement. Despite the (efficiently) causal connection, however, ex hypothesi the latter phase does not constitute a (basic) act-token, as Goldman himself admits.

In another of Goldman's examples, John (1) moves his finger, (2) pulls the trigger, (3) fires the gun, which (4) kills Smith. Event (1) is John's basic act-token; (2) through (4) are nonbasic, generated act-tokens. Assume that John intends the behavior through (3); Smith is accidentally killed by a ricocheting bullet. Is John guilty of murder? As was the case in the earlier example, one can again suppose that the occurrent want causally respon-sible for (1) through (3)—and the corresponding neurological pattern characteristic of action—do not extend beyond (3). Although (1) through (3) identify act-tokens, and (4) is causally traceable to the source of (1), Goldman does not show that killing Smith is John's act-token—murder—rather than a consequence of (but not among) John's actions. It may not be murder, but is it involuntary manslaughter? Or accidental homicide?

In contrast to Goldman, Richard Taylor would maintain that the killing is not John's act-token at all. Of "I move my hand, causing the stone to move," Taylor (1970b, 275) states, "though I move my hand, and thereby, as it happens, cause the stone to move, it does not follow that I move the stone with my hand—moving the stone might be inadvertent and unin-tended, a consequence of what I did, but no part of what I was doing." Even though the cause of the behavior was within the agent, if the con-tent of John's intention were fully specified, the desire activating his body was not "to kill Smith," only "to fire the gun." Since John did not repre-sent the intended outcome as killing Smith, Smith's death did not serve as final cause activating John's desire. Accordingly, Aristotle would agree with Taylor that John's killing Smith was not voluntary. But would Aris-totle maintain that it was still John's action, albeit involuntary (like that of the shipwrecked captain?). What if John believed on good grounds that the gun was loaded with blanks? Would he be off the hook "by reason of ignorance"? That would make only (1) and (2) intended. What would our puzzled jurors say? And these are precisely the sorts of issues jurors are called upon to decide.

Both Goldman and Donald Davidson (1971) recognize that certain descriptions of behavior can refer either to actions or to mere bodily movements. One can mention a person and an event and yet leave open the question of whether he was the agent of that event, as in "Smith fell down." Davidson (1971, 5–6) notes, for example, that "if I spill the coffee because you jiggle my hand," what I have done is not properly an action, yet "it is not incorrect, even in this case, to say 'I spilled the coffee.'" In the previous example, had John's finger moved (thereby pulling the trig-ger) because someone jiggled his hand, even Goldman would agree that since no basic act was performed, neither killing Smith nor "pulling the trigger" is among John's actions. Neither event is an action despite the fact that they are describable as exemplifying the property "pulling the trigger" and "killing." Goldman admits that not all exemplifications of act-type properties are act-tokens. Nevertheless, he insists that all nonbasic events qualify as act-tokens in virtue of having been generated from an intentionally caused basic act.

What Goldman or any other author espousing a causal theory of action needs—and which Goldman tries unsuccessfully to provide with the phrase "in the characteristic way"—is uninterrupted control and direction of the behavior by the intention that originally produced the basic act (and indirectly by the agent whose act it is). One way around this problem might be to build the necessary causal flow into the very concept of intention. In an early work on action theory, John Searle (1983) suggested just that. The unique feature of intentions-in-action (the intention-to-do-x, which causes x to come about), Searle argues, is that the intentional-level description of an intention-in-action includes as part of its content its own conditions of satisfaction. The intention that causes action x has as part of its very content (as the intention-to-do-x) that the behavior *be caused by that very intention*. Motivating Searle's claim, I suspect, is modern philosophy's inability to explain how causes can provide continuous, ongoing monitoring and directing of their effects. Since (in Goldman's example) what caused the killing was not the intention to kill Smith, Searle could maintain that killing Smith was not among John's acts. Alfred Mele (1992), however, objects to Searle's proposal on the grounds that human intentions are usually not specified to that degree of detail. And in any case, Searle leaves cause an unanalyzed notion. Subscribing to the traditional view of cause, Mele himself prefers to think of intentions as events that take place prior to the acts they cause. But he then adds a feature at odds with the standard philosophical model and in the same spirit as Searle's proposal: intentions, Mele states, are able to guide, direct, and sustain the effects they trigger. Other authors (Brand 1984; Heckhausen and Beckmann 1990) have also called for such a double role for intentions, one that not only "triggers" but also guides, sustains, and directs behavior to its completion. But that ability requires a very different metaphysics of causality, one in which causes can provide ongoing "control," "direction," and "monitoring." Although we can sympathize with the rationale behind those attempts, no philosopher has provided a satisfactory analysis of this kind of causality. Neither Mele nor the others offer an account of how this kind of cause operates. Nor does any other philosopher of action or philosopher of cause.

In short, a theory claiming that action is behavior caused in a particular manner requires a concept of cause that not only triggers but also structures and sustains behavior in an ongoing fashion. But none is forthcoming in contemporary philosophy. Action theory has uncritically adopted the standard billiard ball model of Newtonian science: one particle bumps into a second, which it activates even as it disengages. The event that constitutes the discrete want-and-belief complex triggers (efficient cause–like) motor processes which constitute the basic act-token and from which the causal want-and-belief complex disconnects as soon as it triggers them. Since Aristotle's concepts of final and formal cause were discarded, this bump-and-run understanding of efficient cause has, in fact, been the only model of cause with which Western philosophy was left!

Volitionists

Other causal theorists replaced intentions and want-and-belief complexes with volitions (willings) as the requisite cause of actions. Of these so-called volitionists, H. A. Prichard (1949) is the earliest, and Ginet (1990) and McCann (1986) the most recent. Prichard claims that the mental event (the willing) itself is the act-token, which then causes a bodily motion. Only because it is caused by something that is already an action does the behavior (derivatively) qualify as an act-token. But the volition itself is the primary action. The bodily movements, which are the neurological first link in a chain of physical effects, are contingently connected to action but they are not part of the act-token itself. Because causing neurological events itself requires activity, neurological events cannot be acts; only volitions are the real act-tokens.

The volitionist theory has often been accused of circularity: whence volitions? If the explanation is that volitions are caused, what efficiently causes them? Another volition? The threat of an infinite regress looms, an objection, incidentally, which itself rests on assuming a necessary "separation" between volitions and the behavior they cause, as well as between volitions and whatever causes them. Since volitions cannot turn themselves (or flow) into behavior, the charge also presupposes that nothing can cause itself. As mentioned earlier, the possibility of spontaneously generated volitions (free will) is often touted as the way out of this objection, but that is a questionable move. If an act of will is a random event unrelated to the agent's lifestyle, purposes, etc., that pops into existence for no reason and yet is able to direct behavior, is action theory any better off?

L. H. Davis, a modified volitionist, offered an account of action that he maintained avoids some of these problems. Behavior qualifies as action, Davis claimed, if and only if it is the result of a volition. Davis insists that since volitions themselves, unlike intentions or wants and beliefs, are already action, any behavior they cause is automatically action, even if the causal link from the volition to the behavior is circuitous. If Sam, for example, wills to move his arm but unknown to him "some diabolical neurophysiologist has . . . 'rewired' Sam's nerves so that as a result of the volition his *leg* moves" (Davis 1979, 21), the motion of Sam's leg, Davis insists, is Sam's action, albeit unintentional.

Davis's odd and counterintuitive claim can be dismissed with a reductio ad absurdum. Davis does not even require that the entity whose body moves be the same entity to whom the volition belonged; indeed, he does not even require that it be human behavior at all. If it were possible to reconstruct a domino-like chain of efficient causes such that my willing to move my arm results in an event that begins well after I die, according to Davis, *I* performed that event. On this view, any event linkable to anyone's volition through a chain of efficient causes is automatically that person's action.[8] Such a claim is easily dismissed with a variation of Chisholm's uncle example. At least Goldman saw the need to emphasize that the want-and-belief complex must cause behavior "in the characteristic way." Davis seems to think that by making the cause itself an act-token he can avoid that proviso. It is unclear why.

Noteworthy for our purposes is that by insisting that volition-causes are already action, volitionists implicitly acknowledge the problems that requiring that causes be separate and distinct from their effects has occasioned for action theory. Lacking the conceptual framework to do so, however, Davis (like Goldman before him) cannot guarantee that volitions continue to sustain and direct behavior throughout its performance, any more than intentions or wants and beliefs could. Once again, the snapshot nature of the traditional view of causes as occurrent events, separate and distinct from their effects, flaws this view.

That agents must somehow both be aware and in control of the direction and the course of their behavior is an important component of the concept of action. The notions of control and direction, however, imply that someone (the agent causation claim) and/or some processes ongoing during the course of the behavior, not prior to it, maintain and guide it. However, the ability to direct and guide, and thereby control, is foreign to a view that understands cause as the instantaneous impact of a force wholly external to its effect. As a result, the volitions-as-causes theory suffers from the same flaws as those that claim that other events (wants, beliefs) cause action.

One exception to the standard volitional approach is McCann, whose position on volitions is similar to Mele's on intentions. Calling for the agent of an intentional action to be "continuously engaged in the activity of producing," McCann (1986, 262) claims that volitions can provide the ongoing direction that intentions cannot. How so? How or why does willing possess continuing causal powers that intentions do not? McCann is right in rejecting causes that just operate as triggers, but he too fails to provide a substitute account of volitions as sustaining and directing causes. Simply stipulating that volitions provide that ongoing support won't do. A theory of cause that backs up that position is necessary.

Logical Connections and Causality

The literature in the early decades of action theory also offered much discussion about whether the relation between originating mental events and actions is causal (and therefore contingent) or logical (and therefore not causal). Volitions and intentions, some argued, cannot be volitions and intentions for mere bodily happenings; they must be volitions and intentions for actions. "Of what action is this alleged motive a motive? By the hypothesis this motive cannot be a motive for the rising of the arm since this is a bodily happening, and whatever else they may be, motives are motives for actions. Can the action of which this constituent motive is the motive be the raising of the arm?" (Melden 1961, 76–7).[9] Surely not. If so, motives would presuppose actions and the alleged explanation of action would be "hopelessly circular." Separation between cause and effect must be scrupulously maintained if causality is to operate at all. Most theorists, except a few such as Goldman and Davidson, took the disjunction— either causal and therefore contingent, or logical and therefore not causal —to be exclusive. Those who argued that the relationship between an action's cause and the behavior is a logical one maintained that since it is impossible to identify a want or desire except by reference to its object, intentions and other such mental phenomena cannot be causes.

A. I. Melden is probably among the earliest advocates of this view, the so-called logical-connection thesis, that since the connection between volitions, intentions, and the like and the behavior they allegedly bring about is a logical connection, it cannot identify a causal one. Melden pointed out that descriptions either of the reason for acting or of the volition that is the act's alleged cause necessarily refer to the action itself. If we tried to determine what an intention or a volition *simpliciter* is, we could not. A volition can be identified only in terms of the event it supposedly causes (the volition to do x as opposed to the volition to do y). So, too, reasons for action can be described and individuated from each other only as the reason to do x (rather than reason to do y). Since there is no way to individuate reasons, volitions, or intentions except by reference to the action for which they are the reason, volition, or intention, and since philosophy's understanding of cause requires that cause and effect be separate, neither reasons nor volitions nor intentions can be causes of action.

As we saw earlier, Richard Taylor is among those philosophers who uncritically accepted the principle that cause and effect must be separate and distinct. If volitions are causes, it should be possible to identify them as distinct events over and above the action itself. But this cannot be done: "Let us suppose ... that the volitional theory were true. What then would one actually *find* whenever he performed a simple act? He would, obviously, find not merely that he was performing an act, but that he was performing *two* of them.... What, accordingly, one would find or certainly should be able to find, anytime he performs an observable act, is both *events*.... [But] there are not two things I do in each such case ... but just one; or at least, that is all I can *find*" (R. Taylor 1970a, 57). Since Taylor is unable to find two separate events—that is, he cannot identify spatiotemporally distinct entities—he infers that no causal relationship is present. (Recall that earlier I turned the tables on Taylor and demanded that he find the agent in the agent causation relation.) Taylor concludes not that the presuppositions about cause may be at fault, but that there are no volition-causes—all because of the taken-for-granted prohibition against self-cause.

A second reason for holding that intentions, volitions, and the like are not causes is that straightforward causal relationships are transitive: if *a* causes *b* and *b* causes *c*, then *a* causes *c*. But transitivity is often absent in the relationship between mental events and the behavior they allegedly cause. I may intend (and actually do) *x*, and *x* causes *y*, but that does not imply that I intentionally do *y*. Because of this intransitivity, action descriptions are said to be *intensionally opaque*: when describing intentional action, coextensional substitution does not work. The general conclusion drawn is that none of the mental events proposed as causes of action (intentions, reasons, wants and beliefs, desires, volitions, and the like) qualifies as a legitimate cause.

The logical-connection thesis fell in disfavor after Davidson (1963) argued as follows: Melden may be correct in claiming that the description "A did *x* because he willed to do *x*" (or intended to do *x*, or had a reason for doing *x*) cannot identify a causal connection because logical connections cannot be causal. But suppose it were possible to identify an event extensionally identical to the event picked out by the intentional, volitional, or reasons description. Suppose, that is, that the agent's intention or reason for doing *x* is identical to a particular neuron's firing. Since a neuronal event can be described intrinsically, the relationship between the neuron's firing and the behavior could be causal. So once it is understood that descriptions in terms of reasons, volitions, or intentions are merely shorthand descriptions for those neural events, phrasing it as "the reason, intention, or volition caused the behavior" would no longer present a problem.

A particular neuron's firing, however, is a discrete event and as such runs into the same sort of objection as any occurrent cause would: some acts take a long time to perform, and no single neuron is active that long. The possibility of deactivation in midstream appears here as well. So Davidson's claim would need rephrasing in terms of populations of neurons. If each neural pattern of a population of neurons were uniquely paired with one intention, Davidson might be on solid ground. However, the same neurological pattern can likely be implicated in different mental events at different times (and conversely, the same type of thought or intention can be instantiated in more than one neurological pattern). If the intention to raise my arm can be realized in more than one neurological pattern, the causal relationship between intention and behavior would have to hold, not between behavior and neurological processes as neurological, but between behavior and neurological processes *in virtue of their content, as* the intention *to raise the arm* (see Kim 1984, 1995; Sosa 1980, 1984; and van Gulick 1995). The causality would hold, that is, between the behavior and the neurological events as mental, i.e., insofar as those neural processes represent "raise arm." But because empirical studies show that that content cannot be extensionally identified (1:1) with a particular neural pattern, the logical connection problem that Melden pointed out is therefore not so easily circumvented as Davidson supposes. As Alan Garfinkel has noted in commenting on the possibility of reductionism: whenever a macrostate can come about as a result of any number of microstates, microlevel explanations are useless.[10] If Q might have come about as a result of a bundle of Ps, "citing the actual P that caused Q will be defective as an explanation" (Garfinkel 1981, 58). And since modern philosophy forbids self cause, it has no way of explaining how bundles of P's can cause changes in themselves such that Q results.

As Mele's (1992, 1995), McCann's (1986), and George Wilson's (1989) work shows, not all philosophers have been satisfied with causal accounts of action formulated in terms of separate and distinct events as causes and effects. Those who have wanted to retain the idea that something about a behavior's origins qualifies it as action but have been dissatisfied with the atomistic model's externality include the more recent Danto (1979a, 1979b). Like Davidson, Danto tries to defend the traditional causal view against a logical-connection attack. After claiming that actions issue from a representational cause, Danto points out that whereas a volition or other intentional state cannot exist without reference to an object, the "state cum object" can exist without a cause corresponding to that object. My fear of flying, for example, need not be caused by flying itself, so the cause and its object are not extensionally identical, and causality holds. Even after defending the separation between cause and effect, however,

Danto (1979b, 15) feels uneasy: "There seems to be something more to episodes involving representationalistic causes and effects [actions and cognition, respectively] than a frequent constant conjunction of the sort naturally supposed ... for the representational properties of cause (or effect) tend to indicate what sort of effect (or cause) to expect, whereas nothing like this is implied by the familiar concussion of billiard balls."[11] Whether or not billiard ball B moves when constantly conjoined to billiard ball A is merely a matter of "external coincidence," Danto accepts, but this externality is absent when my arm moves when I will it to. The logical connection between "willing to raise my arm" and "raising my arm" reflects that closeness. In part, Danto is chafing against Aristotle's views on the possibility of self-cause. But instead of recognizing this, Danto turns to another possibility: that this "something more" between representational cause and behavioral effect is the semantic relation that exists when, in the case of action, the effect (the behavioral component) "semantically satisfies" the (representational) cause. Roughly, a behavioral effect "semantically satisfies" the content of an intention that caused it if the behavior was represented as such in the intention. If I intend to telephone Mary but do not know that Mary is John's girlfriend, I can telephone Mary as an action because "Mary" semantically satisfies the content of my intention-to-call-Mary. Although "John's girlfriend" and "Mary" identify the same person, because "John's girlfriend" does not semantically satisfy the content of my intention, I cannot telephone John's girlfriend as an action. Norman Malcolm (1968), too, is well known for similarly describing action as behavior performed "under a description."

Danto's added semantic requirement was meant to do the job of circumventing wayward chain objections. But can it? As the Mary and John's girlfriend example shows, the criterion does rule out potential counterexamples that arise due to the "intensional opacity" of representational causes: S intends to do x; x is extensionally identical to y; but because y does not semantically satisfy the content of S's intention, S did not do y as an action. Danto's semantic-fit requirement thus also takes care of the following example: I intentionally take a photograph of the morning star. The morning star is extensionally identical to the evening star. But I do not take a photograph of the evening star as an action. Danto's requirement can also handle Davis's example in which Sam, by intending to move his arm, moves his leg as a result of the neurophysiologist's rewiring. On Danto's view Sam did not move his leg as an action because of the lack of semantic fit between representational cause and behavior.

In yet a third article Danto (1979a) suggests that when they act, agents make the world fit their representations. He fails to explain, however, how the "fit" is brought about. How do intentional (or volitional, and so forth) causes cause such that the behavior semantically fits the content of that cause? Goldman's requirement, mentioned earlier, that the behavior must come about "in the characteristic way," as we saw, got us nowhere. It is too vague to handle satisfactorily the paradigm vexation, Chisholm's example in which the causal link connecting the representational cause and the "semantically fitting" effect is interrupted by accidental events. "Killing the uncle" semantically satisfies the content of the intention that unleashes the chain of events; the nephew's reaching the intention to kill his uncle causes the uncle's death. But the death was accidental. The coincidence drives the rich uncle counterexample and supports our intuition that the nephew did not kill his uncle as an act-token.

It is not enough, therefore, for behavior to "semantically satisfy" its representational cause fortuitously; as we saw, the interference of the nephew's nervous agitation prevents the intention from causing the behavior "in the characteristic way." The content of the intentional cause must therefore not only activate the behavior; it must also guide and control that behavior such that the outcome fits its semantic source as a result of that guidance and control. And yet it seems too strained to require that the agent's onboard intentional cause include every detail of how the behavior must be brought about; that was Mele's objection against Searle.

Danto (1979b, 16) proposes that in the same way that "knowledge ... is a matter of bringing our representations into line with the world ... action [is] a matter of bringing the world into line with our representations." Guiding a plan of action to completion, however, as implied in the gerundive "bringing the world into line," requires the operation of a cause that, far from disengaging at the onset of the action, persists throughout the performance of the act and monitors and directs the behavior. Inasmuch as that type of cause would identify the action's origin, the label "cause" would still apply (Sosa 1980). But it would not be a Newtonian forceful push. The intentional content according to which the agent shapes the world is not related to its behavioral effect the way a Newtonian cause is related to its effect. A proximate intention is an action's origin or source. But it is not a discrete event that precedes the action and yet is not itself part of the action. Nor, as we shall see in the next chapter, is it an impotent Humean "antecedent."

Despite the drawbacks of Danto's positive suggestions, what is significant for purposes of action is that even someone wanting to defend a causal theory finds something not altogether satisfactory about the traditional view of cause in which the relation between cause and effect is one of "external coincidence." Searle was right: the intention must be in the action. So we need an account of the metaphysics of that type of cause. Still, the reluctance to countenance any kind of self-cause persists.

Aristotle wrote *De Anima* to counteract the approach of earlier philosophers who had conflated explanations of action in terms of reasons with explanations that identify the material and efficient causes of behavior. But he also laid the grounds for many conceptual difficulties with his insistence that even in the case of intentional actions, nothing causes itself. Twenty-five hundred years later, the shift in contemporary action theory, from talking about causes plain and simple to talking about reasons, volitions, and intentions-in-action as causes of action, reflects the growing dissatisfaction with causal theories that rely on externally related events for their analysis of action. There is a much closer connection between whatever originates action and the action itself than between billiard balls. That closeness serves as the ground for the appropriateness of certain behavior given an agent's reasons or intentions. The closeness is reflected in the description of an intention as the intention-to-do-x. Danto referred to it as a semantic fit between representation and action. Malcolm claimed that action is behavior performed "under a description." Searle described it in terms of intentions-in-action incorporating their own conditions of satisfaction. But advocates of traditional causal relations balked at all this talk precisely because it appears to violate the required separation between cause and effect, a dogma that remains unquestioned, as does the dogma that all cause is efficient cause.

Chapter 3

Action and the Modern Understanding of Explanation

Action theory has been adversely affected not only by a flawed understanding of cause; a similarly deficient understanding of explanation has been just as detrimental. In the next three chapters I will examine how Hume's model of explanation makes an appearance in the guise of behaviorist accounts of action.

Aristotelian Science and Practical Wisdom

Aristotle is also implicated in modern philosophy's belief in explanation as deduction, but with a twist. Instead of simply providing a definition the way Plato would have, Aristotle's logic of scientific explanation consisted in deducing the *explanandum* from a syllogism with a universal major premise. Unlike Plato before him, who excluded change from ultimate reality, Aristotle believed in the reality of change, as we saw. But he agreed with Plato that those temporal and contextual idiosyncrasies that individuate organisms are irrelevant to scientific reasoning (*episteme*). Despite his claim that individuals are the only true substance, Aristotle insisted that philosophical discussions about contingent beings must not be concerned with "this or that particular contingent being as such, but with contingent being in its essential nature" (Copleston 1962, 47). The object of science is preeminently the universal, "because it is the essential element and so has reality in a higher sense than what is *merely* particular" (46). So explanation qualifies as scientific only when trafficking in the universal. As a result, *episteme* cannot explain the contingent and individual as such.

Biological changes and morphogenesis are therefore proper subjects of scientific explanation only insofar as their dynamics and goals are prefigured from the start. The task of scientific investigation is to discover and articulate accurate descriptions of the universal regularities governing those unfolding processes. At best, therefore, Aristotle's science of change applies only to what biologists call "development," the unfolding of pre-established potentialities. The idea that totally new and unexpected traits might appear and become established in the population is entirely foreign to Aristotle's thinking (Depew 1997). *Episteme* cannot explain truly emergent qualities.

If the temporal and contextual contingencies responsible for individuation, which are so central to human life and behavior, are foreign to science, what form of explanation is appropriate to human affairs? If *episteme* cannot explain specific events in all their idiosyncratic individuality, must reasoning about human conduct also treat particular circumstances as irrelevant? This, too, Aristotle thought unacceptable.

Unlike modern science and philosophy, Aristotle did not claim that the type of reasoning appropriate to science was the only proper way to reason (although he did claim that it was the highest form of reasoning). Whereas the universality of deductive logic characterizes science, the form of reasoning concerned with the human problems of ethics, law, and medicine—practical wisdom (*phronesis*)—must be *pros ton kairon* (as the occasion merits). Although at times sounding Platonic, as when he says that "every wicked man is ignorant of what he ought to do and what he ought to abstain from, and it is by reason of error in this kind that men become unjust and in general bad" (*EN* III.1, 1110b17ff), Aristotle did not believe that those who truly know the Good will automatically do it. Contrary to Plato, as far as human behavior is concerned, the unavoidable intromission of circumstances, of our awareness of them, and of awareness's role in bringing about the behavior make explaining action a much more complicated affair, as the shipwreck case illustrates.

If practical reasoning is unavoidably temporal and contextual, deduction from abstract universals, or even inference from probabilistic laws, is out of the question either as a way of predicting what action someone will perform next or of explaining what he or she did. To complicate matters further, chance and luck as well as human volition add their mischief to the mix (Nussbaum 1990). References to will and choice, absent in Plato, are commonplace in Aristotle. Unlike Plato and his modern heirs but like the contemporary Russian author M. M. Bakhtin (1993), that is, Aristotle acknowledges the messiness of human life by pointing out how difficult it often is to determine in concrete cases what in fact happened. Because explanation must be appropriate to its subject matter, the contextually embedded reasoning of *phronesis*, or practical reasoning, is as legitimate as the universal abstractions of *episteme*.

Aside from the difficulty of establishing what someone knew and when he knew it, determining whether (or how much of?) a given behavior issued from (within) the agent's will and desire, and in consequence qualifies as voluntary action, requires sophisticated skills. Identifying behavior that can be the object of moral judgment, as reflex or compulsory behavior cannot, requires a long training period of moral education. How much did the agent contribute? How much did the environment? Learning to make these kinds of judgments is not something the formulas of *episteme* can provide. For Aristotle, as mentioned earlier, there is no Platonic Form of the Good that, together with initial conditions, offers a practical syllogism with a deductive conclusion. Instead, moral education into practical wisdom, *phronesis*, teaches through example (not formulas). Through habituation, a youth acquires the requisite sensibility to recognize subtle nuances in people's circumstances, motivation, frame of mind, and the like. And this long educational process, Aristotle would say, is the only way to learn to tell a wink from a blink!

This asymmetry between science and practical wisdom would not be exploited for many centuries. During the early Renaissance, the recovery of ancient history and literature only intensified the "feeling for the kaleidoscopic diversity and contextual dependence of human affairs" (Toulmin 1990, 26). Phrased in Aristotelian terminology, *phronesis* ranked above *episteme*. During the late medieval and early Renaissance, and in stark contrast to the modern era, legal casuistry was the ideal of rational thought. Under the influence of the rediscovered classics, time and circumstance reigned, as late medieval Aristotelians such as Aquinas and early Renaissance thinkers like Montaigne acknowledged that universal, foundational principles cannot be applied to such practical matters as law, medicine and ethics; the role that context and history play in those areas prevents it. Even the fractured space of competing vanishing points so characteristic of triptychs reflects the late medieval and early Renaissance toleration of ambiguity and multiple perspectives (Ermarth 1992). As the writings of Marcellus Ficino and Pico della Mirandola show, however, Plato's influence began to revive in the late Renaissance. After Galileo and Descartes, *phronesis* would lose not only its superior status but even its respectability as a legitimate form of rational thought. As occurred in painting, where the single vanishing point became the norm, the logic of *episteme* would become the sole model for rationality. Once again, difficulties with the concept of cause are to blame. Let us see how.

Kantian Teleology

Despite having been awakened from his dogmatic slumbers by Hume, Kant refused to follow his awakener in matters causal. Kant's understanding of causality owes more to Leibniz's notion of force than to Hume, primarily because Leibniz's idea of *vis viva* was more compatible with Newtonian science, which studies acceleration by means of the various active "forces" acting on the system under examination. As a staunch Newtonian, Kant opted for a potent version of causation as one of his categories of the understanding. Since in the operation of cause as characterized by the second law of mechanics, nothing causes itself to change, the causality that Kant's Understanding discovered in those mechanistic causal forces of physics is exogenous: "The existence of certain things, or even only of certain forms of things ... [is] only possible by means of *something else as their cause*" (Kant 1980, 116, §87, AK.V, 448, emphasis mine). Newton thus upheld Aristotle: no self-cause.

Kant was troubled, however, by the fact that in apparent contradiction to Newtonian mechanics, for which all causal forces are external to the system upon which they act, organisms exhibit a built-in formative force. According to Kant, things or objects possess two kinds of objective finality, relative and intrinsic, the former pertaining to the object's adaptability as a means in the pursuit of other ends, the latter issuing from the relation in which a cause stands to its effects. Those natural things possessing merely relative (objective) finality Kant calls extrinsic physical ends; he cites as examples both sandy soil, which is favorable for the growth of pine trees, and rivers, whose course and alluvial deposits benefit the growth of plants (which in turn benefit man). An intrinsic physical end, in contrast, is such that it is *"both cause and effect of itself"* (18, §64, Ak.V, 371). As an example of an intrinsic physical end Kant cites a tree: "in the genus, now as effect, now as cause, continually generated from itself and likewise generating itself, it preserves itself generically." Growth and maturation are examples of this particular type of self-organizing causality. The tree develops itself "by means of a material which ... is its own product"; thus the preservation of its parts depends on the preservation and production of the whole, and vice versa. A tree's leaves not only are produced by but also maintain the tree. It is this type of causality, wherein a physical end is both cause and effect of itself, that is properly termed "final." Only living things exhibit intrinsic finality, and they do so in virtue of their self-organizing capacity. Organisms, that is, are living examples of the operation of self-cause.

To consider a living thing an intrinsic physical end, the first condition "is that its parts, both as to their existence and form, *are only possible by their relation to the whole*" (Kant 1980, 20, §65, Ak.V, 373, emphasis mine). Although the principle of finality is derived from experience, the idea that determines it incorporates all that is contained within it, and is in that sense a priori. And therein lies the integrity of living things, for by being reciprocally cause and in effect of the whole, the parts form a unity and not just an aggregate. The organic integrity of living things makes it difficult to accept that we are no different from a heap of organic molecules. Since living things both are produced by and, in turn, produce the whole, each part exists in virtue of the agency of the others and the whole, and in turn exists for the sake of the others and the whole. "Only under those conditions and upon those terms can such a product be an organized and self-organized *being,* and as such, be called a physical end" (22, §65, Ak.V, 374). For Kant, teleology or goal-seeking *is* self-organization.

But the unity of principle found in organisms and evidenced in their form's growth, maturation, and development is not explicable through "mere mechanism," Kant realized. The causal connections implicated in intrinsic physical ends "involve regressive as well as progressive dependency" (Kant 1980, 20, §65, Ak.V, 372) and are a priori in the sense mentioned earlier. An organism is not a machine and therefore cannot be understood mechanistically precisely because machines lack formative power, that is, they neither produce nor reproduce themselves, nor do they self-organize. "Organization" and its cognates, such as "organism," Kant noted, refer to a structure wherein a member is not only a means but also an end; it both contributes to the whole and is defined by it (20–23, §65, Ak.V, 373–75). No machine exhibits this kind of organization, for the efficient cause of a machine lies "outside" the machine in its designer, and its parts do not owe their existence to each other or to the whole (22, §65, Ak.V, 373). A machine, unlike an organized being, exhibits solely motive power. Organisms, on the contrary, self-organize.

In short, since Kant viewed the time-reversible mechanistic principles of Newton's physics as the only ones providing scientific knowledge (they are also the principles determined by the categories of the Understanding), accounting for the recursive self-organization of living things becomes problematic. Organisms' purposive behavior resists explanation in terms of Newtonian mechanics and is likewise a major impediment to unifying science under one set of principles. These considerations convinced Kant that natural organisms cannot be understood according to mechanism in general or its version of causality in particular.[12] Since only external forces can cause bodies to change, and since no "external forces" are involved in the self-organization of organisms, Kant reasoned that the self-organization of nature "has nothing analogous to any causality known to us" (Kant, 1980, 23 §65, Ak.V, 375). Kant thus upheld Aristotle: causes are external to their effects; self-cause, and therefore, self-organization, are phenomenally impossible.

Although organisms cannot be explained mechanistically because of this strange kind of recursive causality unknown to us, Kant concluded that the impasse is due to a limitation of reason. His solution: relegate teleology and purposiveness to the "regulative judgment" by virtue of the self-organization that is their hallmark. By appealing to the critical turn, Kant thereby avoided an antinomy between mechanism and finality while allowing that mechanism and finality can perhaps be reconciled in the supersensible, a reconciliation, unfortunately, that we will never know. The assumption that only external forces can bring about change thus continued to deny causal efficacy to nonlinear feedback loops, and therefore to self-organizing processes, which were accordingly dismissed as a form of causality unknown to us.

Even though Aristotle's *Posterior Analytics* was the first systematic attempt to examine the concept of cause, modern science summarily dismantled his system of four causes, and it is since mentioned for the most part only with a certain embarrassment. Despite opting in the end for a mechanistic understanding of causal relations, at least Kant recognized and addressed the problem of self-cause. Philosophers since, however, have for the most part ignored Kant's third *Critique*, the *Critique of Judgment*. By discarding Aristotelian appeals to formal or final cause while at the same time retaining his prohibition against that unknown form of causality, self-cause, modern philosophy of action effectively boxed itself into a corner. When action theorists have had to think of cause as forceful, they assume it works the way Newton said it did: one particle impressing its force on another, to which it is only externally related. We have seen the relentless influence of this perspective on contemporary causal theories of action. Modern and contemporary philosophy of cause, however, begins with and follows David Hume in his insistence that potent causes can be reduced to patterns of constant conjunctions. Action theorists have often followed Hume's approach. Let us see why.

David Hume

After the middle of the eighteenth century, Hume's views on causality came to dominate philosophical discussions of the subject matter. Sections 4–7 of *An Enquiry Concerning Human Understanding* dealt a major blow to the classical understanding of efficient cause by arguing that all notions of power and necessary connection must be severed from efficient cause, the only one of Aristotle's four causes still discussed after Newton.[13] In opposition to the Newtonian thesis that forces are potent causes that necessitate their effects, Hume reasoned that since sense impressions do not detect any forceful—much less necessitating—connection between cause and effect, causality is simply not an ontologically verifiable category. Our concept of (efficient) causation, Hume concluded, amounts to nothing more than the psychological anticipation of a previously experienced constant conjunction: we come to believe that A causes B after experiencing numerous individual b's regularly following a's. The experience of one event a constantly followed by the experience of a second event b leads our mind to associate them and identify A's in general as the cause of B's.[14]

Once humans recognize that we never directly sense the necessitating force attributed to cause, we must conclude that it is not real. In contrast to the Aristotelian-Newtonian interpretation of efficient causes as external forces imparting change, therefore, Hume's analysis of cause as psychological constant conjunction renders cause an impotent and subjective phenomenon. Despite removing causal relations from the realm of reality and relocating them in the mind, however, Hume's analysis of cause implicitly retained Aristotle's principle that causes must be other than their effects. Attributions of causal relations presuppose the prior experience of two separate events in a particular sequence, a sequence that then becomes associated in the mind as a cause-effect relationship.

Explanation Is Deduction

Several important consequences that follow from Hume's understanding of cause as constant conjunction have had as significant an impact on action theory as did the mechanistic, billiard ball view of cause. The most important for purposes of the theory of action was the fact that the adoption of Hume's reduction of "cause" to constant conjunction assured the entrenchment of a particular account of explanation in which *episteme* totally eclipsed *phronesis* (Toulmin 1990).

Since from a Humean perspective it would never occur to us to think "A causes B" unless we experienced several a's regularly followed by b's, it follows that individual attributions of causality logically imply a lawful generalization: "a_1 caused b_2" implies "Whenever A, B." As a result of Hume's dismissal of even efficient cause as an ontologically real necessitating force, philosophers began to analyze what appear at first glance to be potent causal relations in terms of lawful regularities. From a universal law (which, according to the science of the time, was assumed to be strictly deterministic, and often still is; see Davidson 1995), together with a statement specifying initial conditions (x happened), the past occurrence of any event should be deducible and thereby explained. And better yet, future events would be predictable.[15] After Hume, the implicative relationship between premises and conclusion thus became what counts as explanation *tout court*. Deductive reasoning, which Aristotle had thought proper to *episteme* only, came to be seen as the only legitimate form of rational thought. Explaining an event came to be identified with predicting it: the whole point of science and a very valuable feature indeed. Explanations in terms of lawful regularities subsequently replaced ontological pronouncements about causal processes. The ability to explain by deducing would be taken as the feature that not only distinguishes the hard natural sciences from the soft human sciences but also (since strict laws are apparently not forthcoming in the latter) discredits them (Snow 1964). The upshot? The ancient concept of practical wisdom slowly disappeared from mainstream—and academic—philosophy, as freshmen students note to their dismay.

By mid–twentieth century, deducing an *explanandum* from an *explanans* formulated as a universal law became the received logic of explanation (Hempel and Oppenheim 1948): the deductive-nomological (D-N) or "covering-law" model of explanation.[16] Other theories of explanation have been proposed since the D-N model. Carl Hempel (1965) himself suggested that the law from which the *explanandum* is inferred might be statistical: the explanatory argument need not render the conclusion necessary, only probable. This modification came to be known as the inductive-statistical (I-S) version of the covering-law model. Wesley Salmon (1965) countered that explanation is not a matter of rendering the conclusion more probable than not: what is important is for statistical explanations to make a difference to the probability of whatever is being explained. Whether deductive or inductive, however, all remain covering-law conceptions of explanation, as is Nicholas Rescher's analysis (1970) of explanation in terms of evidence, despite its criticism of Hempel and Oppenheim. And action theorists have uncritically retained this covering-law model of explanation. Here's why.

Behaviorism

Without Hume and the ensuing covering-law model there would have been no Gilbert Ryle, J. L. Austin, or B. F. Skinner. Ryle's now classic formulation (1949) articulated the principles of logical behaviorism. Ryle argued that appealing to mental events as cause and defining characteristic of action is no more than a vacuous appeal to a "ghost in the machine," an explanatorily fruitless concept devoid of content. Instead, cognitive terms such as wants, desires, intentions, and the like must be reinterpreted as dispositions to behave in specified ways, given certain empirically determinable conditions. According to Ryle, the statement "*S* is ambitious" can be unpacked into a series of conditionals that reveal the recurrence, over time, of an identifiable pattern of behavior. Whenever circumstances *a*, *b*, and *c* occur, *S* is disposed to behave in ways *p*, *q*, and *r*. Unpack the phrase "Lydia knows how to add" and all you will find is that Lydia behaves in particular ways when presented with certain stimuli under certain circumstances. Claims that an instance of behavior constitutes action because it was consciously or intentionally performed mean only that the agent behaved or was disposed to behave in certain ways given such and such circumstances and stimuli. In bypassing any internal mental state, behaviorism claimed that the only difference between winks and blinks is whatever gets filled in for *a*, *b*, *c*, the antecedent of the very Humean, lawful regularity. So the regularity, "Whenever a pretty girl walks by, John's eyes close rapidly" constitutes a wink; the regularity, "Whenever there is a lot of swirling dust, John's eyes close rapidly" constitutes a blink. The organism's "inside"—its constitution or "mind"—was thought to be a black box of no importance.

Looking at things this way seemed to offer several advantages. It promised a satisfactory explanation of intelligent, purposive, voluntary behavior—that is, action—by removing the *explanans* from the sphere of the private and cognitive and relocating it in an empirically determinable pattern of stimuli-responses. Behaviorism would thereby avoid talk of forceful and unseen mental causes in favor of properly Humean, law-like generalizations. Subsuming a particular instance of behavior under a universal law describing those stimulus-response patterns would finally turn the study of behavior into a science, allowing deductions and predictions; in short, it would finally be capable of providing explanations of behavior. Both psychology and philosophy of mind aspired to a scientific, that is, to an impartial, objective methodology. Mimicking physics, the goal of a third-person perspective was thus to eliminate point of view, intentionality, and other such mysterious and inner ghostly states altogether in favor of publicly observable Humean regularities. "Find those universal, deterministic stimulus-response laws!" This B. F. Skinner (1953) experimentally attempted to do.

According to Skinner's experimental behaviorism, organisms acquire dispositions (shorthand for propensities to respond to certain stimuli in regular ways) as the result of continuous reinforcement (positive and negative). Despite acknowledging that organisms learn through conditioning, Skinnerian behaviorists, like their logical behaviorist kin, held that it was unnecessary to postulate any ontological grounds for the stimulus-response patterns. "Disposition" was not supposed to refer to any structural property inside the organism; it was only a shorthand characterization of the stimulus-response regularities themselves. Experimental behaviorists, too, claimed that once universal behavioral laws specifying the stimulus-response patterns were finally discovered and fully specified, there would be no reason to suppose that organisms even possess such an "inner environment"; the mental ghost in the machine would have been exorcized as contributing nothing. Indeed, this was behaviorism's most loudly advertised contribution: by emphasizing publicly identifiable regularities among events, behaviorism prided itself on not requiring private and therefore unobservable mental items such as intentions or volitions that, moreover, took place prior to the behavior and allegedly but inexplicably caused it and thereby made it action. The recently arrived Martian does not take his umbrella when it is cloudy because he has never learned to connect the presence of clouds with the possibility of rain. The behaviorist asks us to believe, however, that nothing has changed inside those of us who have made that link.

For purposes of action theory, behaviorism's insistence on the lawful character of intelligent, goal-directed behavior is interesting. The mold into which behaviorism was cast clearly reflects the Humean requirement of constant conjunction as the basis of any legitimate explanation: all singular, allegedly causal attributions imply a lawful generalization involving two public, empirically observable and testable *relata*: "Whenever *A*, *B*." As always, implicit in this approach was the goes-without-saying determinism that pairs causes and effects in a one-to-one relationship. Even though most philosophers of cause have recognized the need to think of causality in a way that accommodates the special sciences, where multiple realizability is common, the assumption that causal relations must be one-to-one deterministic links between causes and effects still pervades action theory. For example, Davidson to this day (even see, e.g., 1995) refuses to call any relations "causal" unless they exemplify a strict, deterministic law. Although (1) no strict psychophysical laws linking mental events such as intentions or volitions with behavior have been discovered, and (2) evidence shows that different neurophysiological processes can carry out the same type of mental event, the assumption persists that strict laws linking neurophysiological processes to behavior will be discovered and the brunt of the work explaining action, therefore, will in the end be borne by the neurophysiological events as physical (van Gulick 1995). Since those philosophers who disagree with this position (Kim 1984; Sosa 1980), have lacked an adequate theory of either cause or explanation to support their claims that neural events cause (and explain) action by virtue of their content, that is, as mental, the task of explaining actions as the effects of mental causes—*as mental*—has for the most part been shelved.

In short: by replacing those internal, mental events that were traditionally thought to cause action with observable and separately identifiable "situations" of regularly conjoined stimuli and behavioral responses, behaviorists hoped that both the requirement of externality and separation between antecedent and consequent, as well as the requirement of lawfulness, would be satisfied.[17] As a bonus, philosophy would even get a logic of explanation for action that conformed to the received model! The next chapter explores in detail Hume's influence on action theory.

Chapter 4
Action as Lawful Regularities

Following a Humean perspective, behaviorist theories of action analyzed intelligent, purposive behavior in terms of lawlike regularities. This chapter examines how action theory adopted this covering-law approach.

Performative Theories of Action

J. L. Austin's "performative theory" (1961) is probably among the earliest logical behaviorist accounts of action. Certain events qualify as actions, he claimed, if they consist in (1) "uttering certain expressions" (2) in "suitable circumstances." Whenever agent A utters expression B in circumstances C, action X has been performed.

Like their kin the causal theories of action discussed in chapter 2, behaviorist analyses such as Austin's are vulnerable to characteristic and recurring objections. For example, even if (1) the act-type "marrying" requires the "uttering of certain expressions in suitable circumstances," and (2) a particular instance of behavior satisfies that requirement, there is no guarantee that that particular token of behavior will constitute an action. The trouble with performative theories of action is illustrated in a real-life case reported by Dascal and Gruengard (1981, 111–112):

> A man puts a ring on Hannah's finger, and utters the ritual words a Jewish bridegroom says to the bride in a wedding ceremony. The man's intention, however, is only to amuse himself and his friends. Hannah, as everybody else present in the room, is perfectly aware of the fact that he is only joking. In fact, she is not interested in marrying this man, because she intends to marry someone else, Mr. Cohen. Yet, somebody acquainted with rabbinical law, who was present in the room, explains to them that they are actually married because all the conditions for a Jewish wedding have been satisfied by the event that just took place (both are free, legally to marry with each other; they are Jews; the ring is valid; the ritual words have been pronounced in the right way; and there are enough male witnesses present). They laugh at this remark, but when Hannah goes to marry

> Mr. Cohen, the rabbi, to whom the event in question had been reported, demands that Hannah first obtain a divorce from her "previous husband"! She gets the divorce, but even this does not help her because Mr. Cohen, being allegedly a descendant of the "Kohanim" (priests who are supposed to serve at the temple) is not allowed to marry a divorced woman. Clearly ... quite independently of the intentions of the participants, a marriage was consummated and another prevented.

On January 1–2, 1987, United Press International carried a similar story from Islamabad, Pakistan, about an on-screen divorce of a television couple (who happened to be married in real life). A group of Moslem leaders subsequently ruled that the actors were no longer really married and would be committing adultery if they lived together. The grounds: an Islamic law stating that once a husband pronounces the word *talaq* ("I divorce you") three times, the marriage is dissolved. The Moslem leaders cited numerous juridical precedents that affirm that once the words are said, even in jest, they cannot be dismissed. To make matters even worse, the couple cannot even remarry unless the wife first marries another man and then divorces him (see Juarrero-Roqué, 1988b)!

The religious rulings in these examples are reasonable only if in each case the parties are Jewish and Moslem, respectively, and can be expected to be aware of their religion's tenets. In the first example the bridegroom was Jewish and thus, had he been more careful and attentive, would have been aware (however faintly) of the religious rule that an actual marriage is consummated whenever the speech act takes place. However, had the alleged bridegroom been born a Jew but never instructed in Judaic traditions and law, his complete ignorance of his behavior's implications and social significance would render the behavior nonaction, rather than an unintended action, as Dascal and Gruengard (1981) suggest. By "reason of ignorance," Aristotle would say.

If, say, partygoer Hannah (let us rename her Peggy O'Neil) could not have been expected to have the slightest inkling of the significance of her words and conduct, our pretheoretic intuitions would say that her behavior does not qualify as action at all. To claim that certain social, empirically determinable conditions, followed by a certain behavior, constitute action is plausible only on the condition that the agent is aware of the meaningful import of the situation. The same is true, mutatis mutandis, of the Moslem example. Austin's behaviorist conditions may serve as necessary conditions, but they are not sufficient to guarantee the performance of an act-token. For that, agents must be minimally aware of the pertinent social circumstances and regulations that in part make the behavior an action of that type. But awareness is precisely what lawful regularity was supposed to replace.

Action as Rule-Governed Behavior

R. S. Peters, also an early logical behaviorist, pointed out that action proper is not the behavioral effect of external forces. Signing a contract, Peters correctly noted, will never be completely explained through causal specifications of the impact of forces on bodily movements. Offering an explanation of a particular instance of behavior in terms of mechanical causes, he argued, is to concede that no act-token was performed. "Movements qua movements are neither intelligent, efficient, nor correct. They only become so in the context of an action. There cannot, therefore, be a sufficient explanation of actions in causal terms because ... there is a logical gulf between nature and convention" (Peters 1958, 14). Action must therefore be understood as rule-governed, intelligent behavior. Action is lawful, and the laws to which it conforms refer to social patterns, standards, and conventions. Our explanations and predictions presuppose this. A rule-following model of explanation is therefore unlike a mechanical model. Behavior can be explained as action only if set in the context of socially delineated means-ends conventions, Peters maintains.

This last requirement, however, is ambiguous. On the one hand, Peters might be pressing a point similar to one John Rawls makes in the classic (1955) article, "Two Concepts of Rules." In that article, Rawls notes that sometimes "constitutive rules" define "practices," which in turn specify a new form of activity. The acts of hitting a home run, signing a check, and incarcerating someone, for example, cannot logically be performed unless the relevant practice (the institution of baseball, a monetary system, and a penal system) specifying the act-type has previously been socially defined.

Rawls's point, although well taken, will not do as a satisfactory theory of action. He is correct, of course, in noticing that in some cases, behavior cannot (logically) exemplify a particular act-type, much less actually be performed as an act-token, unless that act-type has already been socially defined and established. You cannot (logically) even describe behavior as "signing a check," much less intend to or actually sign a check, before the practices of banking and check writing have been instituted. It is true that action theory must be able to account for act-types like these. However, once act-types have been defined, criteria must still be formulated that demarcate whether a given instance of behavior is an act-token of that type or simply an exemplification of that particular act-type but no act-token. The marriage and divorce examples mentioned earlier illustrate just that, as did the various objections raised against Goldman in chapter 2.

The central task of action theory is not only to specify the conditions that define an act-type; it is also to determine whether a particular example of behavior is an act-token.

Even if some nonbasic acts such as signing a contract, hitting a home run, and marrying logically presuppose a conventionally instituted practice defined by a socially defined pattern of rules (and the behavior can only be understood in light of those patterns and conventions), basic actions such as my raising my arm do not implicate such formally or convention-ally defined standards. And yet raising my arm is as much an act-token as hitting a home run or signing a contract. Indeed, socially instituted non-basic acts like hitting home runs or signing contracts are generated from basic actions such as my raising my arm, as we saw in chapter 2. Any analysis of action must therefore provide necessary and sufficient con-ditions that account for my raising my arm as an act-token (as opposed to my arm rising as a result of electrical stimulation, say) as well as for those behaviors instantiating socially defined act-types such as those described by Rawls.

A. I. Melden

As mentioned earlier, since it impossible to identify mental events such as volitions and intentions independently of their behavioral effects, A. I. Melden found no reason to suppose that they exist as mysteriously inner events. Together, these considerations led him to conclude that mental events do not cause action. Enter Melden's logical behaviorism: to explain and identify behavior as action is to redescribe the behavior in terms of the pattern of what agents do, how they do it, the circumstances in which they do it, and so forth. These empirically determinable conditions and circumstances in which the bodily movements occur "constitute or define the bodily movement as the action it is" (Melden 1961, 210). Those cir-cumstances include the agent's character, interests, wants, and desires[18] as well as the social context in which the behavior patterns are or are not appropriate. By recognizing regular patterns of behavior performed under specifiable circumstances, one comes to "see" a person as an agent and bodily movements as an action in the same way one sees marks on a piece of paper as words. To identify and explain an action, then, is to redescribe the behavior in terms of the all these behavioral and contextual factors. Hume's strong influence is clearly discernible.

On Melden's account, voluntary action thus reduces to an empirically ascertainable pattern of behavior performed under certain conditions. Are the agent's wants, interests, desires, and character (all of which are included in his list of circumstances that enable us to see persons as agents, and their behavior as action) causally efficacious or simply along for the ride—

epiphenomenal accompaniments to the behavior? What if those wants, interests, desires, and character are absent, "by reason of ignorance," as Aristotle would put it? Does behavior performed "by reason of ignorance," however appropriately patterned, qualify as action?

It is easy to construct examples in which appropriate behavior occurs in the right circumstances, yet the subject's mental state is such that no act-token can plausibly be said to have been performed. Considerations pertaining to the agent's inner mental state can always be adduced to show that despite appearances, something very different "really happened." The following objections apply to Rawls and Peters as well.

Suppose a chess player, because of a muscle spasm, inadvertently bumps his arm against a particular chess piece, thereby moving it to another square. Suppose, furthermore, that this move was, in context, the appropriate move to make. That is, it was the most fitting or appropriate move given the game's progress. It might be the move that the player usually opts for under those circumstances; it might even be the move he started to make before the spasm hit. As long as the behavior is appropriate under the circumstances, behaviorist approaches to action offer no way of qualitatively distinguishing between spastic or unwitting behavior, on the one hand, and voluntary actions in which the agent is in control of what he is doing while he is doing it, on the other. What disqualifies the behavior in this chess example from being an act-token, as noted earlier in our discussion of wayward causal chains, is that the agent lost control of the behavior in midstream.

Change the example somewhat. The "chess player" is now a Martian who, despite total ignorance of what a "game" is, much less what "chess" is, is instructed to "play chess." Not having the foggiest notion of what is happening—once again, "by reason of ignorance," in Aristotelian language—the Martian moves each chess piece that is on the mirror-image square of that moved by his opponent. In contrast to the player in the previous example, who meant to move the chess piece but accidentally bumped into it instead, the Martian does move his arm and the wooden figures as actions. But the Martian is not playing chess (as non-basic action).

Whenever lack of awareness is so significant, no act-tokens are performed even if the behavior happens to fit the appropriate pattern. Although it may be necessary for attributing action, behavior with an identifiable pattern is therefore not a sufficient condition of action. If the difference between action and nonaction is a function of the state of mind from which the agent's behavior issued, not just the state of mind that a witness infers from the agent's pattern of behavior, the announced goal of substituting a Humean, lawlike regularity for the agent's internal (mental) states fails.

The behaviorist confusion is due in part to an ambiguity in the meaning of "pattern." (1) There exist patterns of socially understood behavior: people in similar circumstances behave in similar fashion. In both of the previous examples an observer might "see" the raw behavior as "chess playing." Yet in the spasm case, no basic act was performed at all. As we saw in chapter 2, when no basic act is performed, no nonbasic event qualifies as an act-token. In the second example, a basic act was performed, but the nonbasic event does not count as "playing chess." The Martian moved his hand as basic action, but did not "checkmate" (as action).

The appropriate consciousness and awareness must be implicated in bringing about the observable behavior pattern to which Melden and Peters refer. Where there is action proper there is not only intending and initiating, but also monitoring, directing, guiding, and controlling the behavior such that it carries out the intention. The sense of pattern here is that of "patterning after," that is, behavior molded or fashioned by the deliberate and ongoing adherence to a pattern. The empirical pattern that act-tokens exhibit might provide evidence of the presence of an intention. But the pattern is not constitutive of the intention.

There is also (2) the subject's own characteristic pattern of behavior. Behavior we are unable to fit into an socially acceptable pattern would be called "mad," Melden says. However, the behavior might not be mad if it fits the subject's own typical pattern of behavior. This is why Melden refers to and includes the agent's wants, desires, and so forth in those characteristics we consider when deciding whether behavior qualifies as action. But how are these wants and desires to be discovered or determined? Melden's behaviorism reappears: not by looking inside the agent, but by identifying an overall pattern of empirically determinable behavior and circumstances.

But this Humean move gets the behaviorist nowhere, for similar objections to the chess-playing ones above can once again be raised. Even if we allow, as we surely must, that the individual's pattern of behavior is what observers use to attribute inner states, and assuming that chess-playing Martian counterexamples do not arise, the logical behaviorist is still not out of the woods. For if a specific instance of behavior must fit the agent's overall pattern of behavior to qualify as action, it would be logically impossible for agents to perform actions that were uncharacteristic but nevertheless quite intentional. Personally uncharacteristic behavior of a once-in-a-lifetime sort would not qualify as action on any behaviorist account no matter how deliberately intended and carefully executed. By definition, once-in-a-lifetime behavior fails to conform to any pattern, system, or practice whatsoever. A fortiori, it could not exemplify the regularity of a strict law. Once again, logical behaviorist analyses of action betray an allegiance to the Humean thesis that singular events imply a strictly deterministic law.

The problem of action is not only a problem of explanation; it is primarily an ontological matter. It is not a matter just of how or why we come to see behavior as action; it is a matter of what makes some behavior action. Just because a particular token of behavior can be seen as instantiating a pattern does not mean that the behavior was performed to fit the pattern. For an act-token to be performed, the stimulus-response regularity must not just happen: it must be made to happen. But because behaviorists agree with Hume's reduction of causality to constant conjunction, they attempt to reduce that which causes the pattern to the regularity of the pattern itself.

Contrast idle doodling with tracing. In the latter, because the motion of the writing instrument is made to follow the design being traced, the pattern that emerges is no accident but rather was caused to appear using the original pattern as template. In the case of doodling, on the other hand, whatever particular pattern is externally discoverable after the fact is accidental (unless one subscribes to orthodox Freudian theory). It is senseless to characterize what was, in fact, doodling as a "faithful rendering" of, for instance, a house, even if the drawing does indeed look like a house.

Earlier I mentioned Peters's claim that action involves rule-following: but following a rule is not the same as conforming to a rule, that is, behavior that simply fits a rule. Searle makes this point time and again against advocates of classical artificial intelligence by insisting that computers do not "follow" rules. To follow a rule is deliberately to pattern one's behavior after a rule, a very different phenomenon from behavior that just "satisfies a rule." Following a rule presupposes action, and therefore, on pain of circularity, cannot serve as its *analysans*.

Finally, behaviorism's attempt to force the explanation of human action into a Humean covering-law mold also encounters an objection that parallels Chisholm's murder-of-the-uncle example. Suppose I am ordinarily disposed to behave in x, y, and z manner whenever conditions a, b, and c occur. If I do x, y, and z, however, because I was pushed—not because the disposition was activated— x, y, and z are not my actions. To qualify as an act-token, behavior must be the manifestation of the agent's disposition, not brought about forcefully or accidentally. As Aristotle recognized, the process must route through the agent. But according to both logical and Skinnerian behaviorism, dispositions are not internal to the agent. And in any case, even if behaviorists could be convinced that dispositions are internal, modern philosophy would still have no way of explaining how these become manifested such that the content of the disposition flows into behavior, and we'd just be back to the problems described in chapter 2.

Action as Plastic and Persistent Behavior

Another equally well-known logical behaviorist account of action goes as follows: act-tokens are instances of intelligent behavior, defined as "the ability to vary movements relative to a goal in a way which is appropriate to changes in the situation necessary to define it as a goal and in the conditions relevant to attaining it" (Peters 1958, 13). In short, plasticity of behavior with respect to an end defines intelligent behavior.

Goals and ends, however, differ from end states, those internal states of quiescence and satisfaction that psychologists often postulate as ultimate motivators. The difference between goals and end states is basic to any teleological account of action. Stones and avalanches persist in rolling downhill no matter what obstacles they encounter. Pendula, too, "tend" to achieve an end state of rest. But stones and pendula have neither goals nor ends; nor do they act in order to reach them. Moreover, purposive human behavior is not always followed by such end states; sometimes, despite trying their hardest, agents fail to achieve their goal. Goal-directedness is thus not a generalized tending toward an end state.

Could goals themselves be analyzed in terms of persistence and plasticity? Something would be a goal, it might be argued, "not because it is the terminating point of movements but because movements persist towards it and vary in accordance with perceived changes in it and conditions that lead to it" (Peters 1958, 112). Ignoring for the moment the likely circularity in this definition, of note for our purposes is Peters's recognition that neither adaptiveness nor plasticity can be explained simply in terms of mechanistic causes. According to Peters, the prototypical example of behavioral conditioning, Pavlov's dogs salivating in response to a bell, is not purely causal (mechanically causal, that is). The dog's response was not unintelligent, "for the dog came to change it in light of differences in the situation." Insofar as it shows intelligence, the dog's behavior cannot logically be explained by reference to forceful causality

> [f]or the *explicandum* [the salivation] can only be adequately described by means of concepts like "relevance" and "appropriateness" to an end. Processes ... like the melting of ice or the movements of glass when struck by a stone do not require such concepts in their description. They just happen. They are not recognized or described in terms which related them to some kind of means-end nexus. For they do not vary in light of situations related in this sort of way to them. They therefore can be sufficiently explained in causal terms. (113)

It is difficult to determine precisely what Peters means by the dog varies its response "in light of differences in the situation." If "in light of" means "as a function of the dog's awareness of differences in the situation" (Peters does say "perceived changes"), then the account is circular. Peters's behaviorism assumes some level of cognition in its analysis of it.

In contrast to Pavlovian conditioning, whenever a sequence of events exhibits plasticity and persistence toward an end condition, concepts like "relevance" and "appropriateness" apply to the relationship between the mediate and final events, Peters maintains. As a result, mediate events can be described as the means, and final events as the goal of the sequence (the reason why the former happened). Such features cannot be adequately explained as the effect of forceful causes, or even of classical conditioning. The means-end relationship so central to action, in other words, cannot be reduced either to Newtonian causality or simple conditioned response (as a result of constant conjunction), Peters claims, because the notion of correctness is involved in what is to count as a goal. But Peters then proceeds to analyze correctness in terms of the pattern of norms and means-end relationships, which in turn are analyzed in terms of plasticity. So plasticity, in the end, is reduced to behavioral pattern over time. As a good behaviorist—and subscriber to a deductive-nomological understanding of explanation—Peters reduces correctness, relevance, and appropriateness to regularity in stimulus-response patterns.

One final problem for any behaviorist analysis is the fact that the entailment or stimulus-response relationship does not hold as tightly for human actions like winks as either logical or experimental behaviorists would require. "Glass is brittle" can be unpacked as meaning that whenever struck in manner a, b, and c, glass will break and shatter. This strict regularity may hold for things like glass and reflex behavior like blinks; not so for winks. "Mary slammed the door because she was angry" may be true in this particular instance but it is happily not true that whenever she is angry she slams the door, as Jonathan Cohen (1950) has remarked. The higher on the phylogenetic ladder an organism is, the greater the variety of responses available given the same stimulus. Even Pavlov's dogs do not salivate at the ringing of the bell when they are not hungry (a not insignificant fact that behaviorists rarely mentioned)! There is no tidy, linear pairing of causes and effects in human action as there is in the realm of classical mechanics. Despite conditions a, b, and c, people inevitably surprise us by doing the unexpected—not the expected x, y, or z.

It might be argued, however, that to circumvent this objection, the behaviorist conditional must be specified in more detail: "Whenever circumstances a, b, and c exist, behavior x, y, and z will be performed, *unless* $1, 2, 3, \ldots, n$," with every "unless" qualification that counterfactually affects the entailment fully spelled out. If, however, as I argue in part II, human beings are complex dynamical systems, this is a hopeless dream. Their exquisite sensitivity to initial conditions would require that these be specified with literally infinite precision. Each "whenever" and "unless" clause would require infinitely precise qualification, the result being a "universal law" that in fact refers to only one case.

For some time now biologists have had to face the same choice: give up the principle that explanation is inferential or conclude that biological and behavioral phenomena are inexplicable because their sensitivity to time and space places them in the category reserved for psychology and history, that is, in the category reserved for phenomena for which time and context matter, for which relations are not secondary and accidental. In the case of action, however, philosophers have stubbornly refused to abandon the principle that explanation is (or ideally should be) deductive.

Where Are We?

Chapters 1 and 2 documented the Aristotelian-Newtonian understanding of cause that pervades causal theories of action to this day. In chapters 3 and 4 I showed how behaviorist analyses of action follow Hume in matters of explanation. In chapter 5 I will present arguments and evidence supporting the claim that contemporary theories of action that concentrate on the purposiveness and goal-directedness characteristic of action have also tried to reduce teleology to patterned behavior.

Chapter 5

Action and Reductive Accounts of Purposiveness

Behaviorist Reductions of Teleology

Descriptions of intentions, reasons, volitions—even Ryle's dispositions—include a one-way, forward-looking component: someone wills or is disposed to do x, or has reasons for y, or does a in order to b. In chapter 2, I mentioned that several action theorists have noted that one mental event can be distinguished from another only by this anticipatory content—"to do x" as opposed to "to do y"—which also provided, as several action theorists pointed out, the necessary "closeness" between intentional cause and behavioral effect. This closeness posed a problem insofar as contemporary action theorists, because of their assumption that causes must be external to their effects, are forbidden from appealing to either formal cause or self-cause and can rely only on efficient causes. In response to this difficulty, as we saw in chapter 4, behaviorist theories attempted, unsuccessfully, to reduce the appropriateness and fittingness characteristic of action, which even Socrates and Aristotle had noted, to various stimulus-response patterns, including plasticity around a goal object. Let us now turn to those theories that primarily focus on the purposiveness of actions.

Act-tokens must be explained by referring to the agent's purposes and ends, and, as we have seen, to the appropriateness of the behavior given those purposes and ends. This directed flow of events contrasts with the in-principle reversibility of Hume and Newton's accounts of causality, according to which it is possible for any sequence of events to go backward as well as forward. In mechanics, event a could be followed by event b as well as vice versa. According to Hume, since one experiences no necessitating, directed force between two events, their order, too, is also in principle reversible.

In the case of action, on the other hand, the very concepts of intention, disposition, agents, reasons, and the like have a built-in one-wayness: they imply that these concepts issue in behavior, not vice versa. Not all one-way behavior is purposive, to be sure. As we saw, pendula tend toward a resting state, and avalanches persist in reaching the valley; but although both phenomena exhibit plasticity and persistence toward an end, neither pendula nor avalanches have goals. With the role assigned to *orexis*, a one-way reaching out to the world through the intentional object of desire that serves as the behavior's goal, Aristotle's concept of final cause could capture this directional quality of action. Although philosophers today would look askance on an appeal to final causes, any acceptable theory of action must still satisfactorily account for this apparently directed flow of information or meaning from cognitive source to behavioral terminus.

Theories that emphasize the teleological component of action focus on this vectorial quality: behavior flows in one direction toward a particular terminus or end condition—a goal, moreover, that is anticipated in the intention or volition that serves as the source of the behavior. As we saw in our discussion of Kant, however, belief in nonreductive teleology disappeared from metaphysics after Newton. As a result of Hume's influence, many philosophers of action have also tried to reduce the purposive features of action to lawful but nonpurposive elements. Let us see how.

Reductive analyses of purpose can be traced to the rise of classical dynamics in the nineteenth century, according to which all change can be reduced to and thereby explained in terms of point masses. In this century, R. B. Braithwaite (1946) and Ernest Nagel (1953) are two of many well-known philosophers who, by accepting the standard model of efficient causality and explanation, argued that teleological behavior can ultimately be accounted for in terms of nonteleological processes.[19]

Charles Taylor

Following Nagel's lead, many contemporary philosophers of action attempted to reduce teleology to lawful regularities. Charles Taylor has been one of the few who disagreed, insisting that whether I am performing an action at all and what particular action I am performing do not depend only on whether the behavior has a goal or purpose; that goal must also play a role in bringing about the behavior. It is characteristic of human action, Taylor states, that the goal the behavior is designed to bring about is involved in the production of the behavior itself. To claim that action is purposive, that is, is to claim that "the events productive of order in animate beings are to be explained not in terms of other unconnected antecedent conditions, but in terms of the very order they produce" (C. Taylor 1964, 5). Teleological explanations thus account for behavior "by laws in terms of which an event's occurring is held to be dependent on that event's being required for some end" (9). The event's being required to achieve the goal is a sufficient condition for its occurrence.

The similarity between Taylor's description of purposive behavior and Kant's characterization of intrinsic physical ends is noteworthy. Both describe the effect as participating in its own production, a form of self-cause. And Taylor, like Kant, also proceeds to reject the possibility of circular causality. Let us begin, however, by noting Taylor's (1964, 10ff.) claim that teleology is antiatomistic. This is so, he states, because any teleological characterization "identifies the antecedent condition of the event to be accounted for, B, as the state of affairs in which B will lead to G. Thus the antecedent is identified in terms of its lawlike connections with two other events, B and G, i.e., as the state of affairs in which, when B occurs, G will follow" (12). In other words,

$$(G \longrightarrow B) \longrightarrow B.$$

Taylor points out that reducing the connection within the antecedent transforms the law into a nonteleological one. But since the antecedent of the overall law (B's being required for G) can occur independently of the consequent and vice versa, he explicitly notes that teleological laws satisfy the standard causal requirement that antecedent and consequent must be distinct from one another. What teleological laws cannot satisfy, he claims, is only the mechanist's other requirement: that each of the two terms mentioned in any explanatory law in which they figure be separately identifiable. This stronger logical requirement in any case arises out of the tradition of atomism, Taylor states, and rests on the notion "that the ultimate evidence for any laws we frame about the world is in the form of discrete units of information" (C. Taylor 1964, 11). Although insisting on an ontological separation between antecedent and consequent, that is, he denies only the possibility of a logical separation in their descriptions. Shades of Davidson. Teleological explanations are holistic precisely because no description of the antecedent can be given without referring to the consequent. Taylor thus appeals to teleology to account for the logical connection between intention and behavior that Melden had emphasized.

Criticism of Taylor's theory has ignored its anti-atomism. Yet it is interesting that despite his objection to the stronger requirement of atomism, Taylor seems almost relieved to be able to satisfy mechanism's other requirement, that causes be spatiotemporally separate from their effects. Although he insists on the need for a connection in the descriptions of the items in the causal relationship, Taylor is at pains to reassure readers that antecedent and consequence are empirically independent. Taylor remains, in other words, very much a follower of philosophical orthodoxy: alleged causes and effects must be discrete and independent units; only in their description does teleological holism enter. But as Davidson would insist, events cause; descriptions don't.

Furthermore, and despite its avowed purpose to the contrary, Taylor's account of the teleology of action is also implicitly behavioristic.

Teleological descriptions, he says, are conditionals whose antecedents are characterized as "B being required for G." But this antecedent could also be described in terms of the mechanical state of the system plus the state of the environment (let us call this alternative description E). Whereas $(G \longrightarrow B)$ may always be followed by B, however, E may not be. It is logically possible that two cases may obtain, in which the system and environment [E] are in precisely the same state, intrinsically characterized, but in one the teleological description holds, in the other it does not. That is, two persons might be in the same neurological state, but only one would be intending to B. If so, how can we know, given that the two intrinsically characterized situations are identical, whether the teleological description applies to one of them? The only evidence that the teleological description was justified would be the occurrence of B, the event we seek to explain.[20]

Taylor's response lands him in a quasi-behaviorist position. We must look, he says, not at single $(E \longrightarrow B)$ or $[(G \longrightarrow B) \longrightarrow B]$ events, but at sets of such events over time, and choose between them according to their scope and explanatory power. The lawful regularity might hold in one case but not the other. That is, the teleological description $[(G \longrightarrow B) \longrightarrow B]$ will sometimes be lawful even though the causal description $(E \longrightarrow B)$ is not. In short, consistency over time (regularity) becomes the grounds for choosing teleological explanations over causal ones. By making lawfulness a defining feature of teleology, teleological ascriptions depend on implicit generalizations. We have here, once again, a variant of Hume's claim that individual attributions of causality imply a generalization: if and only if a particular attribution of teleology implies a generalization from which it can be inferred will the purposive behavior be explained. As was the case in behaviorist analyses mentioned earlier, the regularity captured in the "whenever G then B" antecedent conforms to the Humean requirement of constant conjunction.

L. Wright

Unlike Braithwaite and Nagel but like Charles Taylor, Larry Wright, another of action theory's warhorses, has argued that teleological ascriptions of behavior qualify as legitimate explanations. Unlike Taylor but like Davidson, on the other hand, Wright maintains that teleological explanations are compatible with mechanistic, neurophysiological accounts of behavior. Wright claims that his behavioral analysis of teleology avoids the errors of the other theories. Although it is the most sophisticated account of its genre, it, too, fails to explain intentional action.[21]

Wright treats what he calls "etiological explanation" as the genus term, with causal and teleological varieties comprising the narrower species. His use of "etiology" corresponds to that used in medical contexts: to provide the etiology of a disease or a biological function is to identify whatever is responsible for the occurrence of the disease or function. Since teleological characterizations such as "*A* in order that *B*" explain etiologically "Why *A*?" by saying "something in general about why behavior of this sort takes place" (Wright 1976, 25), the distinction between teleological and causal explanations "is a distinction among etiologies" (27), not a distinction between etiological explanations and something sui generis.

Wright's own analysis of purposiveness is a modification of Taylor's, which, as just mentioned, showed how "consequences of teleological behavior can function in its own etiology" (Wright 1976, 34–35). According to Taylor, as we just saw, behavior is teleological if it occurs because it is required for an end. Wright correctly objects to the condition of requiredness. If the animal can flee by either running through a door or jumping over a fence, neither alternative is exactly "required" for the behavior to be goal-directed. Classical reductive analyses of teleology by Rosenblueth, Wiener, and Bigelow (1943), Braithwaite (1946), and Nagel (1953) are also unsatisfactory, Wright claims, because they cannot accommodate, for example, unsuccessful attempts to flee from an attacker. As noted earlier, attempts that fail to reach their goal are nevertheless teleological. "Trying behavior" is still purposive behavior.

In response, Wright (1976, 38) substitutes a "consequence etiology" for Taylor's requirement etiology. Behavior is teleological if it occurs because it is the "sort of thing that tends to bring about a certain goal":[22]

> $T =$ "*S* does *B* for the sake of *G* iff
> (i) *B* tends to bring about *G*;
> (ii) *B* occurs because (i.e., is brought about
> by the fact that) it tends to bring
> about *G*." (39)

By using mazes, changing the paths within mazes, and so forth, Wright claims, it is possible to make repeatable and intersubjective tests that will determine whether the behavior satisfies *T*. Thus the ascription-explanation that *B* occurs in order that *G* can be empirically tested by a procedure that is methodologically like that establishing standard causal relationship, since it proceeds by eliminating alternative accounts. Although teleological behavior must be analyzed dispositionally, it differs from behavior resulting from nonteleological dispositions because the latter are dependent on "straightforward antecedent conditions" (58) such as Newtonian forceful causes. Teleological dispositions, on the other hand, are less precise and depend on results or consequences. The dependency, however, is "exactly the same: it is the usual sort of causal link" (58). It is what Wright means by "the usual sort of causal link" that is important for our purposes.

Testing whether B exhibits dispositional characteristics enables us to "discover what something is *trying* to do," Wright (1976, 47) states. To be "objective enough to function in an experimental test," however, conditions must be "repeatable and intersubjective" (45). Using T to determine whether behavior is teleological, in other words, requires constant conjunction. The purposive character of a rat searching for food can be empirically tested by devising and conducting experiments in which, for example, the design of the maze is altered, food pellets are replaced by inedible items, and so forth. So, too, can unsuccessful but still teleological behavior be detected empirically by observing whether the behavior exhibits "systematic organization of the movements about the goal-object" (49). The similarity to Peters's claim that intelligent behavior reduces to plasticity and persistence around a goal-object should be apparent, as is the subtle shift from analyzing what is constitutive of purposiveness to describing requirements for attributing purposiveness. As I pointed out earlier, determining that behavior is teleological may very well require constant conjunction, but whether purposive behavior itself does is another matter. Because Wright's analysis of function is widely accepted (Godfrey-Smith 1993), it is important to determine whether his parallel analysis of intentional action succeeds. The following are four counterexamples to T.

1. The first condition of T requires that B tend to bring about G, a condition meant to account for behavior that is "appropriate, given the goal, though unsuccessful," such as the above-mentioned trying behavior of an animal's desperate but unsuccessful efforts to flee from a predator. T, however, cannot account for behavior that is teleological despite being inappropriate given the goal, irrespective of whether it is successful or unsuccessful (trying) behavior. Here's why.

Suppose behavior-type B never brings about G except just this once; ordinarily B is just the wrong sort of thing to try (in order that G) in these circumstances, and S knows it. For example, S, a student with nothing to lose, flatters his teacher to get a higher grade even though S is well aware that flattering is for the most part the wrong sort of thing to try, especially with this teacher. Yet S has a hunch it might work just this once, and it does! (Even if it hadn't, S's behavior would still count as teleological, trying behavior.) Or consider a psychotherapist who makes an unorthodox remark to a patient to get the patient to reevaluate his situation. Suppose that every psychotherapeutic theory counsels against such comments on empirical grounds: research has shown that they tend to be counterproductive. Not only does the therapist know this; she is well aware that such comments haven't worked in the past with this particular patient. However, being an Aristotelian and not a behaviorist, the therapist has developed an appreciation of and a sensibility to the nuances of the dynamics of the present situation, including the patient's psychological state. She judges that this is a unique crossroads, a singular opportunity—and it works! Once again, even if it didn't, the behavior would still constitute teleological trying behavior.

I emphasize that in these examples G does not just happen as a fortuitous by-product of B; S does B specifically in order that G. Wright claimed that his analysis could account for trying behavior; condition (ii) is meant to do just that. The counterexamples show, however, that situations in which condition (i) of T does not hold can still constitute trying behavior. The behavior is purposive even when the situation does not satisfy the first condition of T. That is, B did not occur (was performed by S) because it tends to bring about G since, ex hypothesi, B does not tend to bring about G and the agent knows it. And yet the agent purposively did B in order to G. Dispositional criteria are inadequate as *explanantia* of unique or atypical situations that do not conform to a regular pattern. And there is nothing in the meaning of "S did A in order to B" that requires regularity, even though the attribution of purposiveness might.

2. Wright's emphasis on the empirical quality of T requires that the subjects under consideration intend a certain goal for at least the time span necessary for tests to be conducted. One can only test for the presence of goal-directedness by examining behavior that exhibits the same direction over a period of time. Suppose S is ordinarily (always has been and always will be again) a peaceful fellow. Just this once, however, he fires a gun fully intending to kill A. S never has before and never will again do B-in-order-that-G, but he does this once. If, to repeat, this is once-in-a-lifetime behavior, no empirical tests could be devised that would determine that S meant to kill A rather than, say, that the gun fired accidentally. There is no "systematicity" or plasticity over time around a goal-object that can be tested for that would clearly identify the behavior as goal-directed. A variation on this example would be a subject who continuously changes his mind. The behavior, although intentional and teleological, would exhibit no systematicity around a goal-object.

"[T]o demonstrate to a skeptic that a particular B ... occurs *because* it is the one that will bring about G ... [requires] the elimination of alternative accounts of the phenomenon" (Wright 1976, 41). But how would one eliminate alternative accounts of unique behavior without appealing to "mental life"? Different goals can be pursued by the same type of behavior and quite different types of behavior can share the same goal. Granted that someone exhibits dispositional tendencies to act in certain ways, "it is still open to us to ask what is his motive for so acting. His actions are quite consistent with his wanting to gain kudos or his having his eye on the postwar political scene; and they are also consistent with his wanting

to help his country. And it is only in this last case that we should call him
'truly patriotic' since patriotism consists in doing things for the sake of
one's country. As Aristotle would have said, this 'for the sake of' clause
is part of the essence of every motive, and it is just this clause that distinguishes a motive explanation from a dispositional explanation" (Nowell
Smith 1954).[23] In cases like (2) in which a mental state (such as a motive
identifying a given instance of behavior as being, for example, in-order-
that-G rather than in-order-that-H) is not amenable to a dispositional
analysis, alternative explanations cannot be ruled out solely through
the behaviorist tools of T. Appealing to these mental items themselves
becomes the only way of eliminating alternative accounts. Wright (1976,
144), however, claims that "mental items are forced on us only as a way
of characterizing in an intelligible way the incredible complexity of the
(largely teleological) dispositional state of affairs that manifests itself in
typical human behavior." Since the impact of mental items can be characterized dispositionally, reference to mental life itself is superfluous, Wright
insists. Wright requires that "intent be *inter alia* a disposition" (134).[24]
Case (2), however, illustrates that once-in-a-lifetime intentions are by definition not dispositions. Their causal impact, therefore cannot be characterized dispositionally. Even though this second counterexample might be
construed in such a way that it appears to meet both conditions of T—
shooting a gun does tend to kill and is performed because it tends to
kill—the example is formulated in such a way that the impact of the specific intention responsible for the behavior is not amenable to dispositional analysis in virtue of its once-in-a-lifetime character.

It might be objected that this second case actually satisfies both (i)
and (ii) of T. Although it might be difficult to obtain evidence for (ii), lie
detector tests, hypnosis, and other exotic alternatives exist that allow
testing T empirically in "unique" cases in which testing for systematicity
is barred. But such an objection succeeds only by ignoring Wright's
repeated claim that the value of T is its ability to bypass reference to
mental life itself, even in determining that S does B (B is performed)
because it tends to bring about G—condition (ii). Appeals to lie detector
tests and hypnosis do not avoid such references. Because polygraph tests
and attempts to hypnotize people can fail, testing devices must first be
calibrated. How would one go about doing so without appealing to
"mental life" itself? Resorting to another (second-order) empirical test to
determine whether, for example, the lie detector (first-order) empirical test
is accurate would simply launch us on an infinite regress.

Nor could one assume that consistent test results automatically establish
the test's validity. The point of the proposed counterexample is that the
validity of any empirical testing procedure to determine whether S did B
because of (or in order to) G presupposes or indirectly refers to S's mental

life. Only if the test accurately reports an independently confirmed intentional state is the test considered valid. Not referring to these mental states carries with it the inability to distinguish between accurate and inaccurate tests.

Cases (3) and (4) show that T can misidentify the behavior's goal.

3. Suppose that at time t_1, S does B-in-order-that-G—say S runs a maze in order to reach food he genuinely desires at that time. As soon as he completes the first test run, however, he suddenly realizes that he is a subject of a laboratory experiment testing for teleological behavior by means of T. The teleological end-condition being tested, let us suppose, is that S's goal is to eat the food (G). Also, suppose that S is an easygoing type who likes the experimenter and wants to please her. As the experimenter goes about altering the maze and other conditions, S continues to do B-"in-order-that-G," even when he becomes satiated and would prefer never to see another morsel of food. S, however, is not doing B "in-order-to-get-food (G)" but rather "in-order-to-please-the-experimenter (H)," but there would be no way to discover this goal empirically.

4. Finally, imagine that S is a mischievous character determined to confuse and mislead any experimenter. S is always able to discover what the test is for, and methodically performs whatever behavior B will appear *not* to be in-order-that-G. Even when the experimenter becomes suspicious and begins to test whether S is doing B-in-order-to-confuse-the-experimenter, S changes his behavior accordingly and makes it appear amenable to testing. Where no consistent pattern of overtly repeated behavior exists, no intersubjective tests can be run, and there would be no way to determine that any teleological orientation is present or, a fortiori, that the goal is G rather than H.

It might be objected that these last two cases of experimental deception are just examples of a well-known problem with an equally well-known solution: carefully disguise either the experiment's real purpose or even the very fact that an experiment is being conducted. Doing so makes the in-order-to-please or the in-order-to-mislead behavior impossible. Although a practical problem, these examples nevertheless do not establish a theoretical flaw in the dispositional analysis of teleology, the objector might claim.

However, for this counterobjection and its proposed solution to hold, it must be possible once again to determine incontrovertibly and without appealing to mental processes that the disguise has succeeded on any given trial. Is that possible? Again, one must test for the disguise's success only with empirical behaviorist techniques. But as was the case in the earlier counterexample and for the same reasons, either an infinite regress will be generated or one will find oneself begging the question. The empirical test designed to bypass any reference to the agent's mental life must, to be valid, accurately make reference to that very mental life. And at the risk of being repetitive, that is exactly what Wright argues is unnecessary.

Wright's (1976, 48) disclaimer that "in each case it is *possible* that we are deceived" does not succeed. Part of his criticism of Nagel and others is that their analyses of teleology "cannot accommodate a substantial range of clear and objective goal-directed behavior" (29). The four counter-examples I have offered are not so far-fetched that they can be compared to saying, "Well, it is possible that the vase was already broken and just held together by a fortuitous magnetic field that dropped in intensity coincidentally with the jolt" (48).

Wright, it was mentioned, claims that whereas beliefs and motives need not be dispositions themselves, their impact must be amenable to disposi-tional analysis. However, two different beliefs, motives, and so forth can become manifest in the same disposition to behave in a certain way. However much one alters the environment and similar factors, A and B's tendency to behave similarly might remain even though the motivation behind the two behaviors is different. Different motives such as gratitude (M_1) and enlightened ambition (M_2) might become manifest in a disposi-tion, D_1, to behave similarly, B_1. To borrow Nowell Smith's example, two quite different motives, ambition and patriotism, might become manifest in the same disposition to seek public office and donate large sums of money to charitable organizations.

Suppose the dispositions to behave in a certain way are indistinguish-able even though the two sets of behaviors spring from very different motives. Two different nonbasic actions will have been performed even though the overt behaviors may be indistinguishable. Explaining a specific instance of behavior as a particular type of action (and not another) is therefore crucial if the behavior is to be explained at all. Empirically detectable tendencies to behave in certain ways alone won't accomplish this goal, for stimulus-response patterns of behavior are often silent, so to speak, about the motive through which they route, as we saw in the pre-vious chapter. Contrary to Wright's claim, then, reference to behavioral dispositions alone fails to explain purposive behavior; reference to mental life itself is necessary to determine whether a particular purposive behav-ior is an action and, if so, what type. Because dispositions to behave in certain ways are not uniquely correlated with mental items, a strictly em-pirical, behaviorist account of purposive action will not do.

According to Wright, we appeal to mental items only to be able to characterize S's (otherwise unintelligible) behavior intelligibly. But in situ-ations such as cases (3) and (4) above, how would the experimenter even know in a particular case that appealing to mental items is necessary? How would the experimenter be able to determine that he even needs to appeal to mental items when the subject's overt behavior exhibits such apparently straightforward "systematic arrangement about a goal-object"? We do not appeal to mental states to explain the incredible complexity of behavioral patterns that one has (antecedently) recognized. On the contrary, we come to believe that there is a "complexity" to be resolved in the behavioral manifestations because we already suspect that there is (or might be) a difference in the agent's motivation, that is, in the agent's mental life. We do not infer a difference in mental states to characterize differences in the dispositional tendencies themselves because, as the example is formulated, there are no empirically detectable differences in the stimulus-response patterns. On the contrary, we can characterize the two examples of behavior as "different" (actions) only because we have independently identified a difference in the mental states in which the behavior originated.

In conclusion, like Melden's, Wright's analysis (1) cannot take into account behavior that is unique but nevertheless purposive, (2) cannot accurately identify the precise goal of teleological behavior, and (3) will often be unable to identify behavior as purposive even though it is. I conclude that Wright's *analysans* does not successfully analyze the *analysandum*.

Behaviorist accounts described in these last two chapters attempted to reduce intelligent action to persistent yet plastic behavioral patterns. In analyzing away the concept of goalhood, behaviorists tried to bypass such ghostly and private notions as having a goal, awareness, and intention. Instead, Humean regularities—empirically determinable, persistent and plastic convergence of behavior toward an end—were offered as constitutive of goalhood and intentionality. However, as we saw in connection with theories that emphasize plasticity of behavior as a mark of goal-directedness, the appropriateness of varying purposive behavior often diminishes as it closes in on the goal. Often, in fact, behavior is appropriately goal-directed precisely because it is, at the right moment, no longer plastic. Even in such cases, however, the behavior continues to exhibit means-end purposiveness. In addition, as mentioned earlier, agents often try to reach a goal but do not succeed. The end toward which the behavior is aimed need not actually be attained; the behavior would nonetheless qualify as an act-token (even if characterized as "trying" behavior).

A final objection to behaviorist approaches to action should also be mentioned: as Charles Taylor noted, behaviorist treatments of persistence betray an implicit mechanism and atomism: "The concept of diachronic persistence [is] constructed out of a series of synchronic plasticity conditionals" (Woodfield 1976, 96). It is therefore logically possible that whereas the organism's behavior is goal-directed at t_1, t_3, and t_5, it is not goal directed at t_2, t_4, and t_6, no matter how appropriate that behavior is to the goal, if, as the spastic counterexample showed, the behavior performed on even moments was accidental. Observers would no doubt attribute goal-directedness on the basis of the overall pattern revealed over time, but they would be mistaken: extraneous factors can always intervene between the discrete units into which persistence has been analyzed, producing a variation of the nervous nephew–type wayward causal chain objection, and thereby disqualifying the analysis. The same can be said of Wilson's (1989) claim that actions are goal-intended, but not necessarily caused by intentions.

To summarize: behaviorists' analyses of both the intentions that cause actions and of their purposiveness are vulnerable to objections that turn on the agent's state of mind, or at the very least, on the agents' minimal awareness of what they are doing, and their ability to guide and monitor their behavior in light of this awareness. Just because behavior can appear to fit a pattern does not guarantee that it constitutes intentional action; the pattern might just have come about accidentally. The central reason for judging behaviorist analyses of action deficient, therefore, is that implicit in the concept of action is that the agent must have voluntarily and intentionally brought about the pattern. "Bringing about a pattern," however, presupposes the concept of action and thus cannot be its *analysans*.

I close this chapter by noting one positive contribution of behaviorism that is rarely remarked on: behaviorism resuscitated the role that the environment plays in action. Contextual embeddedness had been an important component in Aristotle's understanding of action, but was discarded by modern philosophy's emphasis on primary qualities as the only reality. As discussed earlier, once final and formal causes were also thrown out, the efficient cause of intentional action was held to be entirely "within" the agent, as either a nonphysical mind with free will, or a complex structure or pattern of neurological events that pushed something else (the rest of the body) into action.[25] By suggesting that behavior is somehow connected to and dependent on events in the environment, behaviorism clearly emphasized the role that context plays in the life of organisms. But bringing context back into the picture as behaviorists attempted requires a type of cause much different from the collision-like trigger of mechanics. Lacking such an understanding of cause, and reinforced in their Aristotelian conviction that causes are external to their effects, logical behaviorists never quite embedded the agent in the environment to create an integral organism-context system. They just plunked the organism in the environment and assumed that when the appropriate stimulus occurred, boom! the organism would automatically respond. Even Peters recognized that appropriate behavior cannot be reduced to mere constant conjunction.

The End of Behaviorism

With the Humean view of explanation as deduction firmly entrenched, "if not predictable not explained" remains the reigning standard to which all disciplines aspire. And so, several decades after the heyday of behaviorism but with no strict covering law (not even a probabilistic one) capturing regularities between empirical circumstances and human behavior on the horizon, the conclusion appeared inescapable: "Human behavior is inexplicable." But recent research in nonlinear dynamical systems suggests, on the contrary, that if organisms are more like tornadoes or even "chaotic" systems than like glass or planets, behaviorism's ideal was doomed from the start. The reason is that in open systems that exchange matter and energy with their environment, feedback embeds them in that environment in such a way that they are simultaneously context-dependent and initiators of behavior. As a result, their trajectories are unique.

The type of causal relations required to explain the relationship between organisms and their environment—and its past—must be able to account for the way organisms simultaneously participate in and shape the contextual niche in which they are situated, and to which their dispositions are attuned and respond. Developmentally as well as evolutionarily, parts interact to create systems that in turn affect their components: interlevel causality, in other words. But given contemporary philosophy's inability to provide either a satisfactory understanding of this type of nonlinear causality, a form of self-cause, or to take contextual and historical embeddedness seriously, contemporary efforts in action theory have reflected this flaw. As a result they continue to find the going rough indeed. What is needed, therefore, is an account of causality (1) for which mental cause and behavioral effect are internally related to each other, the way genotype and phenotype are interwoven with each other and into the environment, and (2) that can account for the way causes can flow into their effects. Part II will attempt to offer just such an account of causality.

Before we set out on that road, however, two concepts commonly used by communications engineers, noise and equivocation, offer intriguing applications to the problem of action. A look at the theory behind a development that has dramatically changed the lives of everyday people will therefore be useful. The next chapter is devoted to an examination of some concepts borrowed from information theory.

Chapter 6

Information Theory and the Problem of Action

In 1948, Claude Shannon published two papers that examined the problem of transmitting information. Curiously, the equation he formulated to calculate the amount of information involved was formally identical to Ludwig Boltzmann's (1877) thermodynamic equation. Despite repeated warnings that the information of information theory has nothing to do with meaning (a warning to which we will return later), the similarity in the form of the two equations led many thinkers to postulate a connection between the two. Boltzmann even called entropy "missing information."

Why is information theory an important first step toward understanding the way intentional causes issue in action? The flaws of both causal and behaviorist accounts of action described in chapters 1 through 5 highlighted the importance of and need for a casually efficacious cognitive source that doesn't disengage once it triggers behavior, but rather guides and directs (in-forms) by flowing into behavior. To understand action, that is, we need an account of the way an intention's meaningful content constrains behavior such that the former flows uninterruptedly into the latter. Teleological characterizations of intentional behavior respected this information flow. Attempted behaviorist reductions of teleology, on the other hand, did not; they placed no importance on the mental state from which action originates and flows. And neither behaviorism nor the view of cause as the instantaneous forceful impact of intentions or volitions on motor processes was able to account for the ongoing direction and monitoring that intentions and volitions exercise on behavior.

Unlike behaviorist theories but like causal ones, on the one hand, information theory emphasizes the way decision processes generate a message. On the other, in contrast to theories that think of causes as instantaneous impacts, information theory is also centrally concerned with the need to transmit those messages without error. By tracking information flow, communications engineers can determine the extent to which message received is dependent upon message transmitted. The relationship is calculated by measuring two quantities: noise and equivocation. The appeal of looking to information theory, therefore, comes from the way it can offer action theorists a useful way of thinking of action as an unequivocal trajectory. By providing a way of measuring the waywardness of deviant causal chains, it can also show (1) why behaviorists failed to account for the importance of the cognitive source in which the behavioral trajectory originates and (2) why volitionists and other causal theorists failed to account for the importance of the flow of meaning from intention or volition to behavioral outcome. In this chapter I describe the way information theory handles information flow.

Information Theory: A Brief Introduction

Consider the following situation:

> There are eight employees and one of them must perform some unpleasant task. Their employer has left the nasty business of selecting the unfortunate individual up to the group itself, asking only to be informed of the outcome once the decision is made....
>
> Imagine that the group agreed to make their selection by flipping a coin. In order to accomplish this, they divided themselves into two groups of four and flipped the coin to determine the group from which a further selection would be made. Once this was decided by the first flip, they subdivided the unlucky group of four into two smaller groups, each consisting of two individuals. A second flip of the coin determined from which of these two groups the final selection would be made. A third toss of the coin settled the matter between the two remaining contestants, and Herman was the unhappy survivor. If we treat tosses of the coin as the number of decisions or choices that are made in reducing the competitors from eight to one, we get the number 3.... It takes three *binary digits* (bits), one binary digit (0 or 1) for each flip of the coin ... to completely specify the reduction of eight possibilities to one. The amount of information associated with the fact that Herman was selected is 3 bits. (Dretske 1981, 4–5)

Let n be the number of possibilities available. Let s (the *source*) be "some mechanism or process the result of which is the reduction of n equally likely possibilities to 1." Let $I(s)$ be the amount of information associated with, or generated by, the employees' decision procedure at s. $I(s)$ is calculated by

$$I(s) = \log n,$$

"where log is the logarithm to the base 2" (7). In the Herman example, $I(s) = 3$ bits.

The employer receives a note with the name "Herman" written on it. Since the note could have had any one of eight names on it, the amount of information the employer receives, $I(r)$, is also 3 bits. In this first case: $I(s) = I(r)$. Now

> [c]hange the example slightly. The employees scrawl the name "Herman" on the memo and give it to a new, careless messenger. On his way to the employer's office the messenger loses the memo. He knows the message contained the name of one of the employees but does not remember which one. Rather than return for a new note, he writes the name "Herman" on a sheet of paper and delivers it.... No information is transmitted from (s) to (r).... Another way of expressing this is to say that there is no information at (r) about (s). (Dretske 1981, 15–16)

The 3 bits of information that the employer receives in the careless-messenger case happens to be equal to the amount of information generated at the source. But the former did not come from the decision procedure that generated the latter. The example recalls the wayward causal chains described in chapter 2.

Noise and Equivocation

So if we want to track the flow of information from s to r, more important than "How much information did the employer receive?" is the question, "Of the information generated at s, $I(s)$, how much of it arrives at r?" (15). How much of the information available at r depends on what happened at s?

We can think of the information available at r that depends on whatever happened at s as information that flowed from source to receiver. Call it $I_s(r)$. In contrast, *noise* is a measure of the amount of information available at r—$I(r)$—that is independent of s, that is, that did not flow from s. Similarly, *equivocation* is a measure of the amount of information generated at s—$I(s)$—that does not reach r.

Let r_i represent the name that appears on the note to the employer, and s_i the name that is selected by the employees. Suppose there are eight alternatives at s, and the seventh one is that Herman's name is chosen; suppose there are eight alternatives at r and the seventh one is that Herman's name appears on the note. The conditional probability that Herman's name appears on the note to the employer r_7 given that Herman was selected by the employees s_7 is computed by $P(r_7/s_7)$. The conditional probability that Herman was selected by the employees given that his name appears on the note is computed by $P(s_7/r_7)$. s_7's contribution to noise (N) is calculated with the formula

$$N(s_7) = -\sum P(r_i/s_7) \log P(r_i/s_7).$$

Since in the original example the conditional probability of $P(r_7/s_7)$ is unity (and the logarithm of 1 is 0), $N(s_7)$ is 0. s_7 contributes nothing to noise.

Average noise N is calculated by summing the contributions to noise of each of the individual s's and weighting them according to the probability of their occurrence. In the careful messenger scenario, there is no possibility that a name other than "Herman" might appear on the note. Since the probability that any other name will appear is zero, given that Herman was autually selected by the exployees, and since all other s's contributions to noise also equal zero, average noise is zero. There is no noise.

By calculating average noise we can establish whether a given source, say s_7, uniquely issues in one particular outcome r_7. When average noise equals zero, we know that the information generated by a particular source flowed to only one outcome (since the conditional probability of that outcome, given the particular source, is one). Since the conditional probability of any other possible outcome equals zero, we also learn that no other outcome was possible, given that particular source.

The equation for computing equivocation is similar. The conditional probability that Herman was selected by the employees (s_7) given that his name appeared on the note (r_7) is the probability that s_7 was the source given that r_7 was the outcome, $P(s_7/r_7)$.

r_7's contribution to equivocation (E) is calculated with the formula

$$E(r_7) = - \sum P(s_i/r_7) \log P(s_i/r_7).$$

Since in the original example the conditional probability of $P(s_7/r_7)$ is unity (and the logarithm of 1 is 0), $E(r_7)$ is 0. r_7 contributes nothing to equivocation.

Average equivocation E is calculated by summing the contributions to equivocation of each of the individual r's and weighting them according to the probability of their occurrence. In the careful messenger scenario, the information the employer receives could not have come from a source other than the employees' decision procedure. Since the probability that any other source might have produced the note (given that the name "Herman" appeared on it) is zero, and since all other r's contributions to equivocation also equal zero, average equivocation is zero. There is no equivocation.

Determining the presence of equivocation allows us to calculate whether information available at a particular outcome, say (r_7), is uniquely attributable to the information generated at a given source, say (s_7). When equivocation equals zero, we learn that the information available at the output flowed from a particular source (since the conditional probability of that source is one, given the actual outcome). Since the conditional probability of any other possible source equals zero, we also learn that no other origin was possible, given that particular outcome.

By using a calculus of conditional probability, it is therefore possible to estimate the extent to which information available at the output was constrained by information generated at the source. The presence of equivocation and noise, that is, provides a way of tracking what can be called information flow. It does so by calculating how much of the information available at the outcome depends on information generated at the source. It is important to emphasize that the concept of information flow does not reify information. Information flow is only a measure of the relationship between an outcome and a given source: if all the information generated at s is received at r, no equivocation is present. If all the information available at r came from s, there is no noise. If some (or all) of the information generated at the source fails to get through, or if the information available at r is noise that did not flow from the source, then $I(r) \neq I_s(r)$. The information flow described by $I_s(r)$ is therefore a measure of the constraints that the origin imposes on the outcome.

There will always be extraneous noise at the output. Suppose that the note on which the name "Herman" was written is on black-bordered white paper. Suppose also that the employer believes that the employees have a choice of eight paper colors. According to information theory, the information at the receiver's end (I_r), carries three additional bits of information about the memo's paper. The employer concludes: "The employees chose white paper with a black border around it—mourning stationery. Hmmm, they must be very disgruntled." Suppose, however, that the employees had just run out of all other paper, so $I(r) \neq I_s(r)$. The information about black-bordered white paper is in fact noise because no such "reduction of possibilities" took place at the source. No such information was generated at s.

The presence of noise at the receiver's end, however,[26] need not interfere with the transmission of the full message as long as equivocation = 0, in other words, as long as none of the relevant information generated at the source is lost in transmission. Noise can contribute to equivocation. For example (Dretske 1981, 21), the radio report "There will be rain on Sunday (snap, crackle, pop, hiss)" has noise but no equivocation. The original message gets through intact. In contrast, "There will be rain on (snap) nday (crackle, pop, hiss)" has the same amount of noise; but it is also equivocal: given the actual sounds, it is unclear what message (Sunday or Monday?) was transmitted by the source. Because in the careless-messenger version both equivocation and noise are at a maximum, none of the information generated at the source flows to the output, and none of the information available at the output came from the source. In that case $I_s(r) = 0$.[27]

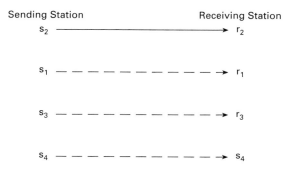

Figure 6.1
The solid arrow between s_2 and r_2 indicates a causal connection; the broken lines indicate causal connections that could have existed but do not actually take place.
Source: From Dretske 1981, p. 28. Reproduced by permission of MIT Press.

Cause versus Information

The concepts of noise and equivocation have significant application to the problem of action. Consider the classic example discussed earlier: I move a finger, thereby flipping a light switch, which turns on the light and in the process startles Smith. Suppose I did intend to turn on the light by moving a finger, but did not intend to startle Smith. Are these all the "same event"? Are they all "among my actions"? As we saw earlier, the answer is often given in terms of the role played by causality: I moved my hand as an act-token if an intention (belief, motive, reason) caused my hand to move. As we saw in chapter 2, however, the received understanding of efficient cause makes a classically causal approach to action vulnerable to the "wayward causal chain," "infinite regress," and "reasons are not causes" objections. Each of these difficulties disappears if actions are understood in terms of the uninterrupted flow of information from intention into behavior, $I_s(r)$.

The difference between informational and causal relations explains why causal models do not succeed (as causal) in explaining action. Consider figure 6.1. The solid line indicates the causal connection that actually took place. The broken lines represent causal connections that could have occurred but did not. Since four possibilities at the source are reduced to one, 2 bits of information are generated at the source. $I(s_2) = 2$. For the same reason, the outcome also carries 2 bits of information. $I(r_2) = 2$. Since only s_2 could have produced r_2, there is no equivocation. Since only r_2 could have come from s_2, there is no noise. Now consider a second variation, as shown in figure 6.2. As was the case in figure 6.1, since four equally probable possibilities exist at the source (s_1 through s_4), $I(s_2) = 2$

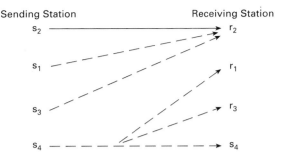

Figure 6.2
Source: From Dretske 1981, p. 28. Reproduced by permission of MIT Press.

bits. Unlike figure 6.1, however, although there is no noise in the case of r_2, equivocation (1.6 bits) is present because r_2 could also have come about as a result of s_1 or s_3.

> Hence, r_2 carries only .4 bits of information about s. Given what *actually* happens, and the causal relationships that *actually* obtain, this situation cannot be distinguished from the previous one. None-theless, in informational terms they are quite different. The causal story … does not tell us how much information is transmitted because it fails to tell us whether the causal sequence is embedded in a network of possibilities similar to that depicted in Figure [6.1] or [6.2]. (Dretske 1981, 29)[28]

Because r_1, r_3 or r_4 could come about only as a result of s_4, each of those three outcomes (unlike r_2) carries the full amount of information generated by its source. That is, each carries complete information about the decision procedure at s_4. In cases r_1, r_3, and r_4, there is no equivoca-tion, but since s_4 does not uniquely identify its outcome, there is noise. What have we thus far?

> 1. Information generated at a source may be lost in transmission; when this happens the output will be equivocal. Conversely, infor-mation available to the receiver may be information which was not generated by the transmitter (noise).
> 2. The signal picked up by the receiver may or may not carry infor-mation about the source of the signal.

Equivocation and Wayward Causal Chains

The "wayward causal chain" objections discussed earlier are vivid illus-trations of the mischief equivocation and noise can occasion. Chisholm's nephew, it will be recalled, after much deliberation finally resolves (while driving) to kill his uncle. The decision causes him such agitation that he accidentally kills a pedestrian—who happens to be his uncle! The example was meant to show that although the killing can be causally traced to (and semantically satisfies) the intention to do so, the young man did not murder his uncle.

Performing the appropriate calculations on Chisholm's example shows why. Because the outcome does not uniquely determine its source, equivocation is present: the conditional probability that another possibility (the nervous agitation) caused the uncle's death is greater than zero. Despite being able to *causally* trace $I(r)$ to $I(s)$, and even if the amount of information available at $I(s)$ equals that at $I(r)$, in this case the noise introduced by the accident brought on by the nephew's nervous agitation *has* compromised information flow. As a result, the uncle's death cannot unequivocally be attributed to the nephew's intention. That is why we are uncomfortable with saying that he killed his uncle as an action. The distinction between informational dependence and cause can thus explain why we intuitively disqualify the outcome of wayward causal chains as act-tokens. Wayward causal chains are the result of extraneous generators of information that make one or more of the other terms in the expansion contribute positively to average equivocation.

Trying Behavior

Analogously, the concepts of noise and equivocation can account for trying behavior. A semiparalyzed patient's unsuccessful attempt to move his legs is due to noise and equivocation. The conditional probability that he will move his legs, given his efforts, is less than one. The conditional probability that his volition will be ineffective given the semiparalysis, is greater than zero.

Equivocation and the Self-Referentiality Thesis

We saw in chapter 2 that several authors tried to preempt those wayward causal chain objections by what Mele (1992) called the "self-referentiality thesis." Searle (1983, 85), for example, claimed that the content of my intention to raise my left arm includes as a condition of its satisfaction that I perform the action of raising my arm by way of carrying out this intention. Similarly, Gilbert Harman (1976, 441) maintained that the intention responsible for intentional action is "the intention that, because of that very intention, one will do A." Intentions-in-action, that is, specify in their very content the conditions of satisfaction of those intentions. The point of incorporating the intention's causal role into its very content was to guarantee that the behavior issued from that intention and no other source. The idea was to ensure that no deviant causal chains occur. Mele (1992) correctly objected to this approach, however, on the grounds that people's intentions are not usually that explicitly specified. Instead, it will be recalled, Mele attempted to explain action as the effects of ongoing intentions. However, he provided no account of causality that incorporates the sustaining and guiding features that such intentions would require.

Viewed from an information-theoretic perspective, appeals to self-referentiality are attempts to ensure that equivocation does not compromise information flow from intention to execution. Requiring that action be unequivocal accommodates the spirit of the self-referentiality thesis, as does thinking of action as information flow. By defining action not as the effects of a special type of efficient cause, but as the unequivocal flow of an intention's content from cognitive source to behavioral terminus, wayward causal chain objections can be preempted. In part II, I will flesh out this idea in more detail, but before doing so, it is important to show how thinking of an action as an uncompromised trajectory from intentional source to behavioral outcome—a flow whose integrity can be determined by calculating the presence of noise and equivocation—can satisfactorily handle many of the problems on which causal and behaviorist accounts of action have floundered.

Basic Acts as I(r): The Behaviorists

By thinking of action as a trajectory $I_s(r)$, and by calculating the interference of noise and equivocation in terms of the relationship between output and origin, it is possible to explain what is wrongheaded about both the behaviorist and volitionist approaches to action. Behaviorism emphasizes lawful regularities between an environmental stimulus and ensuing behavior. Information theory, in contrast, holds that the import of events at the receiver's end is conditional upon their informational heritage. Message reliability depends on the output's unequivocal link to or dependence upon an informational source, not mere constant conjunction.

So too with action. The meaning of a mouse's behavior—that it is fleeing from a predator, say—depends upon its relation to the mouse's "internal states" (the rodent's analog of belief). Classifying behavior as "flight" requires determining the behavior's "appropriateness" to the perceived situation, as Aristotle had pointed out. As we saw in chapters 4 and 5, appropriateness as flight cannot be determined without referring to the relationship between the behavior and an intentional source: the animal's internal state, fear, for example. In contrast to reflex behavior such as twitches, actions are conditional upon their origin, that is, on the behavior's unequivocal dependence on an intentional source. Behavior $I(r)$ constitutes an act-token only insofar as its performance was dependent upon and constrained by the agent's intention, that is, only insofar as the behavior embodies the *flow* of that meaningful intention: $I_s(r)$.

Larry Wright's attempted behaviorist reduction of the purposiveness of action was discussed in chapter 5. Wright insisted, correctly, that it is necessary to determine that the behavior issued from a particular cause and no other. But that is impossible if only events that are independent of each other are involved, even if they are constantly conjoined. From the point of view of information flow, we can now appreciate why: explanations of action that identify only the information available at r, excluding both information generated at the source and $I(r)$'s dependence on $I(s)$, will be unsatisfactory, the reason being that from an information-theoretic perspective, as figure 6.2 illustrates, the possibility of equivocation shows that "[a]n effect ... may or may not carry information about its cause" (Dretske 1981, 31).[29] But for behavior to qualify as action, that uncompromised flow must be assured. The only way to do that, we now see, is by making the behavioral outcome dependent on the intentional source. Doing so satisfies Wright's claims about the etiology of actions without running into the problems that independent events encounter.

Basic Acts as $I(s)$: The Volitionists

Volitionists like H. A. Prichard insisted that acts of will are the basic act-tokens. In contrast to the behaviorists' emphasis on both the information available at the receiver's end and the stimuli that trigger it, volitionists made the mistake of stressing only the role of the internal, cognitive source, the willing. Viewed from an information-theoretic perspective, that is, radical volitionists held that, regardless of all other considerations, $I(s)$ of a particular sort automatically constitutes action. Volitionists seemed to believe that what you will when you will cannot or does not flow into behavior. In doing so, volitionists, too, ignored the flow of the content of that volition into behavior. They ignored $I_s(r)$; that is, they paid no attention to the way the behavior is dependent on or constrained by its source or origin. That is why volitionists like Davis (1979) claimed that whatever behavior the volition causes automatically qualifies as an act-token: it is an effect of a cause that is already an act-token. But as we saw, Davis placed no requirements on the integrity of the flow between volitional source and behavioral terminus. And why should he have, if all causes are supposedly instantaneous Newtonian events? As such, they cannot inform behavior.

In other words, volitionists placed no restrictions on whether or how the content of volitions flows into behavior. As a result, Davis was willing to call "action" behavior that we would intuitively consider non-action. Recall his example of a diabolical neurologist who rewires Sam's nerves so that when he wills to move his arm, his leg moves. Conceptualizing action as a trajectory $I_s(r)$ explains not only what goes wrong with Davis's view but also what truth there is to it. First, since despite his willing to move his *arm* it was the subject's *leg* that moved, equivocation and noise are at a maximum (i.e., none of the original message—"move arm"—makes it through, and the message received—"move leg"—is completely independent of what the source transmitted). $I_s(r)$ equals zero. Although there may have been a causal chain between volition and leg movement, the latter is not dependent upon the former (i.e., "move leg" could have been the received output whether the source's input was "move arm" or "move leg"). That is, the information carried by the behavior is not unequivocally about the decision procedure that took place at the source. $I(r)$ is independent of $I(s)$ and thus does not carry information about the process that generated the volition "move arm." In short, the behavior does not carry reliable information about Sam's act of will. Hence, the leg movement is equivocal, and it is therefore not action. In informational language, in short, moderate volitionists failed to take into account the potentially disruptive influence of noise and equivocation. What and how much information generated by the volition actually flows into behavior was dismissed as unimportant.

If the diabolical neurophysiologist is absent, and Sam's neurological condition is normal, once Sam wills to move his arm, he will move his arm, not his leg. In the absence of extraneous interfering factors, the conditional probability of other possibilities at s will equal zero. Under normal circumstances, that is, equivocation is presumed to be absent. Both the alleged logical connection between intention and action, and the consensus that basic actions must be intentionally performed, suggest that the conditional probability of a particular intention s *given* behavior r must equal one. They imply that the conditional probability of any other possibility at the source—that is, interference by a neurologist, paralysis, and the like—must equal zero.

In examples like that of the neurophysiologist's rewiring, $I_s(r)$ is zero even if the limb the subject willed to move is the one that actually moves, that is, even when $I(r)$ equals $I(s)$. Why? Because the neurophysiologist's activity (or the paralysis) introduces noise and equivocation. A traditionally causal connection between an act of will and its behavioral effect, and the fact that the cause is a volition (as opposed to an intention), do not prevent the flow of information from source to output from being compromised. Because of the noise introduced by Davis's neurologist, Sam's behavior (r) is not unequivocally dependent on his act of will. Because of the noise caused by the paralysis in the second example, the agent's act of will does not flow into behavior. If Sam's movements are conditional upon the neurophysiologist's rewiring, whether he willed to move his arm or his leg is a moot issue. The behavior does not qualify as Sam's basic action because it was not dependent on his volition. A basic action thus tells an informational, not an efficiently causal, story: intention flowed into behavior without equivocation. Because of an outcome's informational dependence on a source (a relationship that can be calculated in terms of conditional probabilities), intention and action are therefore not just externally or accidentally related.

I conclude that (1) no traditionally causal account of action will tell us whether behavior is like figure 6.1 or 6.2. Furthermore, (2) no detailed examination of only the nature of the cause (that is, whether it is a volition, belief, intention, motive, purpose, reason, or any combination thereof) will satisfactorily account for action if it ignores the flow of information generated from that source. That is, if the actual behavior's relationship to and unequivocal dependence upon that volition, intention, and so forth, is not established, the behavior will not have been explained as action, because actions, as I will argue in part II, are networks of relationships. And (3) wayward causal chains between intention (s) and basic behavior (r) as well as examples of so-called trying behavior are cases in which $I_s(r)$ is less than one. It is for these reasons that none of the resulting behaviors qualifies as action.

Basic Actions and Neurological Activity: The Communications Channel

I cannot move my hand as a (basic) action unless certain neurons and muscles are activated. Activating the neurons and muscles themselves, however, is normally not my action because neuronal and muscular processes are not (and often cannot be) the objects of intentions, volitions, and so forth. Following Dretske (1981), we can call the link joining the source and the receiver the *communications channel*. Whether physically embodied or not, communications channels, by definition, generate no information of their own; they merely transmit the information generated by the source. They provide only the conditions that "qualify as the framework *within which* communication takes place; [they are not] a source *about which* communication takes place" (116). $I(r)$ therefore includes no information about the channel along which the information is transmitted.

If basic act-tokens are conceived as the most fundamental level in which behavior (r) carries full information about its cognitive, meaningful origins (s), the concept of a communications channel explains why those lower-level neurological and muscular processes by means of which we perform a basic action are not themselves components of the act-token. By merely transmitting and not generating any new information on their own, lower-level neuromuscular processes constitute the communications channel, which, in this case, happens to be physically embodied. The fact that information can be carried by a vehicle or medium that itself does not generate information explains why I can know that I did *what* I willed (intended, and so forth) without knowing *how* I did it. I may be aware of the reduction of possibilities at the cognitive source from which information was generated, but know nothing about the channel along which that information was transmitted.

Consider another semiparalyzed patient undergoing physical therapy. The therapist moves the patient's legs, one after the other, all the while reminding the patient, "keep trying to do it yourself." At some point the patient's own effort suffices to move the legs, even in the absence of the therapist's activity. From that moment on, because the leg movements are dependent on the agent's effort, the behavior qualifies as "action." The movements occurred in virtue of the informational content of the appropriate source: the agent's volition.[30]

Now consider yet another case. A patient wakes up in a hospital bed to find that both legs have been amputated and he has been fitted with sophisticated prosthetic devices. The first few steps the patient takes are caused not by his intention but by the therapist as she electrically activates the prosthetic devices so that the patient will "get the feel" of it. No basic act-token is performed. After months of intensive physical therapy, however, the patient can intentionally activate the prostheses and walk. In time it becomes "second nature" such that he is not even aware of walking by activating the prostheses; he "just walks" as a basic action.

The earlier steps were not dependent on the same source as are the patient's movements once he becomes adept at utilizing the prostheses. Once that happens, however, if the effort he makes is faithfully routed through the prosthetic devices, is the patient's intention "move leg" sustaining the behavior? Is it action? Clearly, in the absence of the prosthetic devices the intention would not suffice for the actual walking movements. So are we not in the same situation as in the diabolical neurophysiologist example mentioned earlier?

I believe the correct answer is that in situations like this prosthetic devices can become part of the communications channel, about which they generate no information. What counts as a communication channel is a relative matter: "[conditions] function as part of the channel for as long as their [persistence] in the fixed condition generates no new information" (Dretske 1981, 118), and channel conditions generate no information when *"there are no (relevant) possible alternatives"* (115, emphasis mine). That is why the diabolical neurophysiologist example is different from the prosthesis example: Insofar as the rewiring itself causes the movement, the neurophysiologist's presence and activity introduce relevant

new possibilities, thereby generating additional information—noise—
that in this case does compromise information flow. This was also true,
however, of the early stages of the prosthesis example. So why not allow
that, in time, so will the neurophysiologist's patient?

It *would* be allowable if, after some time, the patient in the neurophysiologist rewiring case "got the hang of it" and realized, for instance,
that to move his leg he must (ostensibly) will to move his arm. For behavior generated in this manner to constitute action, however, the rewiring
must be permanent and persist in a fixed condition. If not (as was the case
in the original example), the rewiring would itself generate new information and the behavior would again become equivocal—and nonaction.
Once the rewiring becomes a channel condition, however, the corresponding term in the equation would equal zero, and the term corresponding to
the volition would equal one. So once the rewiring contributed nothing to
equivocation, the behavior would indeed qualify as an act-token because
it would be uniquely dependent on and related to the agent's intention.
And this is the kernel of truth that Davis has going for him. But as Davis
formulates the example, because of the neurophysiologist's interference
and the paralysis, the volition's share is less than one. The interference of
both noise and equivocation explains the uneasiness we feel in calling the
behavior of Davis's patient "action."

The Agent's Privileged Access

Information theory can also account for the relatively privileged status of
an agent's truthful claim of what he did as action. "What makes $I_s(r)$ [the
amount of information reaching the receiver that is known to be reliable]
a relative quantity is ... what the receiver knows about the situation *at*
the source about which he is getting information" (Dretske 1981, 81). In
similar fashion, the known reliability of the claim that a particular instance
of behavior is action also depends on special knowledge about the
goings-on at the source. When different neurological patterns can underlie
the same thought, multiple realizability decouples those brain processes in
which mental events are realized as neural from the contents of those
mental events. If several different neurological patterns can carry out the
same type of intention, *to do x*, say, then none of those neurological patterns as such can be equated or identified with the intention to do *x*. The
decoupling effectively turns the neural processes—as neural—into the
communications channel. As a result, neurological processes as such may
be unavailable to introspection, even if the thoughts and intentions are.

What is known about the possibilities at the source is not the same for
all receivers; at times only the agents themselves can precisely establish

the value of $I(s)$. In those cases only they can tell whether the output signal is reliable, that is, whether the message received at the output is a faithful transmission of the message generated at the source: whether $I(r) = I_s(r)$. Since the agents' cognitive states generate the message, they, unlike witnesses, will have special information about $I(s)$. That is, agents sometimes can have exclusive background knowledge about (1) which alternatives were considered, and (2) the method of reduction of possibilities. The agent is thus in a relatively privileged position to determine the value of $I(s)$, and therefore whether $I_s(r) = 1$.

The importance that background knowledge—of what took place at the source, $I(s)$—has for determining $I_s(r)$, and therefore for determining whether or not an act-token was performed, is dramatically illustrated in Wilder Penfield's research (1975) on epileptic patients mentioned at the beginning of the book. With patients under anesthesia, their brains exposed, Penfield induced speech by stimulating specific areas of the patient's brain. The patient's reaction, however, was to exclaim, "I didn't say that; you pulled it out of me!" The patient's knowledge about the situation at the source (that he had not meant to say what he did, that is, that there had been no such reduction of possibilities by a cognitive source) justified his protest that the behavior was not his action. The patient knew that $I(r)$ did not unequivocally identify $I(s)$, and so $I_s(r)$ equaled zero. Often, in other words, only the subject can tell whether and what information available at r is noise and whether equivocation has been introduced. Penfield's cases highlight the fact that behavior is an act-token only insofar as it consists in the flow of information from a cognitive source into behavior.

An observer may come to believe that a persistent pattern of behavior suggests that the agent's motive all along was, for example, ambition. As counterexamples formulated in chapters 4 and 5 showed, however, the agent might legitimately claim, "Yes, yes, I know it looks like ambition, but I can assure you that in this particular case it wasn't!" Another might reply, "You're just deceiving yourself!" When external observers such as psychologists accuse someone of self-deception or unconscious motives, they are claiming that they can more accurately identify what took place at $I(s)$ than the agent can. But how would psychologists go about doing so? Only "ensembles" of empirically observable trajectories display a detectable pattern. If, as I believe is true, the ensemble of a person's actions reflects his or her character, observers can determine that this particular instance of behavior fits or is in keeping with that overall pattern. And when this occurs, we will judge the behavior to be "in character." But, to repeat, as we saw in chapters 4 and 5, unique, once-in-a-lifetime behavior, by definition, does not conform to a pattern.

Act Individuation

Thinking of action as $I_s(r)$ is also useful in handling the problem of act individuation (usually classified as a subset of the problem of individuating events). Davidson (1967) is well-known for having suggested the following criterion for act-individuation: two events, e_1 and e_2, are identical only if they take place over the same time period.

> "I didn't know it was loaded" belongs to one standard pattern of excuse. I do not deny that I pointed the gun and pulled the trigger, nor that I shot the victim. My ignorance explains how it happened that I pointed the gun and pulled the trigger intentionally, but did not shoot the victim intentionally. That the bullet pierced the victim was a consequence of my pointing the gun and pulling the trigger. It is clear that these are two different events, since one began slightly after the other. But what is the relation between my pointing the gun and pulling the trigger, and my shooting the victim? The natural and, I think, correct answer is that the relation is that of identity. (109)

On this view, simultaneity serves as the criterion of act individuation. Claiming that two simultaneous event-descriptions identify the "same" act-token makes Davidson a "unifier."

Applying information theory to action, on the contrary, yields a "multiplier" position. From the informational perspective proposed earlier, act-tokens differ from "mere behavior" insofar as the former consist in the intentional content's unequivocal trajectory $I_s(r)$ into behavior. As event, then, behavior is different than as act-token because the latter describes a different trajectory than the former. Act-tokens should be individuated, I now propose, by the exact trajectory they traverse, beginning with the information generated by an intention, along the particular pathway constrained by that intention, to its expression in behavior. Information captured by (in) that information generation and flow is (part of) the same action; all extraneous information available at the behavioral output is noise and must be excluded from the act-token. Information generated by the intention that fails to flow into behavior signals the presence of equivocation and compromises the trajectory. Thinking of act-tokens as processes that originate in the decision procedure of a cognitive source, flow along a trajectory, and terminate (if completed) at a sink anticipated by the cognitive content of the origin that directs and constrains the behavior has several distinct advantages. First, it provides a principled way to decide whether unintentional, nonbasic behavior is an act-token at all. One example from action theory is provided by those generated nonbasic event descriptions that could not have flowed from or been dependent upon an intentional source because they were not contemplated at all. For example, if I happen to move a lot of molecules of air *in* moving my hand, that event is noise if I did not intend to do so. Hence, although it will always be possible to include "noisy" information in a correct (as $I(r)$) description of the behavior, these additional bits would be excluded from a description of the behavior as act-token (as $I_s(r)$).[31] As noted in the careless-messenger case, any actual performance will be accompanied by extraneous information that was not generated at the source, noise. The trick is to determine whether that noise also compromised the integrity of the trajectory.

Judith Jarvis Thomson (1971) coined the notion of "act stretches" and suggested that the "time" of a killing (carried out in this case with a gun) should include both the time of the pulling of the trigger as well as the time of the bullet's penetrating the victim. The time stretch covering the "shooting," however, is not identical to the time stretch spanned by the "killing"; the former excludes both the bullet's penetration and the death of the victim. In Thomson's example, the time period spanning the flow of information that describes a "killing" is longer than that events described by "shooting." If I intended to kill Bob by shooting him, the act-token "killing" is identical with the information flow that stretches from the time of the formulation of the intention to Bob's death. The act-token identified by "shooting Bob," on the other hand, spans a more limited time stretch, starting with the information generated by the intention to pull the trigger and ending with that of the bullet penetrating Bob's body. If e_2 = shooting and e_1 = killing, $e_2 \neq e_1$ even though e_2 is comprehended within e_1's stretch of time.

The trouble with individuating act-tokens using either the criterion "same time period" or "time stretches" is that, on both accounts, "moving my hand" and "moving a lot of molecules of air" constitute the same act-token since both identify events that span the same time period or time stretch. Individuating act-tokens in terms of information flow $I_s(r)$, on the other hand, can help resolve these difficulties. On my account, in contrast to "I move my hand," "I move a lot of molecules of air" does not identify an act-token because it picks out a trajectory that neither originates in nor is constrained by a cognitive source at all. From an information-theoretic perspective, then, the criterion of act individuation should be: "Two events = same act-token iff their descriptions track the identical informational vector $I_s(r)$ (identical intentional source, trajectory, and terminus)." For example, suppose I intend to turn on the light. Since the lamp has recently been malfunctioning, I jiggle the switch with one hand while simultaneously screwing in the light bulb with the other. These two events share the same origin (the intention to turn on the light) and the same outcome (the light goes on). But they are distinct, if simultaneous, act-tokens because their en route paths are different. Information theory thus yields a radical multiplier position on act-individuation.[32]

On this account, since shooting and killing have different intentional origins (different reductions of possibilities) and different termini, they are different act-tokens. "Shooting" is a success verb: if the bullet had not penetrated, I would not have "shot" Bob regardless of my intention. So, too, "homicide" is a success noun: if there is no corpse there is no homicide, regardless of someone's intention. Success verbs and nouns, however, do not necessarily identify act-tokens. The information they carry is information available at $I(r)$, regardless of what happened at the source. Other verbs—"to move" for example—can identify either an act-token, as in "I moved my hand," or not, as in "My hand moved." Still other verbs, however, such as "to murder" (which could be called "positive act-types"[33]), are correctly applied only if the behavior is an act-token. The meaning of those verbs implies that no equivocation compromised the flow of information from an intentional source. If those verbs correctly capture the behavior, the source from which the behavior issued is thereby uniquely identified. When correctly used, therefore, positive act-types always identify act-tokens precisely by informing us that the trajectory was unequivocal, $I_s(r) = 1$.

Action and the Flow of Information

As a first pass toward reconceptualizing action, therefore, I speculate that a process analogous to the generation and transmission of information as described in communications theory occurs whenever an act-token is performed. First the agent forms a prior intention to act. As in the process that Dretske (1981) postulates for cognition, doing so involves the progressive narrowing of an initially broad and inclusive space of possibilities until a smaller set is culled. From all the options available, the agent (1) considers only some of them, then (2) homes in on one, reaching the decision to do x. But generating an intention is only one component of an action. Once the decision is reached, the meaningful information generated by the intentional source must then unequivocally flow into behavior for that behavior to qualify as action.

Information as Cause: Another Argument against Davidson

As mentioned in an earlier chapter, Davidson's "Action, Reasons and Causes" (1963) is widely held to have put in its place the claim that reasons or intentions cannot be causes of actions because of the logical connection between, for example, "intention to do x" and "doing x." Davidson argued as follows: Suppose "nerve fibers x, y, and z firing" picked out an event extensionally equivalent to that picked out by "intention to do x." The former description would identify an acceptable cause if the relation between neuronal firings and behavior figured in a "strict, deterministic law." Once it is understood that "intention to do x" is merely shorthand for "nerve fibers x, y, and z firing," there would be no problem with saying that the description "intention to do x" identifies the cause of x.

However, because informational and causal heritages are not identical, from an information-theoretic point of view things look different. Information is generated at the source by a decision procedure that collapses a set of alternatives, but as we saw, this information may or may not flow uncompromised into outcome. In the careless-messenger variation of the Herman example, the information the employer received came about by the messenger's fortuitously choosing the same name picked by the employees' decision-making process, not by the faithful transmission of the message generated by that decision-making process. As a result the information that the employer received was equivocal.

What parallels exist in the case of action? The problem of action turns on whether intentions or other such events are causally efficacious as neurological events or as mental. Davidson (1980) has repeatedly claimed that events are causally efficacious or not independent of how they are described. However, it is not a question of description but of relational properties. If the same thought can be realized in different neurological patterns (either in the same person over time or in different persons), a situation like r_2 in figure 6.2 presents itself. Three different neurophysiological patterns, for example, might embody the same intention to raise my arm. If so, my raising my arm as an act-token would be equivocal with respect to the actual neural process that causes my behavior on this particular occasion. If, following figure 6.2 raising my arm is r_2 and s_2, s_1, and s_3 are the neurological processes from which r_2 might have issued, r_2 would be equivocal with respect to those processes. On the other hand, insofar as it is an act-token the behavior would be unequivocal with respect to the intention to raise my arm. Whenever noise and equivocation are absent, $I_s(r) = 1$.

We have seen that it is useful, following information theory, to think of action as informationally dependent and constrained behavior. Those intentions and other cognitive phenomena responsible for action must be robust enough to withstand the mischief of noise and equivocation and to flow into behavior. We can now appreciate, however, that behavior constitutes action if and only if it flows unequivocally from a cognitive structure in virtue of its meaningful content (Audi 1995; Kim 1995). And "it must *be* this content that defines the structure's causal influence on output" (Dretske 1981, 199). That is, the intentional content, not the lower-level neurological processes in which that content is instantiated, determines whether behavior unequivocally constitutes action. If the same intention can be realized in several different neurological processes, the dependence of behavioral output x on origin must hold in virtue of the mental properties of that source, not its neurological realization. It must hold, that is, in virtue of those neurological processes *embodying* an intention. Behavior that constitutes action is unequivocally dependent on an intentional source in virtue of the full information which that output carries about the meaningful content of the intentional source, not its mechanically causal relationship to that source, which is likely to be equivocal. That is, the behavior must be unequivocal with respect to the intention from which it issued, not the neural process in which that intention was embodied. But modern philosophy has offered no account of how meaning can flow into behavior. This failure, I have claimed, is due to fundamental flaws in the received understanding of causality.

This was the point made earlier in connection with behaviorism. For behavior to count as action, it cannot just fortuitously satisfy the content of the intention, the way it did in the careless-messenger version of the Herman example or in the case of the nephew who killed his uncle with his car. The meaningful information generated by a source must constrain the behavioral output such that the latter actualizes the former. Even if "firing of nerve fibers x, y, z" were coextensional with "intention to do A," on an information-theoretic account of action it is not as nerve fibers' firing that the event is the unequivocal origin of the action. The reason, as we learned from information theory, is that if several different patterns of nerve fibers' firing can realize the same intention, the resulting behavior would not, as action, identify only one pattern of neurological activity. Since whenever one outcome might have come from more than one source that outcome is equivocal, the behavior would be equivocal with respect to its physical (neurological) origins.

Suppose that Davidson is correct: by identifying the event picked out by "intention to do x" with certain neurophysiological events, the logical connection between the description of the alleged cause and its effect can be circumvented, thereby gaining a lawful regularity that satisfies Humean orthodoxy. From the point of view of information and meaning, however, the newly identified (and thus acceptable) efficient cause buys you nothing. It fails to show that those neurophysiological processes—as mental— constrained the actual behavior. The lack of dependence of a particular instance of behavior on a particular intention thus prevents the latter— even if as neurophysiological it served as Newtonian cause—from identifying or explaining action as action. Newtonian causality is irrelevant to the flow of information because Newtonian causality is a relation among externally related events. Information flow, on the other hand, links output to source in such a way that they are no longer independent events. They are now components of a larger, relational trajectory.

Actions thus express the content of an intention that flows into behavior without equivocation. Or, what is the same thing, action is behavior that is fully constrained by the content of a mental structure. This characterization incorporates that feature of action which, following Malcolm (1968), has come to be described as "behavior performed under a description." Insofar as it constitutes behavior performed as an instance of a semantic category, action is meaningful behavior. Those events correctly describable as act-tokens are only those carrying the full, meaningful information that flows from s to r—where $I_s(r) = 1$, that is.

Disadvantages of an Information-Theoretic Account

Despite the fact that, by using the notions of equivocation and noise, an information-theoretic account of action can account for the flow of information from intention to behavior, we are still far from being out of the woods. Framing behavior in terms of communications theory carries with it its own problems, notably those described in the following two sections.

How Is the Pool of Alternatives (n) Established?

The information-theoretic idea of "reduction of possibilities" at the source is important for the theory of action, as we have seen, because it corresponds to our intuitions about the way agents narrow available possibilities to reach one definite intention (Brand's [1980] focusing component of action). But in development as well as evolution, the pool of alternatives expands as we climb the phylogenetic scale. As children acquire new information and skills, behavioral alternatives previously unavailable open up. In particular, new kinds of behavior become possible. Winking is in principle excluded from the pool of alternatives of newborns and animals. Normal adults, however, can wink as well as blink. As we saw in chapter 4's discussion of Rawls and Peters, any acceptable theory of action must address the question of how act-types come to be available for inclusion in the list of alternatives from which the agent selects.

An information-theoretic account is also unable to explain why the space of possibilities available to an agent at a given moment contains the options it does. Aristotle claimed that behavior qualifies as intentional action when the source of movement is within the agent. However, modern philosophy does not allow agents to be embedded in their environment such that the environment can play a role as the behavior's final cause. And self-cause, as always, remains a conceptual impossibility. According to modern philosophy, therefore, the agent's mind or brain must do all the work on its own. If so, which alternatives get included in the set under consideration and why? And if the set of alternatives that the agent considers is a function of the relevance and significance of its members, and if one alternative is selected on the same basis, the decision procedure problem collapses into the problem of meaning, information theory's most serious blind spot.

Meaningful Information

No doubt the reader has concluded by now that I have been quite careless throughout this chapter in using the terms "meaning," "information," and "significance" interchangeably. In information theory, the reader will point out, the penciled squiggles "Herman" do not refer to Herman: they are meaningless. As mentioned earlier, the information of information theory is purely quantitative, not qualitative. The communications engineer deals only in the number of "bits" a message carries, bits that in themselves mean (refer to) nothing. Whatever amount of information a message carries is devoid of semantic interpretation. Significance and meaning are also absent from the mechanism that Herman and his coworkers use to reach their decision. In contrast, the "reduction of alternatives" that guides and informs intentional action, and thus marks it off from mere behavior, is a function of the significance and meaning that the alternatives have for the agent. That is also true of perceptual knowledge: we often literally won't see the mailbox if we don't need to post a letter. In the case of animal instinct and biological function, the selective pressures of evolution have established that dependence. But what about the overall space of possibilities presented for human action, and the way one alternative is selected?

In short, the technical understanding of "information" is unlike the robust, content-filled ideas we ordinarily have in mind when we speak of "information." If human action is meaningful behavior but information theory does not involve meaning, what is it that flows unequivocally from intention into behavior?

In this chapter I have shown how information theory can point the way toward a reconceptualization of action as unequivocal trajectory, with the integrity of the information flow from origin to output measurable in terms of conditional probabilities. For purposes of analyzing meaningful, intentional action, however, the concept of unequivocal information flow must still be supplemented with (1) an account of the way the space of alternatives is partitioned in virtue of their meaning and significance. The procedure according to which the meaningful partitioning takes place must also (2) be physically realizable. Finally, it will be necessary to explain (3) how the meaningful content of an agent's intention can flow into and constrain behavior such that it qualifies as action.

Part II will formulate an alternative to the Newtonian understanding of cause, an alternative that can also handle the problem of meaning as cause. To do so, however, will first require the exploration of territory not previously visited by action theorists: the fields of systems theory, non-equilibrium thermodynamics, and neural networks. The new dynamics that these theories describe will permit us to recast radically our understanding of meaningful intentions and the way they flow into and constrain behavior.

Part II

Dynamical Systems Theory and Human Action

Chapter 7
Some New Vocabulary: A Primer on Systems Theory

Recapitulation

In chapters 1 through 5 of part I, I claimed that a flawed understanding of the concepts of cause and explanation has led to the characteristic and recurrent problems of contemporary action theory. Then in chapter 6, I suggested that two concepts used by information theory, noise and equivocation, offer a way of rethinking the way intentions *flow* into behavior. Traditional information theory, however, was unable to incorporate a robust sense of meaning, and yet it is the meaningful content of intention that flows into action. We therefore still need an account of the way intentions, as meaningful, unequivocally inform and constrain behavior such that it qualifies as action. Since I intend to use complex dynamical systems as a theory-constitutive metaphor for that process, we must first go back and take a brief look at scientific developments since the time of Newton and Descartes. Doing so not only will show that there is no longer any reason for action theory to subscribe to either the Newtonian model of efficient causality or the covering-law model of explanation; it will also point the way toward both a renewed understanding of cause and a different model of explanation.

Thermodynamics

Basic assumptions on which the modern scientific world view was based came under attack over time. In the nineteenth century alone, two challenges appeared to that conceptual framework: thermodynamics and evolutionary theory. Thermodynamic systems can use energy only when "the arrangement of energy is to some extent 'orderly': higher temperature here, lower temperature there, and a clearly marked contrast between the two" (Campbell 1982, 33). The first law of thermodynamics states that the total amount of energy in the universe is conserved. The second states that, over time, the disorderly arrangement of energy, entropy, inexorably increases, and the orderly, usable arrangement of energy decreases. Unlike the phenomena of Newtonian mechanics, the equations for which are time-reversible, thermodynamic processes thus exhibit an irreversible tendency toward increasing disorder, a death march that will ultimately terminate in a state characterized by a complete lack of energy potential, that is, by the uniformization of the universe's arrangement of energy. This equilibrium state constitutes the heat death of the universe.

The trajectories of near-equilibrium thermodynamic systems follow uniform and hence predictable change. Small perturbations cause small changes and the trajectory soon resumes its predictably normal course— emphasis, as always, on *predictable*. For the same reason that Galileo could dismiss friction when studying how balls roll down inclined planes, classical thermodynamics was able to ignore the way in which time and space uniquely individuate objects. As befitted a respectable science, moreover, unique, individual, historical trajectories in near-equilibrium thermodynamic systems remained outside the theory's purview. In certain important respects, every trajectory was like every other. A covering-law logic of explanation therefore made sense.

The inexorable increase of unusable energy (entropy) postulated by classical thermodynamics provided a criterion for differentiating past from present and future. Measuring the change in the amount of entropy tells you the sequence in which events happen: the state with less entropy comes first, the one with more entropy next, the one with total entropy last. In contrast to Newton's time-neutral equations, thermodynamics therefore appeared to return irreversibility and temporal direction to science, vindicating the intuition that whereas you can go from an egg to an omelette, the reverse is impossible. In the end, thermodynamics teaches, you can't put Humpty back together again.

This postulate of an arrow of time did not go unchallenged: Boltzmann (1877) argued that the one-wayness pertains only to macroscopic, statistically averaged-out systems; at the atomic level events remain neatly, time-reversibly Newtonian. The arrow of time thus applies only to the law of large numbers; at the microscopic atomic level, ultimate reality remains properly timeless. Although it is overwhelmingly unlikely that Humpty will ever get put back together again, it is in principle possible, since the atoms that make him up know nothing about backward and forward. In principle, omelettes might also reconstitute into eggs, but don't bet the rent that either of these is likely to happen. In any case, however, by showing that the macroscopic universe was unidirectionally running down and would eventually grind to a halt in the whimper of equilibrium heat death, thermodynamics called the timelessness of the Newtonian model into question, at least as it pertained to the macroscopic realm.

Thermodynamics may have brought time back into the scientific picture, but history still remained absent from the structures of classical, near-equilibrium thermodynamics: their progression toward equilibrium remains ahistorical in the sense that they forget where they came from. The specific location and circumstances from which a system started out, and the particular path it has traversed to date, are irrelevant; whatever its origin, the system will eventually reach equilibrium. Thermodynamic systems near equilibrium are therefore insensitive to initial conditions. Their past does not affect either their present or their future. Since according to the determinism of classical thermodynamics all processes in the universe are converging toward this same end despite their different starting points, determining the state of the system even a few minutes ago is impossible. Whereas Newtonian theory had allowed both for exact retrodiction as well as prediction, nineteenth-century near-equilibrium thermodynamics allowed only prediction. Both classical mechanics and thermodynamics, however, agreed on the deterministic and "machine-like" quality of the universe; they disagreed only on whether motions are reversible.

In any case, every prediction of near-equilibrium thermodynamics also pointed toward a future more disorderly than the present. But experience provides numerous counterexamples to increasing disorderliness: a fetus is more complex and organized than the blastula it was a few moments after conception; a cow is more complex than an amoeba. If thermodynamics is correct, whence the increasing complexity that has characterized both cosmological and biological evolution, not to mention the development of organisms? What went unnoticed at the time was the fact that nineteenth-century thermodynamics deals only with systems as if they were closed and isolated from their environmental context, with which they do not interact. As befitted a properly modern science, that is, near-equilibrium thermodynamics ignored relational, secondary qualities, those properties that appear in virtue of an object's interactions with its surroundings and its past. Unlike the closed and isolated systems of classical thermodynamics (which are near equilibrium and do not exchange matter and energy with their environment), however, living things and even some nonliving ones are neither. And open states of order can be maintained only when the internal state of the system is in nonequilibrium (Zeleny 1980).

Evolution

Enter Darwin. Charles Darwin's theory of evolution appeared to account for the mechanism responsible for the increasing complexity and order that characterize ontogeny and phylogeny. In doing so, Darwin revealed the scientific inadequacy of both atemporal and acontextual frameworks in accounting for biological phenomena. In a blow to Plato, not to mention religious fundamentalism, Darwin undermined the idea that essences exist that universally and eternally mark off this kind of organism from that. Natural kinds are not eternal; species evolve over time. Moreover, by giving the environment in which an organism finds itself (and with which it interacts) a central role as the agent of selection, Darwin's writings returned context to science for the first time in centuries. The specific ecological niche in which an organism is embedded matters greatly, since it determines which organisms live and get to reproduce and which do not. Because organisms are more or less fit relative to the particular environmental niche in which they are located, fitness is therefore a relational property, not a primary one like mass. By his resuscitating the role of context, functional properties, which had been discarded by modern philosophy (MacIntyre 1981), also made a comeback with Darwin. They would come to play an even more central role in the far-from-equilibrium thermodynamics of open systems.

And yet much of the flavor of Newtonian mechanics continued to permeate the theory of evolution (Depew and Weber 1995), particularly in the way Darwin understood explanation. The radical change from Aristotle to Darwin was the recognition that, through the environment's selective pressure on reproductive success, unpredictable, truly novel phenotypic features could be passed on to future generations. Mutations, those events whose role it is to present different and new phenotypes to be selected by the environment, were supposed to happen randomly. However, Newton's heirs found it impossible to allow chance, random events into a deterministic, Laplacean universe. Since mutations are unpredictable events not deducible from what went before, even Darwin believed that evolution proper could not, therefore—even in principle—be scientifically explained. Only development could.

What made Darwin an original scientist was that he articulated a mechanism whereby evolution could occur; many others had suggested that species evolve without explaining how. But when speaking of evolution proper—the origin of really new species—the role of chance mutations meant that a deductive explanation of those qualitative changes was impossible. For Darwin as well as Aristotle, then, science cannot explain novelty or emergence unless that seemingly novel, emergent, and original event is really neither truly novel, nor emergent, nor a radical new beginning, but instead is already there, folded into the dynamics, just waiting to be unfolded and made actual. Darwin was left with telling a story. Isabelle Stengers, Ilya Prigogine's co-author, has said that nothing sounds so much like a novel as the writings of Darwin (personal conversation, 17 October 1991).

Such was the prevailing view in the late nineteenth century when Herbert Spencer coined the term "evolution": the actualization of preformed potentialities. This belief conformed to Aristotelian orthodoxy concerning the nature of *episteme*. But with all causes reduced to efficient cause, the manner of causality whereby the selective pressures of the environment cause species to evolve into truly new forms became a problem in need of a solution, one that is still rarely addressed. I believe that this is because the received understanding of efficient cause does not allow philosophers even to think of that relationship as causal at all. And yet, as even Hume pointed out and David Lewis (1986) reiterates, part of the concept of cause includes "if that weren't so, this wouldn't be." So if one thinks of causal relations in this way, the environmental niche in which organisms are embedded does play a causal role. But it is not the efficient cause of an external force on passive and inert matter.

How external to an organism is the niche in which it is located if, over time, features of that environment contribute to specifying the very primary properties of that kind of living thing? An organism's primary properties are, according to evolutionary theory, both a record of past environments and a conjecture about the current one. The overall species-niche supersystem determines the traits that individual organisms will exhibit. It is known that two animals with the same genotype can be phenotypically different depending on the environment in which they develop. Is this not a form of self-cause whereby the distributed whole influences its components?

An organism's fitness with respect to its environment is measured by its chances of survival, which in turn affect the likelihood that it will reproduce and pass on its genes to the next generation. As the number of some genotypes increases in a population while the number of others decreases, those characteristics that identify the species change until the population constitutes a "different" species. What manner of cause is this whereby the environment alters the probability of survival and reproduction of particular phenotypes, which in turn modifies the probability that over time entirely new phenotypes will appear? What manner of cause is this, in other words, that increases and decreases the repertoire of states and behavior of organisms? With only efficient causality to go on, philosophy found it impossible even to address these questions. Classical evolutionary theory also offered no preferred direction to evolution: in principle the environment could select the less complex just as easily as the more complex (Brooks and Wiley 1988). The time-reversibility of Newtonian science was not questioned.

And so the impasse continued between the second law's claim that everything is winding down, and evidence to the contrary presented by the increasing complexification in both cosmological and biological evolution. Classical thermodynamicists and Darwin agreed that time was real, at least for macroscopic objects. For the thermodynamicists, however, things more and more fall apart. Darwin's ideas, on the other hand, appeared to account for the increasing order and organization in evidence in biological development and evolution. The increasing complexity of living systems, both onto- and phylogenetically, seemed to violate the second law of thermodynamics. But there it is. Open systems far from equilibrium show a reduction in local or internal entropy; they are able, in other words, to create form and order. Human beings are more complex than amoebas, meaning, according to at least one denotation of "complexity," that the former can access a greater variety of states than the latter. The cosmos, too, is much more complex today than just after the big bang: different types of states are available to it now than then.

It was not until the mid-twentieth century that scientists discovered that under certain conditions, open systems that exchange matter and energy with the environment, including organisms, behave quite differently. But the self-organization of such complexity was as forbidden by the principles and laws of classical thermodynamics as by mechanics. And if the focus is on the *self* in self-organization, it was just as forbidden to classical Darwinism, which, like the behaviorism it spawned, viewed the environment as external to and independent of the organism. How to reconcile these contradictory views? A new framework is called for, one that rethinks causality in such a way as to provide some form of ongoing self-cause. To that end, a new conceptual model of the interaction between parts and wholes must be articulated. Aristotle drew from pottery, the fundamental technology of his time, to conceptualize his four causes and related notions on explanation. Freud borrowed heavily from hydraulics for his metaphors. Different aspects of the ideas of Hume and Kant conformed to modern science. Is there a scientific framework today that we might borrow as a "theory-constitutive metaphor" (Boyd 1979) for the ways parts and wholes interact?

Systems Theory

Fortunately, a readily available framework exists from which we can begin. General systems theory was first articulated by organismic biologist Ludwig von Bertalanffy (1981) as a counterpoint to classical science's mechanistic understanding of human beings and nature. Its fundamental claim is that when living things are embedded in a orderly context, properties emerge that are not present when the things exist as isolated individuals. Picking up where Darwin left off, systems theory continued the revival of relational or secondary properties by reminding us that context matters. But it does so very differently than behaviorism.

Like most sciences, systems theory devoted its early years to taxonomy. Unfortunately, the literature still displays little uniformity in terminology. At times, for example, "collection" refers to what I will identify as an "aggregate"; at other times, "collection" refers to what I will call a "system" proper. "Structure" and "organization" are often used interchangeably, and "holism" signifies to some authors what "hierarchy" means to others. A brief survey of the terminology is therefore imperative.

Aggregates versus Systems

The intuitive idea of a *system* as opposed to an aggregate is of a group of things related in a particular way. However, defining a system as "a set of elements and relations between the elements" is so general as to be vacuous (Marchal 1975, 460). Everything might count as a system as long as a relationship of any kind exists between the two elements: the moon and I would constitute a system held together by "distance relations," as would a pile of rocks, which, intuitively, is an *aggregate*, not a system.

To circumvent this objection of vacuity a second characteristic must be added. In an aggregate, the properties of the parts do not change depending on whether or not they are part of the aggregate. In a system, on the other hand, the properties of the components depend on the systemic context within which the components are located. Although components of an aggregate are spatially related to each other, in a system the relation "makes some difference to its relata" (Bunge 1979, 6). Once science discovered that the earth would lack some properties such as tides were it not for its relationship to the moon, our willingness to characterize the earth-moon duo as a system rather than just an aggregate or a collection increased.

Correlation and coordination among the parts confer a peculiar unity on the overall system. Such interrelations into an integral whole, which characterize systems but not aggregates, reinforce our intuition that piles of rocks and sandpiles are just aggregates, not systems. "The root idea of system," Nicholas Rescher (1979, 4) notes, is "of integration into an orderly whole that functions as an 'organic' unity." A strong echo of Aristotle's concept of formal cause can be detected in the concept of a system.

A system's *organization* is different from its *structure*. Poodles come in various sizes and colors. A particular flower can be a token of the type "rose" as well as of the type "peace." The distinction between organization and structure is like that between type and token—both presuppose *multiple realizability*: a type can be realized in several tokens, each different from the next. There is no one-to-one relationship between organization and structure.

A system's organization consists in the "relations among components, whether static or dynamic, that constitute a composite unity as a unity of a particular kind" (Maturana 1980, 48). For a system to retain its identity as a system of that particular type, these relations must remain invariant. Not so a system's structure. Its structure consists in "the actual components and the actual relations among them that at any instance realize a particular composite unity as a concrete static or dynamic entity."[34] For example, the organization of parts that makes an object an "automobile" can be variously realized in different structures: station wagon, sedan, or coupe. Each of these, in turn, is itself an organization realized in the different structures of, for example, Camry, Accord, or Taurus sedans. Ordinarily, as a living thing grows, its structure changes, but not its organization. The metamorphosis of a tadpole into a frog, on the other hand, constitutes a change in organization.

A system's *internal structure* consists in the specific components and the relations among them. Its *external structure* or *boundary conditions* consist in the interactions between the components and the environment, that is, "the set of all things [not components of the system] that act or are acted on by components of [the system]" (Bunge 1979, 6). The environment of interest to the systems theorist, however, is not the total environment but the environment that affects and is affected by the thing in question. At any given moment a particular system is characterized by the structure (both internal and external) that individuates it. Together, the internal and external structure constitute the system's total structure. A system with no external structure—no environment with which it interacts—is a closed and isolated system. Only the entire universe is closed and isolated.

A system's external structure can affect its internal structure and not just as efficient cause. This feature falsifies the thesis that secondary or relational properties are epiphenomenal and subjective. That kind of interaction between open systems and their environment also marks the limits of modern scientific methodology. It is possible to get only so far (pretty far, to be sure, with some processes—but not with others) by isolating a system from the context to which it belongs. The concept of external structure will play an important part in our reconceptualization of cause.

A system's structure should not be confused with its *configuration*, the spatial relations in which the components of a system stand to one another. Aggregates have spatial configuration, but no structure; they lack the peculiar type of interrelatedness that unifies and binds the components in such a way as to make a difference to those components. Configuration, in turn, is not the same as *shape*; social systems, for example, have spatial configuration but no shape.

A system's internal structure can be more or less stringent. Systems whose components are tightly connected often possess a high degree of *integration* "relative to the disintegrating actions of the environment"

(Bunge 1979, 35). However, at times, as with cancer, the *cohesion* (another word used for integration) of the system's subsystems may compete with that of the global system. *Coordination*, on the other hand, is a different, functional phenomenon: if coordination among the components fails, the system undergoes functional breakdown. "There can be integration without coordination but not conversely. A complex machine out of kilter is integrated but not coordinated" (38).

Resilience and Stability

A system's functional efficiency is often related to its integration. The system is called *stable* if it returns to or fluctuates minimally around a constant value. Stability is usually inversely related to integration, that is, to the stringency of the structural bonding. For the most part, the more flexible the coupling between the subsystems, the greater the overall system's stability. Usually, too, the more homogeneous the environment in which the system is located, the more stable the system. Greater variety of internal couplings as well as a larger number of such couplings also tends to increase stability.

The Great Lakes ecosystem is a good example of a stable system, one that also illustrates the fact that very stable systems, when perturbed, may be unable to survive. Because flora and fauna in freshwater aquatic systems are fairly homogeneous and the water tempers extreme climatic fluctuations, lakes are characteristically stable ecosystems. They may be stable, but they are not *resilient*. Fish stocks are often quickly decimated when the lake's ecological balance is perturbed. Resilience is "the ability of the system to absorb changes ... and still persist" (Holling 1976, 83). A system can be quite resilient yet unstable if it persists as that (kind of) system despite wide fluctuations. Resilient systems are able to modify their specific structure so as to ensure the adaptability and survival of their overall organization. Insects and viruses are remarkably resilient: they can mutate dramatically and so persist. Complex systems are usually more resilient than simple ones, with complex open systems that interact with their environment exhibiting the highest degree of resilience.[35] As anyone who has tried to rid his house of cockroaches can confirm, evolution generally favors resilience, not stability.

Facultative and Obligate Systems

Although we tend to think of systems as static and permanent forms of organization, systems can be reversible and disband. These are called *facultative systems*. Those that, once formed, do not disband, are called *obligate systems* (Grobstein 1973). Although most higher organisms are examples of obligate systems, examples of facultative systems include both colonies of bacteria that disperse to form new colonies, and the slime mold, which self-organizes into a slug during times of scarcity to access otherwise inaccessible food sources, and then breaks up again into individual independent amoebas. I will argue that intentions and actions should be taken to be facultative, self-organized dynamical systems.

Allopoiesis versus Autopoiesis

Because their organization is given "from the outside," machines are *allopoietic*. Living organisms, on the other hand, self-assemble, and as such are examples of *autopoietic* (self-organizing) systems. As we saw in an earlier chapter, this self-organizing feature of living things occupied Kant in the third *Critique*. Considering the popularity of theories that have attempted to reduce purposive behavior to cybernetics (Wiener, Rosenblueth, and Bigelow 1943), the significance of the distinction between autopoiesis and allopoiesis should not be overlooked. Unlike the mechanisms responsible for biological homeostasis, a thermostat's function, maintaining a constant temperature, is given to it from the outside by its designer. The expansion of mercury may be a natural sign of ambient temperature. But it was the thermostat's designer and manufacturer who artificially coupled that natural indicator property to the device that controls the boiler. No thermostat originates that function on its own, nor are its parts self-produced. Thermostats do not self-organize.

Concrete versus Property Systems

Mario Bunge calls systems made up of components which are themselves things *concrete systems*. The solar system is a concrete system. Bunge (1979, 7) goes to great lengths, however, to emphasize that "a set of states of a thing and a collection of events, even if ordered, are not concrete systems." "Sets of interrelated properties" (15) are, therefore, property systems, not concrete systems.

Process, Functional, and Information Systems

As mentioned earlier, a system's organization is given by the invariant relations among its components, not those components' primary properties. In some cases, the relationships among the components are processes such as "interaction, production, transformation and destruction" (Zeleny 1980, 5). Joseph Earley (1981) calls these systems "structures of process."[36] Functional systems such as the digestive system, which are "sets of coupled processes" (Bunge 1979, 15), are examples of structures of processes. In process systems, the couplings, being dynamic, are called *flows*. When the interactions flow in a particular direction, they are represented by directed graphs. (I will claim that cognitive systems, including intentions, are dynamical structures of process, and that act-tokens are best represented as vectors on directed graphs.) "If a physical flow happens to carry information, the connection is called informational and the entire system an information system" (9). Persons, intentions, and actions are also information systems, as is the genetic system.

Hierarchical Systems

Systems with nested structures are hierarchies. Because, by definition, all systems consist of at least two organizational levels (the level of the components and the level of the global system), the term *hierarchy* is usually reserved for systems with several nested levels. How are hierarchical systems created? "[W]e know of no natural hierarchical configuration not produced by an irreversible process.... [A]ny irreversible process dealing with discrete units will always be hierarchical, a fact not fully appreciated by biologists until comparatively recently" (Brooks and Wiley 1988, 82).

Decomposable Systems

The levels of organization of some hierarchical systems are as neatly sealed off from each other as ice cream flavors in a parfait. Natural levels of organization can often be identified by their bond strengths and timescales. The sharp separation can often be detected in the energy levels at which components interact: molecules are held together by covalent bonds of approximately 5 electron volts; the forces binding the nucleus are on the order of 140 million electron volts. "An atom interacts at one energy level [with another atom] and molecules interact at [another], and that is how we tell the difference" (Simon 1973, 9). Timescales often allow us to demarcate levels: the components at the lowest level interact the fastest; structures at the highest levels exhibit longer time frames of interaction (Salthe 1997). Systems whose levels of organization are clearly separated in this fashion are called *decomposable systems*.

The fact that the numbers are often sharply separated also allows a description to be constructed for the global level "in ignorance of the detailed structure or dynamics at the next level down, [or of] the very slow interactions at the next level up" (Simon 1973, 11). The ontological basis of decomposability justifies the change in level of discourse: decomposability allows us to think of and study molecules in ignorance of what is happening at the atomic level. Each description specifies more precisely the goings on at the previous level (see Salthe 1993b and its discussion of "specification hierarchy").

Structural and Control Hierarchies

Howard Pattee (1973) distinguished structural from control hierarchies. When levels of *structural hierarchies* do not interact, they can be described by dynamical equations that deal with only one level at a time. In *control hierarchies*, on the other hand, the upper level exerts an "active authority relation" on the components of the lower levels (hence the term "hierarchy"):

> In a control hierarchy, the upper level exerts a specific, dynamic constraint on the details of the motion at the lower level, so that the fast dynamics of the lower level cannot simply be averaged out. The collection of subunits that forms the upper level in a structural hierarchy *now also acts as a constraint on the motions of selected individual subunits. This amounts to a feedback path between levels.* [The description of] the physical behavior of a control hierarchy must take into account at least two levels at a time. (Pattee 1973, 77, emphasis mine)

As a result, control hierarchies are not as tractable as hierarchies whose levels do not interact. When the environment that is part of the system's external structure is also taken into account, at least three levels are simultaneously involved: the focal level, the environmental level immediately above, and the component level immediately below (Salthe 1985)—with feedback paths among them.

Nearly Decomposable Systems

In control hierarchies with this sort of leakage between levels, a clean dynamic theory referring to one level at a time cannot be formulated. Simon calls systems like these *nearly decomposable*. As we shall see in our discussion of dynamical systems, this apparent design flaw can have remarkable consequences: interlevel leakage makes the system robust to noise, context-sensitive, and, in the case of artificial neural networks, able to generalize.

Multilevel, dynamic coupling of components, both at the same level and between levels (such as one finds in the cells, tissues, organs, and so forth of biological organisms) "maintains a certain autonomy at all hierarchical levels" (Jantsch 1980, 247). Components at different levels are not subsumed or fused into the highest level, but they do interact. Such interlevel relationships present tremendous difficulties in explaining these systems, as Kant noted to his dismay. And yet there are many such systems, both mechanical and natural. The crucial questions for purposes of action theory, of course, are, "How do irreversible processes produce natural hierarchical systems?" and, in particular, "How does interlevel, particularly top-down, control operate?"

Entrainment

In the case of mechanical hierarchies, examples in which higher levels control lower ones are familiar. Consider the well-known engineering phenomenon called *mutual entrainment*. Entrainment occurs when "two or more oscillators interact with each other in such a way as to pull one another together into synchronism" (Dewan 1976, 183):

> The most familiar technological example, perhaps, is its use in television. The picture on the television tube is created by a scanning electron beam which goes row by row across the picture from top to bottom. This beam is controlled by two oscillators, one for the vertical and the other for the horizontal direction. The picture remains stationary only when these oscillators are "locked in" or entrained to pulsars originating from the transmitter. As all television viewers know, occasionally the oscillators can "break out" of synchrony, causing the picture to "rotate." The remedy is to read just the natural frequency of the oscillator until it is "close enough" to the input frequency. It then locks in again, or becomes entrained, and the picture again stands still.

Dewan also describes the entrainment of an electrical power system. Each electrical generator is an oscillator with a built-in feedback mechanism "which causes it to stay at 60 cycles per second no matter what the present 'load' may be—a larger load automatically causing a reaction in the governor to increase steam pressure and vice versa" (Dewan 1976, 185). Entrainment confers a measure of stability on the coupled oscillators that they would not have on their own. In thermostats and generators, however, the governor is an external control device added specifically to achieve this effect (which makes generators and thermostats allopoietic).[37] Feedback is the key responsible for entrainment.

Mutual entrainment can also occur when several generators are interconnected: if one generator exceeds 60 cycles per second, the others absorb the excess; "[t]his will increase the load on the generator, forcing it to slow down" (Dewan 1976, 185). Conversely, if it falls below 60 cycles per second, the other generators "pump energy into [the first] so that it catches up." Similarly, two pendulum clocks mounted on a common support will eventually tick in unison. The important point is that in these cases no externally imposed control mechanism exists. Mutual entrainment signals the spontaneous emergence of a *virtual governor*, a distributed, global-level phenomenon that neither is a concrete physical existent nor has spatial location. Nevertheless, it constrains the components that make "it" up. Once again, the key is for the components to be connected.

Entrainment occurs in biological processes such as the circadian rhythm. Like clocks mounted on a common support, menstrual cycles of female students and army recruits also synchronize after a few months of living in the same dormitory or barracks: their individual menstrual cycles are no longer independent events. Cardiac cells, too, entrain and pulsate in unison, "beating as one," a consequence of which is that the overall heart is meta-stable. Entrainment makes individual cells behave much more regularly by reducing the variability of their individual fluctuations. When synchronization fails, life-threatening fibrillation sets in. "*[E]ntrainment is a very simple but instructive paradigm of a holistic property of control which has causal potency, which is emergent, and which supervenes on the behavior of individual units*" (Dewan 1976, 185, emphasis mine).

Near Equilibrium and Far From Equilibrium

Earlier I described those systems studied by classical thermodynamics: closed systems that do not interact with their environment. Changes in those systems always aim toward equilibrium, "the elimination of non-uniformities and the increase of disorder within the system" (Allen and Sanglier 1980, 109). No closed system near equilibrium ever becomes more complex or ordered.

But even crystallization is an order-producing process. And living things, unlike crystals, are not "frozen accidents." They are dynamical, adaptive, and evolving beings that interact with their environment through exchanges of matter and energy. As we climb the developmental and phylogenetic ladders, organisms grow and species become increasingly complex, one mark of which is their ability to access a greater variety of states and behaviors. People can blink but amoebas can't; grown-ups can wink but newborns can't.

The human sciences have often been tempted to model their subject matter after the (idealized) linear, closed systems near equilibrium that the hard sciences studied and that, for those very reasons, were tractable and in consequence produced spectacular results. I take it as self-evident today that human beings are neither linear, closed, nor near equilibrium, nor likely to be understood by models with these assumptions. People are neither isolated from their surroundings nor simply dropped into an environment that pushes them hither and yon. On the contrary, they are embedded in their environment, which they in turn influence. Wanted: a theory that addresses nonlinear, dynamical, nearly decomposable, control information systems. For centuries, however, nonlinear equations that describe these open systems were the mathematical counterpart of the philosophical puzzles of reflexivity. Because these equations were considered intractable, students were counseled to ignore their existence. No longer.

Chapter 8
Nonequilibrium Thermodynamics

More than two decades ago, Ilya Prigogine (recipient of the 1977 Nobel Prize for Chemistry) and his Brussels school formulated the theory of dissipative structures, the fundamental insight of which is that "nonequilibrium may be a source of order" (Jantsch 1980, 28). Through nonlinear processes, self-organization—a higher level of order—can occur in open systems far from equilibrium. This chapter will explore the way nonequilibrium dynamical systems theory conceptualizes the relationship between wholes and parts.[38] I hope to show that precisely as a result of this reformulation, complex adaptive systems can serve as a "theory-constitutive metaphor" that allows us to rethink the philosophical concept of cause, particularly as it applies to causal relations between parts and wholes. In turn, this rethinking will radically recast our understanding of intentional causality and human action.

Nonequilibrium Thermodynamics

Consider molecules in a shallow pan of water at room temperature randomly bouncing against each other. Each molecule is identical to its neighbor, from which it is distinguished only externally and numerically. If the pan is uniformly heated from below,

> [a]t first, the temperature in the layer of liquid is practically uniform; the system [remains] in thermodynamic equilibrium.... But if the bottom of the pan becomes hotter and the temperature gradient in the liquid layer steeper, thermal non-equilibrium increases. At a certain gradient, *convection* starts. At first, smaller convection streams are suppressed by the environment. (Jantsch 1980, 22)

While the interaction with the environment is maintained constant, and as long as the fluctuations occurring naturally are damped, the system remains stable. Taking it even further from equilibrium by altering the boundary conditions (by increasing the heat, or "control parameter"), however, causes the system to become unstable, unable to maintain its present organization. "Beyond a critical temperature gradient fluctuations become reinforced rather than suppressed and the dynamic regime abruptly switches from conduction to convection" (Jantsch 1980, 22). Macroscopic molecular flows of more than 10^{20} molecules acting as if in concert suddenly appear. The spatial symmetry of the pan of water is broken when the macroscopic structure of these rolling columns of hexagonal cells, called Bénard cells, appears. Bénard cells are an example of a *dissipative structure.*

The reorganization that streamlines the disorderly complicatedness of millions of independent molecules of water bouncing helter-skelter into each other into the complexly organized, macroscopic, dynamic process structure of a Bénard cell facilitates dissipating the critical gradient that had built up. It takes an irreversible burst of entropy to achieve the streamlining; external entropy production increases and the second law of thermodynamics holds. But the abrupt transition to order from chaos (Prigogine and Stengers 1984) allows the system to lower its rate of internal entropy production. Local sinks of macroscopic order can thereby be produced without violating the second law.

Orderly pattern and structure can appear where previously absent when discontinuous *phase transitions* (also called *bifurcations*)[39] take the water from a regime in which the molecules are uncorrelated, independent entities to a regime in which the molecules are correlated, that is, to a regime in which the behavior of each molecule depends on the behavior of all the surrounding ones—to a regime, that is, in which context plays an essential role. Each molecule of water is now suddenly captured in a network of dynamic interrelationships, a higher level of organization. The molecules are no longer externally related and independent of each other. They behave differently when captured in the dynamics of the cell than they did before. Increased heat is the order or control parameter that drives the Bénard system away from equilibrium toward a bifurcation: in the case of Bénard cells, moreover, the heat level is altered from the outside. If the amount of heat is reduced, Bénard cells disintegrate; if it is increased further, the water abruptly becomes "turbulent." Scientists used to think that turbulence was disorderly; only recently did they discover that the seemingly "chaotic" behavior of turbulence is in fact a highly complex form of order.

Autocatalysis

Those self-organizing systems that reorganize by altering their control parameters themselves are truly autopoietic. In these systems, the non-linear role of positive feedback is most dramatic. Robert Ulanowicz (1997) notes that positive feedback can arise as a result of two negative interactions. So he labels "mutualism" those cases of "positive feedback comprised wholly of positive component interactions" (42). Autocatalytic cycles are paradigmatic examples of mutualism. To understand the concept of autocatalysis and its role in self-organization, consider the following chemical reaction sequence, the Belousov-Zhabotinsky (B-Z) reaction:

$$A \longrightarrow X$$

$$B + X \longrightarrow Y + Q$$

$$X \longrightarrow P$$

$$Y + 2X \longrightarrow 3X$$

Earley writes: "This sequence of reactions describes the conversion of A and B (the reactants) to P and Q (the products) while X and Y are both formed and destroyed (intermediates). The first three reactions are not remarkable, but the fourth step ... has the unusual feature of being *autocatalytic*" (Earley 1981, 246): X, the product of the process, is necessary for the activation of the process itself. Autocatalytic processes, therefore, are examples of what Kant called "intrinsic physical ends."

As more and more X's are produced, autocatalytic cycles can link up to produce *hypercycles*. The autocatalytic step—X producing Y to produce even more X—fuels the hypercycle. Nonequilibrium reinforces the hypercycle's rotation such that the circle not only renews itself continuously, but *"as a whole acts like a catalyst"* which transforms starting products into end products" (Jantsch 1980, 33, emphasis mine).[40] Instead of damping oscillations the way negative feedback would, mutualist feedback loops of the autocatalytic fourth step increase the system's fluctuations around a reference value.

With the system driven far from equilibrium by the runaway process of its mutualist dynamics, at a certain critical distance an instability occurs, a threshold point at which small, randomly occurring fluctuations can no longer be damped. Instead, the internal mutualist dynamics of the autocatalytic hypercycle can amplify a fluctuation, driving the reaction to a new mode of organization. This new system is characterized, as was the Bénard cell, by the *"coherent behavior* of an amazingly large number of molecules which synchronized to form a moving zone of high concentration of a component—a chemical wave that oscillates from blue to red" (Allen and Sanglier 1980, 110, emphasis mine). A colorful macroscopic structure (the visible evidence of the phase change) has suddenly appeared. True self-organization has taken place because it is autocatalysis's own internally driven dynamics, not an outside source cranking up the heat as in the Bénard cell, that drives the system far from equilibrium and precipitates the bifurcation.

Even though B-Z reactions are chemical reactions and Bénard cells are not, both are examples of homologous, far-from-equilibrium dynamics with the following features. Driven to a critical instability threshold (called a bifurcation point) under favorable conditions of nonequilibrium, a random, naturally occurring fluctuation can become amplified, serving as the nucleation that drives the initial regime into a new dynamical organization. A qualitatively different, higher level of organization emerges when uncorrelated molecules suddenly become correlated in a dynamical system.

Even when the lower-level processes that identify the individual steps of the overall autocatalytic cycle are highly disorganized and unstable, the organization of the autocatalytic loop itself will be meta-stable as long as the fluctuations occurring, because of energy exchanges, in the reaction or diffusion rates are maintained in dynamic (not static) equilibrium. By accelerating the process through its own self-reinforcement, however, the positive engine of mutualism can once again take the system far from equilibrium. At another critical threshold, a normally occurring fluctuation can be amplified and carry the system into a new, even more complex level of organization.

In virtue of its own internal dynamics, self-organization thus spawns even higher levels of self-organization and the system as a whole evolves. That is, dissipative processes self-organize into stable structures that, after again reaching a critical threshold of nonequilibrium, can bifurcate once more and reorganize into an even more complexly differentiated, meta-stable system. And the process repeats. Dissipative structures thus evolve through a sequence of such irreversible phase changes or bifurcations. Each reorganization, it will be recalled, dissipates the nonequilibrium that had built up. The reorganized system is therefore better adapted to current conditions than the earlier one. So dissipative structures are also adaptive systems that show how, over time, complex order emerges from disorder. Because random, contingent fluctuations serve as the nucleus around which the reorganization occurs, the progression of this evolutionary process also marks the trajectory of an increasingly individuated system. Bénard cells can rotate in either a clockwise or counterclockwise direction; which particular direction the system "chooses" depends on the random fluctuation around which the phase change happens to nucleate. Events and singularities thus play a crucial role in the particular direction a phase change takes, and in the way a particular process becomes uniquely specified and individuated over time.

Functional Differentiation

Examining a sequence of self-organizing systems reveals increasing complexity, one measure of which is a system's progressive differentiation into a highly articulated, multilevel hierarchy in which new, functionally defined individuals or components emerge. There are many ways to measure complexity. "[M]easured by the number of interacting functional elements" (Prigogine 1976, 124), complexity (say, of a sand castle) is not an additive measure (as is the complicatedness of, for example, a sand dune) but a measure of organization and order. A system emerges when previously uncorrelated particles or processes suddenly become coordinated and interconnected. In subsequent steps of an evolutionary sequence, components and processes are correlated and interconnected differently —in an even more complexly differentiated hierarchy. What makes each step of a self-organized process new is that its components are systematically interrelated in qualitatively novel ways.

Some thinkers speculate that the underlying homologous dynamics of self-organization (Jantsch 1980, Kauffman 1993) might drive all evolution (cosmic as well as biological). Of more immediate philosophical interest for the study of action, however, are (a) the way new, unpredictable properties emerge with each new self-organized phase change and (b) the manner in which causality (in particular interlevel causal relations) operates in nonlinear dynamical systems. The specific properties that characterize a given level of organization (whether the particular Bénard cell will rotate clockwise or counterclockwise, for example) cannot be inferred from the sum of the properties of the earlier stage. For that reason the covering-law model is clearly inadequate as a logic of explanation for these systems. Also centrally of interest, therefore, is (c) how to explain those phenomena that evolve and adapt in this fashion.

A central claim of this book is that the conceptual framework of the theory of self-organizing dynamical systems has significant implications for the philosophical concepts of identity, teleology, cause, and explanation. In combination with the concepts of noise and equivocation borrowed from information theory, a "theory-constitutive metaphor" taken from the science of complex adaptive systems can renew the study of action by opening up novel questions and avenues for exploration. Let us begin with the concept of identity.

Identity of Self-Organizing Processes

Simplify the illustration of autocatalysis. Suppose that molecule A catalyzes the formation of molecule B, which in turn catalyzes a third molecule C; C catalyzes D, and so on, so that "somewhere down the line you might very well have found a molecule Z that closed the loop and catalyzes the creation of molecule A" (Waldrop 1992, 123). The "organizational closure" that autocatalysis achieves differentiates the autocatalytic web from the background out of which it emerged, partially decoupling them and thereby conferring on the network a particular identity. The decoupling is not simply a physical demarcation; it is primarily informational (Brooks and Wiley 1988).

Because self-organizing systems are dynamic processes, here, too, reification is inappropriate. Self-organizing structures are not concrete things. Dissipative structures and autocatalytic webs are meta-stable networks of transformations, nested, hierarchical arrangements of *organizational* patterns: "structures of process." Whereas before the bifurcation there was only an aggregate of elements (a heap), after the phase change one finds an orderly arrangement of particles or processes: a system. This pattern of coordinated processes appears, for example, as the colorful wave of the B-Z reaction, or the rolling, hexagonal Bénard cell. These emergent phenomenal properties were absent before self-organization. Grobstein calls such set-superset transitions "neogenesis":

> [I]n each instance of neogenesis the properties that appear during the origin of the new set are not the simple sum of the properties of the components that make up the set.... [T]he properties which characterize the set frequently depend upon a new relationship established within the set and upon the context, or superset, within which it functions.... [P]articularly in biological systems, it takes both a transformation and the establishment of a new context for these properties to be manifested. (Grobstein 1973, 45)

The newly established relationship among the components *is* the new external structure for those components. Given this new systemic context, novel properties appear. In the B-Z reaction, the sudden appearance of the new property—alternating blue and red chemical waves—marks the qualitative transition to a new regime. Emergent novelty is a characteristic feature of all complex dynamical systems. Each new step in a sequence of evolving dissipative structures thus represents a qualitative change in the system's organization. Because each of the processes that define an autopoietic system requires the others, the system must be studied as a whole, as the coordination of several process, that is, as a network of activity and relationships. Isolating each of the processes and attempting to reduce the whole to its components (as atomism tried to do) produces "nothing more than that: a series of snapshots" (Zeleny 1980, 17). Moreover, the specific properties of the system as a whole (clockwise or counterclockwise, red or blue wave first) "cannot be inferred from the characteristics of its parts" (Zeleny 1980, 20) because the particular direction it takes or which color appears first will depend on the randomly occurring fluctuation around which the phase change happens to nucleate. Because the rules the network follows describe dynamic and stochastic interactions, they capture relational properties that, *pace* the followers of Newton, cannot be reduced to microlevel descriptions of primary qualities.

As a dynamic system, therefore, an autopoietic system's identity is given by the coordinated organization of the processes that make it up, not the primary material of its components. Bénard cells are Bénard cells whether they are made of water or any other viscous material. Playing a role analogous to that of Aristotle's formal cause, the coordinated relationships make the system one kind of thing and not another. No one molecule or event, however, serves as coordinator. The organization and coordination are distributed relationships that act as a virtual governor. Dissipative processes like Bénard cells and self-organizing ones such as the B-Z reaction are dynamic patterns at a higher level of order. Zeleny (1980, 5) defines an autopoietic system as "a distinguishable complex of component-producing processes and their resulting components, bounded as an autonomous unity within its environment, and characterized by a particular kind of relations among its components and component-producing processes: the components, through their interaction, recursively generate, maintain and recover the same complex of processes [the organization] which produced them."

Formal Cause

Once the autocatalytic loop closes (A via B ... Z, which in turn catalyzes A), the cycle as a whole acts as a catalyst, that is, it becomes a focus of influence, a self-organized eddy that draws matter and energy into itself. As a result of the mutualist feedback of autocatalysis, therefore, the molecules in the network "steadily grow more and more abundant relative to molecules that are not part of the web" (Waldrop 1992, 123). The web grows, "not only in size but in activity and influence" (Ulanowicz 1997, 53).

Because some of the imported energy is diverted to maintaining that internal organization, autocatalytic webs, as Zeleny (1980) points out, are not just passive conduits for energetic forces entering from the environment. Although they are open systems that interact with their environment, their global dynamics renew and maintain the cohesion and integration of their overall organization by actively modulating the intake of materials and energy. Acting as a principle of movement in the thing qua thing, to use Aristotle's phrase, both autocatalytic webs and slime molds *as wholes* regulate the rate of chemical reactions to promote their overall continuity and stability. Acting to preserve and enhance the integrity of the higher level, autocatalytic webs and slime molds—self-organizing processes generally—are thus self-referential: they maintain, streamline, and renew their systems-level organization, not any of their individual components (Ulanowicz 1997). The dynamical framework in which the components are now embedded rules on the components' adequacy by selecting for inclusion those that enhance the global organization. For that reason self-organizing processes can be considered precursors of what might be called a "point of view."

The system's overall organization will be preserved even at the expense of the individual parts that make up its structure at any given moment. Autocatalytic webs select those components that increase the efficiency of the individual catalytic flows (Ulanowicz 1997). Component D might replace component B if the former were a better catalyst; E could replace C and F could replace A, "so that the final configuration DEF contains none of the original elements" (Ulanowicz 1997, 48). The final configuration, a highly pruned and streamlined version of the original, might not even look exactly like the earlier triad.

The system as a whole, to repeat, is not just a passive pass-through for energy exchanges. The dynamical organization functions as an internal selection process established by the system itself, operating top-down to preserve and enhance itself. That is why autocatalytic and other self-organizing processes are primarily informational; their internal dynamics determine which molecules are "fit" to be imported into the system or survive. Brooks and Wiley (1988) call this ability to pursue the integrity of the whole *informational closure*, in the sense that it is actively based on the organization's own internal requirements, not the environment's; as such it supersedes energetic exchanges. Ulanowicz (1997) explicitly identifies it with Aristotle's formal cause: the overarching dynamic pattern that makes an autocatalytic web that kind of process and no other.

The ordered environment in which the components of an autocatalytic cycle—or of any complex dynamical system—exist thus selectively (top-down) constrains their behavior and activities. Such top-down constraints are often "weak": they can be satisfied in many different ways. The pruning and streamlining illustrate why: autocatalytic processes act to preserve their overall organization, but different structures can realize the same organization. A component that may be fit in one context may not be in another; a structure that may be fit in one context or at one time may not be in another. Far from being a primary quality, therefore, fitness is a multiply realizable property (Depew and Weber 1995) that depends on what occurs elsewhere and previously.

Final Cause

The behavior of autocatalytic processes is also *"asymmetric ... imparting a definite ... direction to the behaviors of [such systems] towards ever greater levels of performance"* (Ulanowicz 1997, 46) by streamlining pathways and replacing components as just described. The direction of self-organization is always away from disorganized complicatedness and toward more organized complexity. "Greater levels of performance" thus refers to more efficient processing of energy and matter flows, all in the service of the enhanced integration and cohesion of the whole. Autocatalysis's "goal" is its own maintenance and enhancement in the face of disintegrating pressures from the environment. It is to that extent partially decoupled from and independent of the environment: autonomous.

Commentators on Aristotle's concepts of formal and final cause have often noted how these become entangled in living things. As we saw, Kant identified teleology with self-organization: an intrinsic physical end such as a tree both produces itself and maintains itself as itself, that is, it aims to preserve and promote its overall identity despite a constant turnover of components. This description is obviously true of dissipative, autocatalytic processes. As they select for inclusion in the web molecules that enhance overall activity, autocatalytic cycles "aim" at greater performance by constantly pruning and streamlining their pathway structure. To maintain itself as itself, an autocatalytic web functions as an "attractor" (see chapter 10): a rudimentary precursor of final cause.

It would be anthropomorphic to call this vectorial characteristic of autocatalytic structures "goal-intended" or "purposive"; it would be even more absurd to say that these dissipative structures act as they do "for a reason." And yet a precursor of teleology is detectable in the way such structures of process operate. Whether embodied in physical, chemical, biological, psychological, or social processes, homologous, irreversible dynamics appear to be at work in constructing nature's levels of organization, along with the emergent properties characteristic of each (Salthe 1993b). A naturalized account of purposiveness such as I am attempting must identify other biotic and abiotic processes that are rudimentary, primitive—"proto" goal-directed. Autocatalytic and other self-organizing structures are examples of precisely that.

Self-Organization and Teleology

Brooks and Wiley (1988) state that it is evident today that organisms are dissipative structures. As Kant recognized in the third *Critique*, biological organisms are characterized by this "previously unknown" form of nonlinear causality. Homologous dynamics are also responsible for chemical self-organization: there, too, the products of the whole themselves produce the whole. As a result, neither organisms nor dissipative structures can be understood via mechanistic principles alone, and neither is a candidate for reduction because their identity and integrity are given at a higher, relational level of organization. I do not mean to suggest that Kant understood all dynamical laws and relations to lie outside the scope of mechanics, only those responsible for self-organization. Stuart Kauffman has been quoted (Lewin 1992) as saying that Darwin didn't know about self-organization. Well, Kant didn't either.

Self-organizing systems, however, have no built-in, rigidly specified telos, the way Aristotle's organisms were supposed to, that unfolds developmentally and is preserved through reproduction. Instead, an openness and novelty that Aristotle could not have envisioned characterize complex dynamical systems. As mentioned earlier, Aristotle would not have thought it possible that randomly occurring fluctuations (biological mutations) not previously specified in the genome could be involved in the emergence of a new form that is then transmitted through reproduction (Depew 1997). The dynamic interaction between self-organizing systems and the contingencies of their environment, on the other hand, allows us to understand how both individuation and true evolution (not just development) are possible, something neither Aristotle nor Kant could have accepted.

Interlevel Causality

Once in place, the dynamics of a dissipative structure as a whole "provide the framework for the behavioral characteristics and activities of the parts" (Zeleny 1980, 20). By delimiting the parts' initial repertoire of behavior, the structured whole in which the elements are suddenly embedded also redefines them. They are now something they were not before, nodes in a network, components of a system. As such they are unable to access states that might have been available to them as independent entities. Insect colonies are an example of this phenomenon, self-organizing systems whose complexity "permits the division of functions, particularly the division of labor, as well as hierarchical relationships and mechanisms of population control" (Jantsch 1980, 69). The evolutionary advantage of such systematic hierarchical differentiation is that the whole can access states that the independent parts cannot. The overall hive can do much more than the individual bee. The price is that workers in a hive lose the ability to reproduce.

In short, not only do individual but interacting parts suddenly correlate to create systematic wholes: once organized, the resulting systems affect their components. In other words, self-organizing systems exhibit that previously unknown interlevel causality to which Kant referred, both bottom-up and top-down. They display bottom-up causality in that, under far-from-equilibrium conditions, their internal dynamics amplify naturally occurring fluctuations around which a phase change nucleates. When this discontinuous and irreversible transition occurs, a qualitatively different

regime self-organizes. A new "type" of entity, one that is functionally differentiated appears. In turn, the newly organized hierarchy constrains top-
down its components' behavior by restructuring and relating them in
ways they were not related before. Dissipative structures thus operate on
two levels simultaneously: part and whole, which interact in the manner
of Douglas Hofstadter's (1979) "strange loops," or Kant's "unknown causality." In Chuck Dyke's (1988) great phrase, they are "structured structuring structures."

Systemism versus Holism

An objection commonly raised against systems theory is worth mentioning. Because of claims such as Dewan's (1976) to the effect that
entrainment is an example of an emergent, holistic property of control
that has causal potency, Bunge (1979) charges holism with the false
claim that wholes act on their parts. Wholes cannot act on their parts,
he maintains, since a level of organization "is not a thing but a set and
therefore a concept ... levels cannot act on one another. In particular the
higher levels cannot command or even obey the lower ones. All talk of
interlevel action is elliptical or metaphorical" (13–14). Since there is, on
Bunge's account, no ontological (only an epistemological) relationship
between levels of organization, there can be no actual control by one over
another.

   Complex adaptive systems have proven Bunge wrong; their interlevel
relationships, however tangled, are real, not just epistemological. The
emergence of relatively autonomous levels of organization carries with it
the emergence of relatively autonomous qualities; quantitative changes
produce qualitative changes (Bohm 1971). Once a transition point is
passed, new modes of being emerge, in particular, new modes of causality.
"The most essential and characteristic feature of a qualitative transformation is that new kinds of causal factors begin to be significant in a given
context, or to 'take control' of a certain domain of phenomena, with the
result that there appear new laws and even new kinds of laws, which
apply in the domain in question" (53). Aversion to the possibility that
wholes might act on their parts betrays both the continuing and uncritical
acceptance of philosophy's refusal to countenance self-cause as well as the
prevalent philosophical tendency toward reification: an ontological bias
that favors concrete things over processes and relations, substances over
properties. It is true, of course, that wholes do not act on their components forcefully; but neither are wholes other than or external to the components that make them up. And to claim that they do not causally affect
their components at all begs the question by assuming that all cause must
be billiard ball–like to be causally efficacious at all.

Contradicting Bunge, Zeleny (1980, 20) suggests that the lesson to be learned from the theory of autopoiesis is precisely "the lesson of holism." Far from being an inert epiphenomenon, the dynamics of the autopoietic whole serve as the orderly context that structures the behavioral characteristics and activities of the parts, a clear formulation of one of Bunge's (1979, 39) characteristics of a holistic point of view: the dynamics of the global level control the functioning of components at the lower level. The whole *as whole* most assuredly acts on its parts: self-cause—but not, as some would have it, qua other—one part forcefully impressing itself on another. Instead, complex adaptive systems exhibit true self-cause: parts interact to produce novel, emergent wholes; in turn, these distributed wholes as wholes regulate and constrain the parts that make them up. Bunge (1979) also explicitly rejects the concept of hierarchy because, he notes, "hierarchy" implies a "dominance relation," always by the higher level on the lower one. It is true that, as Bunge notes and Pattee's distinction between structural and control hierarchies reinforces, the word "hierarchy" implies a unidirectional flow of order or authority, always and only from higher to lower (see Dyke 1988). To counteract this connotation, students of complex dynamical systems have coined the neologism "heterarchy" to allow interlevel causal relations to flow in both directions, part to whole (bottom-up) and whole to part (top-down). For stylistic reasons, however, I will continue to use the term "hierarchy," without thereby prejudicing the direction of influence between levels of organization.

Chapter 9

Constraints as Causes: The Intersection of Information Theory and Complex Systems Dynamics

---

Recapitulation

The last two chapters introduced an alternative to a Newtonian model of cause. In those chapters I showed how according to nonlinear, far-from-equilibrium science (and without appealing to any mysterious élan vital), systems are created from interacting components, which they then, in turn, control. As a result of this strange loop relationship between parts and wholes, these dynamical systems are not mere epiphenomena; they actively exercise causal power over their components. Still missing, however, is an analysis of the way this causal influence works. Simply calling it a phenomenon akin to Aristotle's formal and final causes, or Kant's unknown causality, does not take us very far. How can we analyze the type of cause at work in dynamic interlevel relationships, both bottom-up and top-down? Specifically, the problem boils down to the following: how can we both supersede Aristotle's prohibition against self-cause and at the same time go beyond modern science's limited, mechanistic understanding of cause as billiard ball–like? In this chapter I offer an analysis of the interlevel causality of dynamical systems—as the workings of constraint. Doing so will give us a handle on top-down causality, in particular, on how intentions can cause and flow into behavior: how they can inform its trajectory, in other words.

Distributed Control

Dissipative structures are not mechanical processes; in autocatalysis no one molecule pushes the others around. Neither does any one of the brain's neurons. The central nervous system has no localized grandmother control unit that, in the manner of a Newtonian force, activates others by bumping into them. We saw that as structures of processes, autocatalytic webs are distributed patterns of dynamic relations. They are relational and property, not concrete systems. It is therefore a category mistake to think of them as exercising causal power by impressing a force on their components. And yet far from being inert epiphenomena, as traditional science and philosophy would have it, complex systems like macroscopic Bénard cells, as distributed wholes, do indeed affect their components.

How are we to conceptualize this distributed control that complex systems exercise, top-down, on their components? I propose that we analyze those causal relations as the operations of constraint. Doing so allows interlevel relationships, previously intractable, to be incorporated into a more comprehensive understanding of cause, while simultaneously conferring ontological status on the level of the distributed whole. Once barriers against self-cause are broken down, there can be no objection to having wholes act on parts.

Constraints

The concept of constraint was first used formally in physical mechanics to describe the way the motion of a simple pendulum or a particle on an inclined plane is *"compelled by the geometry of its environment* to move on some specified curve or surface" (Lindsay 1961, 239, emphasis mine). To explain oscillations, Lindsay notes that "some of the most important cases of constrained motion are those in which particles are *connected by rods and strings"* and cannot, therefore, move any which way. In his explanation of D'Alembert's principle, Lindsay states, "If the masses were subject to no constraints (i.e., if they were not connected in any way or forced [a synonym for compelled?] to move along certain curves or surfaces) ..." (251). And in his discussion of Gauss's principle of least constraint, Lindsay says, "The system being subjected to certain constraints (i.e., the masses being perhaps connected to each other by rods or cords, or constrained to move along certain curves or surfaces) ..." (254). In physical mechanics, that is, constraints are said to "compel" and "force" behavior. The term suggests, however, not an external force that pushes, but a thing's connection to something else by rods, cords, strings, and the like as well as to the setting in which the object is situated. What do both have in common?

The first point to be made, in opposition to Newtonian science and modern philosophy's dismissal of relational properties as subjective, is that by "constraints" Lindsay clearly means something other than Newtonian forces that is nevertheless causal. As features either of an object's connections with the environment or of its embeddedness in that environment, neither are they "primary qualities"—intrinsic features, like mass, that the object would exhibit regardless of circumstances. Not every environment constrains things in it; aggregates and agglomerations do not constrain their parts, which are related only externally. Independent, disconnected objects change or move only when pushed about by external forces. On the other hand, both the connection to the rod and the curvature of the surface on which the object is located do make a difference to the object.

The orderly context in which the components are unified and embedded constrains them. Constraints are therefore relational properties that parts acquire in virtue of being unified—not just aggregated—into a systematic whole.

For example, the physical link between the tibia and the peronei on the one hand and the knee joint on the other systematically constrains the movement of the lower leg. As a result of the connection, the tibia's physiology is not independent of the knee; the linkage creates an orthopedic system that controls the tibia in ways to which it would not have been limited otherwise. The anatomical tie restricts the lower leg's range of motion. The constraints that the tibia's relationship to the knee places on the tibia limit the number of ways in which the lower leg can move: it can bend backward but not forward, for example. In this example, a constraint represents a contraction of the lower leg's potential range of behavior: the lower leg has less freedom of movement, given its connection with the knee, than it would have otherwise. Limiting or closing off alternatives is the most common understanding of the term "constraint."

But if all constraints restricted a thing's degrees of freedom in this way, organisms (whether phylogenetically or developmentally) would progressively do less and less. However, precisely the opposite is empirically observed. Some constraints must therefore not only reduce the number of alternatives: they must simultaneously create new possibilities. We need to understand how constraints can simultaneously open up as well as close off options (Campbell 1982).[41] To do so, it is helpful to examine another usage of the concept of constraint. Let us return, therefore, to information theory, in which constraints are identified not as in physical mechanics, with physical connections, but with rules for reducing randomness in order to minimize noise and equivocation.

Information-Theoretical Constraints

Lila Gatlin quotes Weaver (of Shannon and Weaver [1949] fame) as saying that "this word 'information' in communications theory relates not so much to what you do say, as to what you could say" (quoted in Gatlin 1972, 48). In a situation of complete randomness where alternatives are equiprobable you could say anything but in fact do say nothing. Random, equiprobable signals are static hiss unable to transmit actual messages.[42] It is true that in situations in which all alternatives are equally likely, potential information or message variety is at its maximum: before the process of selection in the Herman example, any one of the employees could be chosen. Likewise, the equiprobability of static crackle equates with unpredictability and maximum freedom, in short, with the possibility of constant novelty. But a series of totally random or equiprobable signals is meaningless: no pattern or message is extractable from the disorder. There is none.

At equilibrium, message variety is therefore a great but idle potential; actual information is zero. "Capacity is of no value if it cannot be utilized" (Gatlin 1972, 99). Without contrasts there can be no message; television snow is as meaningless as white noise. Transmitting or receiving a message requires a clear demarcation between message and background noise. The transmitter as well as the receiver must reduce the randomness in the sequence of signals to a "manageable" level. Encoding (and deciphering) the message according to certain rules is one way of doing so. Whether in communications or genetics, therefore, actual information content—a difference that makes a difference—requires an ordering process that harnesses the randomness. As we saw in the Herman example, a decision procedure is required to cull one name from the rest.[43] Constraining "the number of ways in which the various parts of a system can be arranged" (Campbell 1982, 44) reduces randomness by altering the equiprobable distribution of signals, thereby enabling potential information to become actual information. Constraints thus turn the amorphous potential into the definite actual: following Aristotle, constraints effect change. And in-form. Constraints embodied in encryption rules also take the signals away from equiprobability and randomness. Shannon's (1948) theorems are two such ordering processes.

Context-Free Constraints

The "most random state is ... characterized by events which are both independent and equiprobable" (Gatlin 1972, 87). When anything is as possible as anything else, and nothing is connected to anything else, however, nothing can signify or communicate anything. Flashes from a lighthouse pulsing regularly three long, three short, three long, on the other hand, can carry information precisely because regular flashes are more improbable than random ones, and can therefore be differentiated from background noise. Even to an extraterrestrial, the improbability of regularly pulsing flashes of light says "Signal," "Signal," "Signal," even if ET cannot tell *what* it means.

The same is true of language: if all sounds were equiprobable and every letter of the alphabet were as likely to show up as any other, no message could be communicated. Hence in any language, some letters appear more often than others. A number on a fair die has the same likelihood of being thrown as any other. The probability that a particular letter of the alphabet will appear in a word or sentence, however, is not like that. Some letters are more likely than others: in the long run they repeat more often (with increased redundancy) than they would in a random distribution. Each letter has a characteristic prior probability: in English, *es* have a higher prior probability than *zs*.

The prior probability of a specific letter is stacked by the conventions of that language. A string of letters with many *xs* and *zs* and relatively few *as* and *es* informs us that the text contains a message. Given that the conventional ordering of English is such that *xs* and *zs* appear very infrequently and given that we know that ordering rule, the string of letters also carries the information that the message is not in English. In each of these cases constraints alter the probability distribution of the available alternatives. They make a system diverge from chance, randomness, or equiprobability. Lila Gatlin calls constraints that function in this manner *context-free*.

The price paid for depending solely on context-free constraints is high, however, because reliability of transmission is inversely related to message variety. Suppose that to avoid the careless-messenger scenario, prevent equivocation, and improve transmission reliability, Herman's coworkers had imposed context-free constraints. What form might such constraints have taken? The employees might have broadcast "Herman," "Herman," "Herman," again and again. By restricting its potential variability to unity, one signal would repeat over and over. At the limit, context-free constraints would transmit only one signal or letter (with probability 1); the rest would be impossible (probability 0). No pattern whatsoever can convey no information, but the same pattern redundantly repeated again and again conveys no new information. There is, therefore, an inverse correlation between imposing context-free constraints so as to be able to transmit a message and the ability to say a lot in that message. Context-free constraints, in other words, are expensive: "if increased too much, they severely curtail the variety of messages which can be sent" (Campbell 1982, 119).

Thermodynamic Embodiments of Context-Free Constraints

A container filled with evenly diffused molecules of gas at room temperature is at equilibrium. Just as the random crackle of static can transmit no messages, thermodynamic systems without a temperature gradient can perform no work. Inserting a piston (an externally imposed, context-free constraint) into the container and moving the piston such that the molecules are compressed to one side takes the system away from the homogeneity of thermal equilibrium to the thermodynamic counterpart of regularly pulsing flashes of light. Individual gas molecules will be located with 100 percent probability on one side, absent 100 percent of the time on the other, an orderly arrangement of energy. Thermodynamically, the system can now do work. But as with any closed thermodynamic system, if pressure on the piston is removed, the system will move back toward equilibrium, thereby conforming to the second law of thermodynamics.[44]

No closed system can spontaneously become differentiated and complex, the thermodynamic analog of increased message variety. The piston's context-free constraint will make the molecules cluster at one end of the container, but no organization, form, or structure will ever appear just because of the piston. Brooks and Wiley (1988) note that if particles are independent of one another, no increase in number will ever produce organization. Heaping more individual and disconnected grains on a sand dune will never turn it into a sand castle.[45]

If nature relied solely on context-free constraints to create form, matter might clump and agglomerate, but differentiation and complexity would not exist. In short, no complex systems would appear. Here, too, encoding rules are needed to limit the amount of randomness in a string of signals. But they should not reduce uncertainty altogether; sufficient leeway must be allowed for novel messages to be expressed. Within the permissible range, the more order (because of its greater improbability than disorder), the more actual information, and the general concept of information therefore treads a fine line "between total constraint and total freedom" (Campbell 1982, 74).

Whether in chemistry, biology, or communications theory, therefore, context-free constraints cannot be the only way to encode information, for if they were, both biological development and evolution as we know them would be impossible. As mentioned earlier, increasingly complex order and structure characterize both cosmological and biological evolution, not relentless disintegration and disorder. The behavioral repertoire of a more complex species is larger than that of the species from which it evolved. Although, as noted earlier, one ordinarily thinks of constraints as limiting freedom, "control constraints must also create freedom in some sense" (Pattee 1973, 85). How to decrease randomness and entropy while simultaneously increasing the potential variety of messages? We need a type of constraint that curtails randomness without eliminating disorder altogether so that the possibility of new messages is retained.

Context-Sensitive Constraints

Shannon's (1948) great contribution to communications theory was to demonstrate that the need to reduce error need not restrict the ability to transmit messages. If encoded correctly, a message can be made as error-free as desired. Whether in dissipative structures, autocatalysis, or communications, the key is to make particles and processes interdependent by correlating and coordinating them. Stuart Kauffman (1991) claims that doing so serves up "Order for Free!" (Well, perhaps at a cost of degraded energy.) Let us look first at how language does it.

"Does the occurrence of X, [whether a letter or a word] alter the probability of the occurrence of Y [a second letter or word]" (Campbell 1982, 36)? The answer in any language is yes.[46] Some letters or words are more likely or unlikely to occur, not just because of the prior probability distribution of letters in that language, but also depending on the letter or sequence of letters, word or sequence of words that preceded them. Spelling, syntactic, and grammatical rules (at the level of the phonetic sequence of letters as well as of parts of speech)—even Morse code—are examples from linguistics of this very different kind of constraint.[47] As every *Wheel of Fortune* player knows, in addition to the relative improbability of *x*s and *y*s and the greater likelihood of *a*s and *e*s, the rules of conventional English dictate that the occurrence of the letter *q* raises the probability that the next letter will be a *u* and decreases to virtually zero the probability that the next letter will be another *q*. *I* before *e* except after *c*—with only some weird exceptions! Gatlin (1972) calls this kind of constraint, which establishes divergence from independence, *context-sensitive redundancy*.

Suppose a die is biased: context-free constraints make the number four appear, say, one out of three times (instead of one in six times, as it would in a fair die). Although the frequency distribution of numbers thrown by that die is no longer equiprobable, the likelihood of throwing a four remains an independent trial. Each number is still unrelated to the number that appeared on the previous try. Each throw of even a loaded die depends only on the die's (loaded) frequency distribution, that is, on its prior probability. In contrast, letters in a text are not independent of one another. The likelihood that the next letter or sequence of letters will be thus and such does not depend solely on that letter's or sequence's own prior probability. It also depends on the letter or sequence of letters that preceded it. Because the probability of any particular letter's appearing at $t + 1$ partly depends on what happened at t—(that is, on the overall environment in which that letter finds itself), measuring the impact of context-sensitive constraints requires a calculus of conditional probability: the probability of *x* at $t + 1$ given what happened at t—$P_x(t + 1/t)$. We can now appreciate that equivocation and noise, those measures of the dependence of outcome on origin discussed in chapter 6, in fact calculate the effectiveness of context-sensitive constraints imposed at the origin in ensuring information flow.

Constraints and Complexity

When the appearance of *q* increases the likelihood of *u*, the two have become related, not just by an external conjunction, but systematically: the pair are now what grammarians call an *i*-tuplet with *q* and *u* as components. Similarly, as relations among *i*-tuplets are constrained, words become possible; additional contextual constraints (on top of the contextual constraints that create words) make sentences possible. Systems, systems of systems, and so on can be assembled. By making the appearance of letters in an alphabet interdependent, contextual constraints thus allow complex linguistic structures to emerge.

As is the case in all complex systems, newly synchronized components pay a price for creating a global system: the number of ways in which they can be individually arranged is correspondingly reduced. In English, once "t-i-o" appear toward the end of a noun, the probability of *a*'s appearing next decreases dramatically. But the payoff trumps the cost: the interdependence context-sensitive constraints impose offers the advantage of permitting unlimited message variety despite limited channel capacity. A contextually coded alphabet yields more *i*-tuplets than its twenty-six letters; there are more words than *i*-tuplets, more sentences than words. To achieve the requisite variety, and because Mandarin Chinese limits words to one or two syllables, for example, the context-sensitive constraints of inflection are sometimes needed. Phonetic, syntactic, and stylistic layers of context-sensitive constraints, added on top of the context-free constraints on the prior probability of individual letters, thus provide a significant advantage over ideograms, pictograms, or hieroglyphs.

Without contextual constraints on sounds and scribbles, communication would be limited to a few grunts, shouts, wails, and so forth that would be severely restricted in what and how much they could express. Language's increased capacity to express ideas rests not on newly invented grunts and shouts but on the relationships and interconnections established by making interdependent the sounds in a sequence of grunts or shouts, that is, by making the probability of their occurrence context-dependent. Context-sensitive constraints are thus as efficient but not as expensive as context-free ones, for they "can be increased by a reasonable amount without cramping the message source too severely" (Campbell 1982, 119). *By correlating and coordinating previously aggregated parts into a more complex, differentiated, systematic whole, contextual constraints enlarge the variety of states the system as a whole can access.*

All of this would, of course, be of minimal interest to action theorists or philosophers of mind if it were a mechanism found only in language. That this is emphatically not so is one of the lessons to be learned from complex dynamical systems. I have used examples from language merely as a heuristic illustration of the process.

Context-Sensitive Constraints in Nature

The emergence of Bénard Cells and B-Z chemical waves signals the abrupt appearance of context-sensitive constraints in mutualist-driven, open processes far from equilibrium. This discontinuous change occurs when previously unrelated molecules suddenly become correlated in a distributed whole. A complex dynamical system emerges when the behavior of each molecule suddenly depends both on what the neighboring molecules are doing and what went before. When components, in other words, suddenly become context-dependent.

The same is true of autocatalysis. Returning to the triad illustrating autocatalysis, assume that you start out with the same number each of several types of molecules (A, B, and C), randomly floating around in a primordial soup and independent of each other: no geometric features enhancing the likelihood of catalysis exist yet. Equilibrium forever. Next, suppose context-free constraints are imposed such that there are more of some molecules in certain areas than in others. Result: possible clumping, but no differentiation.[48] On the other hand (as in the original example), suppose instead that because of their geometrical structure, some of the molecules are catalysts: A enhances B's binding, which in turn increases the likelihood of binding C, and so on. If B is more or less likely to occur given the presence of catalyst A than otherwise, B's conditional probability differs from its prior probability. Being systematically connected to and correlated with A has changed whatever prior probability B had in the overall frequency distribution of molecules before the interrelatedness was established. As physical embodiments of context-dependent constraints, catalysts are therefore one way in which natural processes become subject to conditional probabilities.

Because of their geometry, that is, catalysts can take molecules away from *independence*, not just equiprobability, the way context-free constraints do, by enhancing the likelihood that certain other events will occur. Once the probability that something will happen depends on and is altered by the presence of something else, the two have become systematically and therefore internally related. As a result of the operations of context-sensitive constraints and the conditional probabilities they impose, A is now part of B's external structure. Because A is no longer "out there" independent of B, to which it is only externally related, the interdependence has created a larger whole, the AB system. Insofar as it is part of B's new context or external structure, A has been imported into B.

By making a system's current states and behavior systematically dependent on its history, the feedback loops of autocatalysis also incorporate the effects of time into those very states and behavior patterns. Indeed, precisely what makes these complex systems dynamical is that a current state is in part dependent on a prior one. Feedback, that is, incorporates the past into the system's present "external" structure. Feedback thus threads a system through both time and space, thereby allowing part of the system's external structure to run through its history.

Feedback processes thus embody the context-sensitive constraints of history. By embodying context-sensitive constraints, mutualist feedback renders a system sensitive to (constrained by) its own past experiences. This makes nonlinear dynamical systems historical, not just temporal the way near-equilibrium thermodynamical systems are. Once the system's subsequent behavior depends on both the spatial and temporal conditions under which it was created and the contingent experiences it has undergone, the system is historically and contextually embedded in a way that near-equilibrium systems of traditional thermodynamics are not. The very structure of a snowflake, for example, embodies the conditions under which it was created. Because dissipative structures are not just dropped into either time or space the way Newtonian atoms with only primary qualities are, their evolutionary trajectory is therefore not predictable in detail. Mutualism thus makes a dynamical system's current and future properties, states, and behaviors dependent on the context in which the system is currently embedded as well as on its prior experiences. As a result, unlike the near-equilibrium processes of traditional thermodynamics, complex systems do not forget their initial conditions: they "carry their history on their backs" (Prigogine, Spring 1995, U.S. Naval Academy). Their origin constrains their trajectory.

Operating as enabling constraints (Salthe 1993b), *context-sensitive constraints make complexity possible.* The emergence of autocatalytic cycles and slime molds—of self-organized systems in general—is the phenomenological manifestation of the sudden closure of context-sensitive constraints. As mentioned earlier, the new relationship among the components is the establishment of a new context—a new external structure or boundary conditions—for those components. Once particles and processes are interrelated into a dissipative structure, they become components or nodes of a more highly differentiated whole. By correlating previously independent particles and processes, context-sensitive constraints are therefore one mechanism whereby chemical and biological hierarchies are created.

Context-sensitive constraints, in short, are a mechanism for morphogenesis. Evidence for this claim is plentiful: for example, the position of a cell during the developmental process is crucial for gene expression and differentiation, and the phenotypic manifestation of a particular DNA codon depends on the overall context in which it is located. DNA codons given a particular context become genes, with new properties, rules, and laws that apply to that level of organization.

First- and Second-Order Contextual Constraints

The ability of catalyst A (perhaps because of its geometric shape) to increase the likelihood that B will occur, of B to increase the likelihood that

C will happen, and so on embodies what can be called *first-order contextual constraints*, that is, context-sensitive constraints operating at the same level of organization. In the B-Z reaction, however, once molecule Z catalyzes A and the autocatalytic loop closes, a phase change takes place: the autocatalytic network's organization itself suddenly emerges as a contextual constraint on its components. I call these *second-order contextual constraints*. Top-down, second-order contextual constraints serve as the boundary conditions in which the components are located—and to which they are now systematically, not just externally related. All virtual governors are examples of such top-down, second-order contextual constraints.

Recall the case of Bénard cells. Once they abruptly self-organize, the water molecules that make up the hexagonal, rolling cell are no longer independent of each other: the behavior of each water molecule suddenly depends on what all the others are doing. That is, it depends on its relation to the Bénard cell as a whole. Once self-organization takes place, second-order, context-dependent constraints (from whole to part) suddenly appear on top of any context-free constraints. In the case of the B-Z reaction, for example, once autocatalytic closure occurs, the wave as a whole imposes (top-down) second-order constraints on the behavior of the individual component chemical molecules. Their behavior thus depends on their relation to the overall wave, a part-whole, whole-part phenomenon.

That is, once autocatalytic closure takes place, second-order, context-dependent constraints (from whole to part) suddenly appear on top of the first-order contextual constraints that, say, catalyst A exerts on B, B on C, and so on, and on top of any context-free constraints already in place. The newly created "structured structuring structure" in which the component molecules are now situated as a whole changes the prior probability distribution of their behavioral options and, as such, alters their degrees of freedom. More precisely, the newly created "structured structuring structure" *is* the change in the probability of the components' behavior. There are suddenly ways in which they can no longer behave at all. We saw the process at work in the Bénard cell: a Bénard cell *is* the molecules' concerted pattern of behavior; that is, it *is* the phenomenological manifestation of their conditional probability distribution: how this molecule will behave *given* what those others are doing. Once captured in—entrained by—the cell's overall dynamics, the individual water molecules therefore behave "as if in concert" with the others—as if, that is, they knew what the others were doing and modified their behavior accordingly, without any one molecule giving orders. A control hierarchy has appeared.

Those aspects of the environment with which I am systematically interdependent are therefore part of my external structure. As both a biological and social entity, I extend into the world and am embedded in it. That's the point that both logical and experimental behaviorism missed.

By taking the organism far from equilibrium and precipitating a bifurcation, the persistent interaction of conditioning establishes context-sensitive interdependencies between the organism and its environment. Parts interact to produce a greater organism-environment whole, which in turn affects (top-down) those very parts. Conditioning and learning import the environment into the agent's dynamics by reorganizing and recalibrating those dynamics. In this sense, components are embedded in and not just dropped into an environment, as in an experiment. Once self-organized, the global dynamics of the overall organism-environment system become the control knob of its components—top-down causality, in effect.

The difference in the way individual slime mold amoebas behave while they are independent entities and after they self-organize into the complex slug is not explicable solely as the result of bumping into another amoeba (as mechanics and modern philosophy would have it). The difference is largely a measure of second-order context-sensitive constraints embodied by (in) the whole self-organized slug. So too, the difference in the way molecules of water behave while they are isolated and independent and after they self-organize into the Bénard cell is a measure of the second-order, context-sensitive constraints embodied by (in) the hexagonal cell. That difference is also a measure of each system's complexity or degree of organization (Brooks and Wiley 1988). Top-down constraints that begin to weaken cause a system to become unstable. When this happens, the conditional probability that a component will behave in a certain way given the systematic context in which it is embedded begins to alter, and the behavior of the components fluctuates much more widely. The overall system's integrity (identity) and survival are in danger.

Bottom-Up Enabling Constraints

Contextual constraints thus perform double duty. From the combined effects of context-free and first-order contextual constraints, dynamical structures and patterns at a higher level of complexity self-organize. Parts interact to produce wholes. When context-free and first-order contextual constraints correlate flows of matter (reactants) and energy and thereby take them far from equilibrium and independence, a dynamic dissipative structure of process suddenly emerges. This discontinuous transition to entrainment and hierarchical organization is the sudden establishment of second-order context-sensitive constraints: abruptly, the behavior of an individual cardiac cell, generator, water molecule, or letter of the alphabet is no longer independent of those around it. The renewed repertoire of behavioral alternatives and properties that suddenly becomes available to the emergent system as a whole is the phenomenological counterpart of the sudden appearance of second-order contextual constraints. By coordinating previously independent parts, context-dependent constraints allow a more complex organization to emerge, with novel properties that the isolated parts lacked. Self-organization enlarges a system's phase space by adding degrees of freedom. Enabling constraints thus create potential information by opening—bottom-up—a renewed pool of alternatives that the emergent macrostructure can access. The explosion of potential message variety available to each new global level is its expanded potential. The coherent laser beam can cauterize flesh; the waves of the individual laser atoms, separately, however, cannot. The emergent level is thus qualitatively different from the earlier one. As an integrated organism, the slime mold has properties the independent amoebas that make it up did not. Tissues (which are organized webs of cells) can do different things than independent cells, organs different things than tissues, proteins different things than amino acids, Bénard cells different things than independent water molecules—all because of homologous dynamics at work. Gatlin (1972) argues that the explosion of phenotypes that took place with the appearance of the vertebrates occurred because vertebrates managed to maintain context-free redundancy constant while allowing context-sensitive constraints to expand.

As research increasingly uncovers evidence of context-dependent mutualist feedback in the brain (Edelman 1987; Freeman 1991a, 1991b), we can posit the dynamical self-organization of a neurological hierarchy. Progressively higher levels of neural organization self-assemble, each exhibiting novel properties and greater degrees of freedom. In turn, the higher levels impose second-order constraints on the lower ones. This is what self-consciousness and intentional action are all about. But I anticipate.

Top-Down as Selective Constraints

As a distributed whole, a self-organized structure imposes second-order contextual constraints on its components, thereby restricting their degrees of freedom. As we saw, once top-down, second-order contextual constraints are in place, energy and matter exchanged across an autocatalytic structure's boundaries cannot flow any which way. The autocatalytic web's dynamical organization does not allow *any* molecule to be imported into the system: in a very important feature of self-organizing dynamical systems, their organization itself determines the stimuli to which they will respond. By making its components interdependent, thereby constraining their behavioral variability, the system preserves and enhances its cohesion and integrity, its organization and identity. As a whole it also prunes inefficient components. Second-order contextual constraints are thus in the service of the whole. They are, also therefore, the ongoing, structuring mechanism whereby Aristotle's formal and final causes are implemented (Ulanowicz 1997).

Organization limits the degrees of freedom of a system's components. Once autocatalytic closure takes place, molecules C and D become components in a system. As such their behavioral repertoire is selectively constrained (their degrees of freedom curtailed) by the systematic context of which they are now a part. Unlike electrical generators and other allopoietic devices that require externally imposed governors, however, both autocatalytic closure and biological entrainment signal the spontaneous emergence of a field or dynamic network that is the endogenous establishment of second-order, context-sensitive constraints on the components at the first level. As distributed wholes, complex adaptive systems are virtual governors that give orders to themselves—qua thing, not qua other. The coherent laser beam "slaves" its component atomic waves even though "there is nobody to give orders" (Haken 1987, 420). That is, one particle does not push another around. The orderly relationships that characterize the structure of the overall laser beam as a whole are the context that "gives orders" to its components. The same can be said of individual cardiac cells: the systematic context of the overall heart confers an otherwise absent stability on individual cardiac cells.

Top-down constraints that wholes exert on their components are inhibiting, selectionist constraints. Components that satisfy the requirements of the higher level will be classified as well-fitting. The constraints that wholes impose on their parts are restrictive insofar as they reduce the number of ways in which the parts can be arranged, and conservative in the sense that they are in the service of the whole. But they are also creative in a different, functional sense: those previously independent parts are now components of a larger system and as such have acquired new functional roles. The newly created overall system, too, has greater potential than the independent, uncorrelated components.

Paradoxically and simultaneously, that is, self-organization also constitutes the appearance of the remarkable and unpredictable properties of the global level: the cauterizing ability of the laser beam, the enzymatic capabilities of a protein—or, I speculate, consciousness and self-consciousness—and their attendant states. These emergent properties of the higher level are the phenomenological manifestation of those dynamic relationships. But I emphasize that they are emphatically not epiphenomenal. Although not in a push-pull, forceful manner, the higher level of organization is causally effective: as a second-order, top-down constraint.

Nature's Own Jekyll and Hyde

Context-sensitive thermodynamic constraints operating in open systems far from equilibrium such as autocatalytic cycles decrease the rate at which local entropy is produced. Simultaneously, the imposition of context-sensitive constraints satisfies the second law of thermodynamics by irreversibly increasing total entropy. How is this possible? Thermodynamically the answer is clear and well-known. Local sinks of order are bought at the price of increased total disorder.[49] The self-organization of a new level of complexity renews the system's overall entropy production even as it uses some of the energy to create and maintain a local eddy of order and lowered internal entropy production. Per gram of biomass, an adult consumes less energy than does the blastula. The brain metabolizes almost as much glucose while in a deep sleep as it does while working on a difficult calculus equation.

Acting as Dr. Jekyll, second-order, top-down contextual constraints are thus nature's endogenous Maxwell's demon. By curtailing the components' alternatives, they reduce randomness and create order. Unlike Maxwell's externally imposed demon, however, which produced more entropy in determining the molecules' location than the order it thereby established, the order created by context-dependent constraints is an inside job. Although total entropy production increases with the irreversible creation of order, the streamlining achieved through self-organization reduces the rate of internal entropy production as some of that energy is diverted to maintain its own structure. You and I (as well as tornadoes and slime molds) are just such local eddies of order. Because these processes are local eddies of order in a sea of much higher dimensionality and potential, fewer dimensions are required to describe them; self-organized processes are therefore describable as collective variables: you and I. Folk psychological terms are just that: descriptions of the collective variable level.

Operating as Mr. Hyde, on the other hand, bottom-up, enabling contextual constraints simultaneously renew message variety by enlarging the overall system's state space. The renewed possibilities of the expanded phase space available to the emergent level of organization more than offset (see Alvarez de Lorenzana 1993) the local order that top-down contextual constraints effect by limiting alternatives at the component level. It is important to emphasize that the potential behavioral repertoire that the context-sensitive ordering process creates is at a dynamical level of organization different from that on which the selective constraints operate. The higher level of organization, whether thermodynamic, chemical, biological, psychological, or social, possesses a qualitatively different repertoire of states and behavior than the earlier level, as well as greater degrees of freedom. The global level, which in one sense is nothing more than the combined enabling constraints correlating components at the lower level, is at the same time the locus of emergent properties. *You* can write a book; the blastula from which you developed could not. Increased variety is one way greater complexity is identified. Not only can you or I write a book, we can do so carefully, sloppily, easily, and so forth. As the number of options open to the overall system increases, the potential for disorder is simultaneously renewed. The second law of thermodynamics is thereby upheld as well.

Objection

I have analyzed interlevel causality in terms of the workings of context-sensitive constraints and constraint as alterations in degrees of freedom and probability distributions. It might be objected, however, that "alteration" presupposes causality and so the entire project is guilty of circularity. In reply, consider the following: assume there are four aces in a fifty-two card deck, which is dealt evenly around the table. Before the game starts each player has a $\frac{1}{13}$ chance of receiving at least one ace. As the game proceeds, *once* players A, B, and C have already been dealt all four aces, the probability that player D has one automatically drops to 0. The change occurs because within the context of the game, player D's having an ace is not independent of what the other players have. Any prior probability in place before the game starts suddenly changes because, by establishing interrelationships among the players, the rules of the game impose second-order contextual constraints (and thus conditional probabilities).

Not so, the objector will reply; dealing an ace each to players A, B, and C is what caused player D's chances to change. That reply only buttresses my own case: no external force was impressed on D to alter his situation. There was no forceful efficient cause separate and distinct from the effect. Once the individuals become card players, the conditional probabilities imposed by the rules and the course of the game itself alter the prior probability that D has an ace, not because one thing bumps into another but because each player is embedded in a web of interrelationships. The higher level's self-organization is the change in probability of the lower-level events. Top-down causes cause by changing the prior probability of the components' behavior, which they do as second-order contextual constraints.

Evidence from Biology

Context-dependent dynamics are ubiquitous in biology, neurology, and even developmental studies. John Collier (1986) as well as Brooks and Wiley (1988) take it as virtually self-evident that organisms are self-organizing dissipative structures. In biology the evidence is plentiful and widespread. Having shown that aggregation cannot be understood in terms of discrete sets of individual cells, Alan Garfinkel (1987) developed a model that establishes that dynamic phase entrainment is the key to slime mold organization. Brian Goodwin (1987), too, redefined organisms (not cells) as the fundamental biological entity by reconceptualizing organisms as fields. Doing so makes it possible to explain why cells respond to positional information: "gene products act within an organized context whose properties must be defined before the generated morphology can be described" (179). Studies by Gunther Stent and his colleagues (1978) have also shown how the endogenously produced rhythms required for leech locomotion depend on oscillations that arise from the coupling among the various neurons.

Evidence from Neurology

It has been known for some time that the neurons with which human beings are born undergo severe pruning and organizing during the first year of life. It is not implausible to speculate that the complex neural organization thereby constructed, which no doubt provides the biological basis for the emergence of self-awareness and meaning, occurs in response to entrainment that results from persistent interactions with the environment. These interactions drive the neurological system far from equilibrium and precipitate a phase change. The newly self-organized system in turn imposes second-order, context-sensitive constraints on its components, the individual neural processes.

There is extensive evidence that the activity of individual neurons depends on their place in the overall system. Antonio Damasio's research has shown that each of the various levels of neural architecture (neurons, local circuits, subcortical nuclei, cortical regions, etc.) functions as a structured structuring structure (Damasio 1989, 15). Each depends on its place in the next higher level, which in turn contributes to the functioning of that level. It is also known that the integration of these various units and levels forms a coordinated dynamic map that is, moreover, "not a single contiguous map but rather an interaction and coordination of signals in separate maps" (66). Furthermore, not only is there ample evidence that portions of the brain are organized topographically; there is even evidence that the very topographical arrangement of these dynamic maps alters as a result of the organism's experiences (Merzenich, Allard, and Jenkins 1990).

The human brain is also known to be sensitive to temporal relations. It has become increasingly clear that neuronal activity depends not only on immediate input, but also on the neurons' prior activity. In other words, the brain shows a pattern of "history-dependent unit activity" (Fetz 1993, 188):

> A single pattern of sensory input is represented by different patterns of interneuron activation at different times relative to stimulus onset and offset. Similarly, a single pattern of motor neuron excitation and inhibition is represented by different interneuron activity patterns at different times relative to the stimulus. The concept of time-dependent sensory and motor representations has received relatively little attention because models of sensorimotor integration have tended to focus on static representations. (Lockery and Sejnowski 1993, 132)

Such data strongly support the hypothesis that the nervous system handles excess degrees of freedom dynamically. That is, neurological research suggests a mechanism whereby "higher order inputs can act to shape and modify ongoing activity in response to proprioceptive and sensory feedback, thus utilizing excess degrees of freedom when necessary" (Chiel and Beer 1993, 147).

Auditory Perception

How do we extract the necessary information from an auditory signal so that we are able to recognize it in the future? Port, Cummins, and McAuley (1995) have shown that we do so in two ways, both of which are context-dependent forms of coding. We extract auditory information both from the serial order in which signals are presented and from their relative duration as well. *Serial order processing* relies on the subject's previous experience of a string of signals, the sequence of which is remembered. The drawback of this form of coding, which albeit is context-dependent, is that if several patterns are presented simultaneously, listeners have difficulty keeping the different sequences straight. *Relative duration processing*, on the other hand, also a form of context-dependence, operates by extracting the periodicity internal to the signal itself: the characteristic tempo or beat of a horse's trot or gallop, or of a faucet's drip, for example. The auditory system carries out this process by entraining its own periodic neural activity to the incoming signal, which subsequently allows the person to recognize that particular beat or tempo. The natural periodicity of the neurons resets to that of the incoming signal, which it subsequently represents. When this happens, the context-sensitive constraints established by entrainment in effect import the external world into the newly recalibrated neurological pattern. Entrainment to an incoming signal is therefore one way in which a pattern of neurological organization can acquire an indicator function, that is, can represent something in the outside world. The advantage of this form of processing comes not only from the fact that many signals in nature are periodic but also from the fact that entrainment is highly robust to noise.

Olfactory Perception

On their own, cortical neurons fire randomly: they crackle like static noise. When feedback loops connect them to other neurons, however, dendritic waves, some of which are periodic, suddenly emerge (Freeman 1995, 56). Once that irreversible phase change takes place, neuronal activity is no longer random; the periodicity of the dendritic waves displays a characteristic frequency. By taking neurons far from equilibrium, the connectivity functions as an enabling contextual constraint establishing an emergent but endogenous frequency distribution. This periodic behavior is characteristic of dendritic wave patterns, which serve as the material basis of higher brain functions.

In his studies of olfaction in rabbits, Walter Freeman (1991a) found that the perception of smell can be explained only in terms of the distributed pattern formed by the cooperative behavior of many millions of neurons. Each odor appears on EEG recordings as a coherent pattern of activity, a complex neuronal "attractor" (see chapter 10) that moreover does not record just the incoming stimulus. The wave pattern of an odor associated with a reward is different from one that lacks that association. If this association changes, the wave pattern changes also. The overall EEG pattern, in other words, not only represents the odor; it also represents the meaning that the stimulus has for the animal.

For an incoming stimulus to be perceived as meaningful, the brain must entrain it both to the rest of the animal's memory store (time-dependent contextuality) and to other incoming stimuli (environment-dependent contextuality). Freeman postulates that each sniff is processed and recognized within a complex context that embodies the past history of the animal's experience with that smell as well as the animal's current state of arousal and other internal features. Embedding the organism in time and space in this way can be done only with dynamically changing and updated context-dependent coding. We have already seen that this form of organization is characteristic of dissipative structures in general.

Visual Perception

Recent experimental results indicate that the scanning pattern of human saccadic eye movements is also context-dependent, highly sensitive to the task at hand—e.g., questions about the ages of people in a picture will elicit saccades bringing the fovea largely to the faces" (reported in McClamrock 1995, 136). Eye movements respond to the meaning of the stimulus, not just to light or sound waves! The direction of the eye movements, in other words, is sensitive to the meaningful context established by the questions. The advantage of contextual sensitivity, of course, is that there is no need to scan the entire visual field if you let the questions meaningfully narrow the search space for you. A form of context-dependent coding similar to that operating in olfaction therefore appears to be at work in visual processing.

Summary

Context-sensitive constraints are thus a causal (but not efficiently causal) engine that drives creative evolution, not through forceful impact, but by making things interdependent. The increasingly complex differentiation that has characterized both development and evolution is a function of the operation of contextual constraints. Even if nothing other than parts organized in a certain way, complex dynamical systems are for that very reason more than the sum of those parts, and therefore different from and irreducible to their aggregation. Although a three-dimensional structure is made up of two-dimensional components, one cannot adequately capture its three-dimensional relationships simply by enumerating its two-dimensional components.

I hypothesize that in the same way, high levels of self-organization of the human brain and nervous system can access different states with different properties than less complex and uncorrelated neuronal processes can. We can postulate that the various characteristics of consciousness and self-consciousness, including meaning, intentionality, purposiveness, and the like, are just a few of these novel, emergent properties. Chapter 11 presents evidence that strongly suggests that meaning, too, is embodied in the global properties of high-dimensional dynamical systems. But first it will be very useful to try to visualize these dynamics as graphs and landscapes.

Chapter 10

Dynamical Constraints as Landscapes: Meaning and Behavior as Topology

---

Recapitulation

In the last chapter I argued that, through the imposition of second-order contextual constraints, a dynamical system's global level limits its components' degrees of freedom such that the organization (order, pattern) of the higher level is maintained and enhanced. A complex system's contextual constraints effect this top-down control by altering the prior probability of the behavior of its components. The higher level constrains the lower, for example, by regulating the rate at which its component processes occur, that is, by altering their natural frequency. Given its embeddedness in a systematic setting, the prior likelihood that a lower-level process will be activated automatically alters. That conditional probability is what embeddedness in an systematic whole is. The rates at which autocatalysis, for example, allows energy and matter flows in from and expels them to the environment are constantly updated in such a way as to preserve the organization of the overall network. The regulation preserves the organization's integrated system of values—its invariant relations—that give the overall system its identity. Despite significant variability at the component level, the global level thereby remains meta-stable and robust to perturbations.

To conceptualize actions as behavioral trajectories constrained top-down by an intention, understanding dynamical systems as directed graphs will be helpful. Having the right models makes it possible to visualize the constraints of complex dynamical systems graphically or, better yet, topologically, as a landscape. Doing so also has the advantage of illustrating how some of those systems can embody meaning in their very organization, and how that meaning can flow into behavior.

Picturing Dynamical Systems

Each property of a system can be represented by a separate axis on a graph. Each axis corresponds to a variable in the equation that captures the system's dynamics. A system with two properties is graphed onto a two-dimensional graph, one with three properties onto a three-dimensional graph, and so on. A system's *state space* therefore represents its present potential: each possible state of the system is represented as an intersection of coordinates, a point or region in two, three or, more likely, multidimensional space.

When one of the axes represents time, the graph depicts the system's *phase space*: its potential over time. Changes in state, including behavior, can be represented by arrows on a directed graph of vectors that illustrate the motions of the self-organized system through its multidimensional phase space, the *manifold*. The arrow's trajectory begins at a particular point representing the state and time in which the change began (called the *source* or *origin*), continues along a specific path, and ends at a terminus or *sink*. Multiple trajectories terminating in the same sink and originating from precisely the same source may be possible through different en route nodes. Because of the sensitivity of nonequilibrium complex systems to initial conditions, if the trajectories originate at even infinitesimally different times, radically different trajectories are possible from the same origin because other things have changed in the interim.

Attractors

Trajectories that converge on typical patterns describe what are called the system's *attractors*. Once water molecules self-organize into Bénard cells, those attractors describing a Bénard cell regime pull the individual molecules into their orbit. The apparent goal of each molecule, we said earlier, is to recreate the overall Bénard cell. As a consequence we can also speak metaphorically of individual water molecules' acting "as if they knew" what the others were doing. The contextual constraints or changes in conditional probability embodied in the attractors are responsible for this apparent omniscience.

Consider the pendulum on a grandfather clock; represent its behavior on a Cartesian graph whose x-axis represents the bob's position, the y-axis its speed. Its behavioral trajectory will look like a spiral-shaped arrow converging on the point representing the bob's resting place ($0, 0$ on the graph). No matter where the pendulum starts out, it gradually moves toward its resting point. Attractors are representa tions of natural precursors of final cause; etymologically, even the word "attractor" suggests a pull. Arrows on a directed graph whose flow converges toward an attractor sculpt its *basin*, the watershed surrounding the attractor. Points located within a basin of attraction represent states with a greater than average probability of being visited by the system. Changes of state originating from one of those points will naturally tend toward a lower point in that basin, that is, toward states with an even higher probability. While in a stable regime, a system's behavior converges on its attractor.

Finding oneself within a basin of attraction means that one's future behavior will be *constrained* by that attractor—that is, directed and channeled by the contour of its valley (by its dynamics)—thereby increasing the likelihood of being drawn in one direction rather than another. Unlike preset Aristotelian final causes, however, self-organized attractors embody the constraints constructed by the interplay between the system's own internal dynamics and its environment. Attractors therefore represent a dynamical system's organization, including its external structure or boundary conditions.

Or, to say the same thing, a system's current dynamics constrain its behavior. Given a system's internal dynamics, its current state, and the context in which it is embedded (i.e., its external structure or boundary conditions), the system will tend, for example, to do A. In part, as mentioned earlier, this tendency is due to its internal structure; it is also in part assembled from the system's interaction with the environment.

The pendulum on a grandfather clock is a near-equilibrium system. External perturbations will cause the trajectory to deviate, but the pull of the attractor gradually draws the system's behavior back toward its characteristic motion. The single endpoint toward which the pendulum's behavior naturally converges despite external perturbations—point (0, 0) on the graph—is called a *point attractor*. Once the system reaches its attractor, it takes an external push to dislodge it from that stable state.

The pendulum's motion does not visit the entire space of the graph in figure 10.1, as it would if its behavior were random. Attractors thus provide evidence that the system's overall organization constrains available alternatives (Brooks and Wiley 1988) such that its behavior is character-

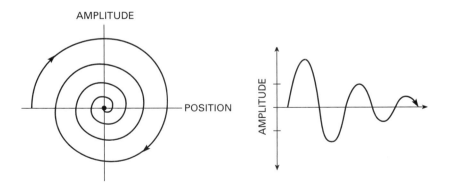

Figure 10.1
Point attractor. The system converges on a point in phase space. Ex: the behavior of the pendulum on a grandfather clock (where the x axis represents velocity or position and the y axis represents amplitude or displacement).

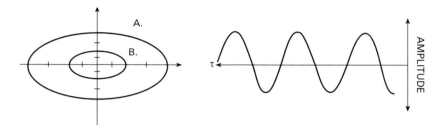

Figure 10.2
Limit Cycle attractor. The system's behavior repeats periodically, producing a cyclical orbit. The behavior of the B-Z reaction waves, and predator-prey relationships can be represented in this manner.

istically drawn to certain patterns. Once again, the difference between random behavior and the actual, restricted trajectory carved out by the attractor is a measure of those second-order contextual constraints emerging from the interaction between the pendulum's inherent dynamics and gravity. The pendulum's attractor portrait captures the relationships that identify the organization of the pendulum-gravity system. The attractor portrait of a pendulum in zero gravity would look quite different.

Those systems (such as the B-Z reaction's chemical wave) that oscillate between more than one stable state (blue to red and then back to blue) are governed by a *limit cycle attractor* and can be graphed as behavior that repeats regularly in a continuous, periodic loop (figure 10.2). Many neurons are natural oscillators. Because the behavior of the pendulum or of the B-Z reaction can be fully described by two variables: position and velocity in the case of the former, red and blue in the latter, they are easily pictured on a two-dimensional Cartesian grid (figures 10.1 and 10.2). Complex dynamical systems like you and me, however, have an indefinitely large number of properties. Representing each by an axis in state space requires an unvisualizable graph with an astronomical number of dimensions. Even the simple recurrent network Jeffrey Elman (1995) designed to predict the next word (one of twenty-nine) of a sentence consists in a state space of seventy dimensions (see chapter 11). It is important to keep in mind that many complex systems and certainly the human neurological system are describable only by a manifold of mind-boggling dimensionality.

Complex, Chaotic, or Strange Attractors

In the last twenty-five years or so, a third type of attractor has been identified. So-called strange or complex attractors (figure 10.3) describe patterns

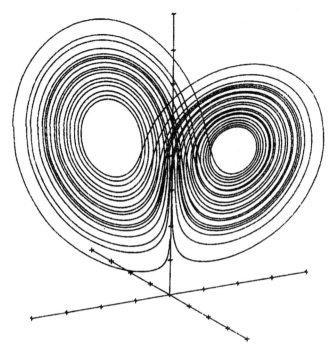

Figure 10.3
A complex or strange attractor, the Lorenz attractor. The crossover from one wing to the other corresponds to a reversal in the convecting fluid's spin direction. Never exactly repeating itself, the trajectory nevertheless stays within certain bounds.

of behavior so intricate that it is difficult to discern an overarching order amid the disorder they allow. All attractors represent characteristic behaviors or states that tend to draw the system toward themselves, but strange attractors are "thick," allowing individual behaviors to fluctuate so widely that even though captured by the attractor's basin they appear unique. The width and convoluted shape of strange attractors imply that the overall pathway they describe is multiply realizable. Strange attractors describe ordered global patterns with such a high degree of local fluctuation, that is, that individual trajectories appear random, never quite exactly repeating the way the pendulum or chemical wave of the B-Z reaction does. Complex systems are often characterized by strange attractors. The strange attractors of seemingly "chaotic" phenomena are therefore often not chaotic at all. Such intricate behavior patterns are evidence of highly complex, context-dependent dynamic organization.

Ontogenetic Landscapes

Another useful way of visualizing the dependencies and constraints of attractors is as *ontogenetic landscapes* (figure 10.4) depicting a "series of *changes* of relative stability and instability" over time (Thelen and Smith 1994, 122).

If a system accessed every point or region in its phase space with the same frequency as every other (that is, randomly), its ontogenetic landscape would be smooth and flat. A completely flat, smooth initial landscape would portray an object with no propensities or dispositions—that is, with no attractors. It would describe a "system" with no identity, a logical impossibility. (On a graph like figure 10.1 such a "system" would look like TV snow.) In contrast, the increased probability that a real system will occupy a particular state can be represented as wells (dips or valleys in the landscape) that embody attractor states and behaviors that the system is more likely to occupy. The deeper the valley, the greater the propensity of its being visited and the stronger the entrainment its attractor represents.

Topologically, ridges separating basins of attraction are called *separatrices* or *repellers*. Sharp peaks are *saddle points* representing states and behaviors from which the system shies away and in all likelihood will not access; the probability of their occurrence is lowered or eliminated altogether. These landscape features capture the impact of context-sensitive constraints over time. Separatrix height represents the unlikelihood that the system will switch to another attractor given its history, current dynamics, and the environment. The steeper the separatrix's walls, the greater the improbability of the system's making the transition. On the other hand, the deeper the valley, the stronger the attractor's pull, and so the more entrenched the behavior described by that attractor and the stronger the perturbation needed to dislodge the system from that propensity. The broader the floor of a basin of attraction, the greater the variability in states and behaviors that the attractor allows under its control. The narrower the valley, the more specific the attractor, that is, the fewer the states and behaviors within its basin.

A system's identity is captured in the signature probability distribution of its dynamics. The organization of the indentations in figure 10.4 represents the shifting probability that the real system will access that state or behavior. The effects of constraints can therefore be represented as a probability landscape like figure 10.4. Since a system's external structure can recalibrate its internal dynamics, probability landscapes also incorporate the role of the environment in which a system is embedded. Since a system's prior experience constrains its behavior, that history, too, is embodied in its ontogenetic landscape. Ontogenetic landscapes, therefore,

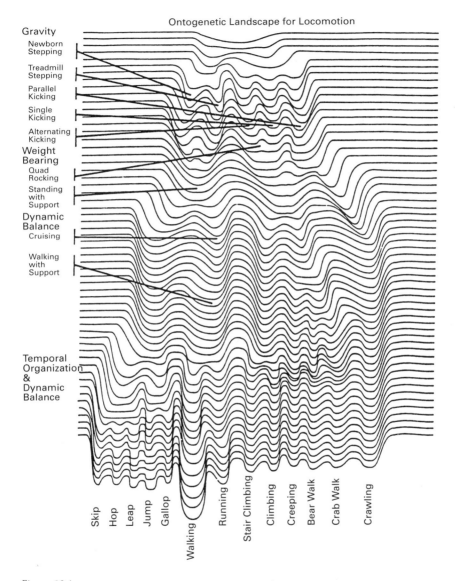

Figure 10.4
Ontogenetic landscape for locomotion created by Michael Muchisky, Lisa Gerschkoff-Stowe, Emily Cole, and Esther Thelen. The vertical axis represents time; different points on the horizontal axis represent different behavior patterns. The relatively flat terrain depicted at the top of the landscape suggests that the newborn shows few strong movement attractors. As development progresses, behavior becomes increasingly canalized into more specific behavior patterns.
Source: From Thelen and Smith 1994, p. 124. Reproduced by permission of MIT Press.

are constantly modified, dynamical portraits of the interactions between a system and its environment over time: they capture, in short, a time-lapse portrait of individual systems. Although complex dynamical systems theory is science, *pace* Aristotle, it can account for the particularity and concreteness of individual cases.

Furthermore, attractors and separatrices of complex systems are neither static givens in the manner of an Aristotelian telos nor external control mechanisms (as was the temperature cranked up from the outside in the Bénard cell example). Nor are they determinants operating as Newtonian forces. Representing constrained pathways within self-organized space, attractors embody the system's current control parameters (its self-organized knobs), which have been constructed and continue to be modified as a result of the persistent interactions between the dynamical system and its environment. The probability that a system will do x next depends on its present location in the current overall landscape, which in turn is a function both of its own past and of the environment in which it is embedded. Attractors thus embody the second-order context-sensitive constraints of the system's virtual governor.

More precisely, attractor basin landscapes describe the effects of those second-order context-sensitive constraints that give a system its particular structure and identity. They identify regions of equilibrium in a system's dynamical organization. As such, a system's dynamical portrait maps the contextual constraints that its attractors and organization embody. The difference between random behavior on the one hand, and the actually observed behavior on the other, provides evidence that an attractor is constraining the latter. Once again, this difference also measures the system's organization (Brooks and Wiley 1988), and confers on it its identity.

Evidence from Developmental Studies

Thelen and Smith's research (reported in 1994) strongly suggests that it is unlikely that either physical or cognitive development is a process of maturation dictated by deterministic codes in the genes. Motor development appears instead to be a process of dynamical self-organization that takes place as a result of ongoing interactions between an organism and its environment. This process can be pictured as an ontogenetic landscape.

Thelen and Fisher (1983) studied the way two infants, Hannah and Gabriel, learned to reach for objects. The infants started out with very different inherent dynamics. Gabriel tended to flail wildly and repetitively; Hannah, on the other hand, was less active, watching and assessing the situation carefully before moving. Because their innate dynamics were different, Gabriel and Hannah in fact faced different spring problems (reported in Thelen and Smith 1994) calling for different solutions. Although both children reached successfully within a few weeks of each other (thereby, from an observer's perspective, apparently conforming to a Piaget-like unfolding of preestablished developmental stages), in fact each infant generated an individual solution to the task at hand. There was no preprogrammed, unfolding pattern common to both. In directed graphs such as figures 10.1 and 10.2, different vectors would represent the trajectories terminating in each infant's successful reach. Drawn as a landscape, the trajectories would be depicted as different chutes which converge on the same point attractor.

Thelen concludes that children begin by exploring their environment through innate, often very different spontaneous dynamics. In virtue of these continuous interactions with the environment, "the activity of the system itself changes the ranges of the parameter values" (Thelen 1995, 91). As in autocatalysis, positive feedback provided by the interaction between the child and its environment takes them far from equilibrium and precipitates a transformation that establishes the second-order context-dependent constraints of a new child-environment system. In combination with the infant's original internal dynamics, those second-order constraints top-down reset the former's parameter values and reshape both the particular attractor pattern and the overall probability landscape in which the child is embedded. As a result, the inborn, springlike attractors of the infants' limbs recalibrate, allowing them to reach successfully for an object.

Studies of why the natural stepping motion of infants gradually disappears during the first year (Thelen 1986) support this thesis even more dramatically. It turns out that the change has nothing to do with maturation: rather, it is a function of weight gain. The growing child's changing ratio of muscle to fat—the changing context in which the leg is located—constrains and thereby resets the child's innate leg dynamics. Just as remarkably, infants placed on small, motorized treadmills produce stepping patterns that are more like adult locomotion than any natural infant leg movement. Adult-like treadmill stepping in infants is elicited by the interplay between the treadmill's motion and the child's own dynamics. The interaction between the child and its environment suddenly self-organizes into adult-like treadmill stepping.

Recent research also points to homologous dynamics at work during development of the brain cortex's folding pattern. It appears that mechanical tension along the axons of the cerebral cortex is responsible for the folding patterns. The combined tension in a particular region (that is, the overall context in which that portion of the brain is located) determines whether that region will fold inward or outward (reported in Blakeslee 1997).

Both of these studies support the conclusion that

> patterned motor behavior emerges from the ongoing interactions
> between a neural network and the periphery that it controls.... The
> range of gaits produced by the controller emerges from the inter-
> actions between sensory inputs and the central neural network, and
> this in turn causes the controller to be extremely robust to pertur-
> bations that would completely incapacitate a more centralized con-
> trol architecture (Chiel and Beer 1993, 161).

Bifurcations as Catastrophes

During stable states between phase changes, a complex system is in a
given dynamical regime: an overall landscape of attractors and separatrices. Under those conditions its behavior can be pictured as a "thick"
and convoluted trajectory governed by both the combined constraints
that identify that regime's dynamics and its initial conditions. But the
landscape of a dynamical system, by definition, is never static. Although it
remains qualitatively the same between phase changes, it continually
shifts in response to the system's interactions with its environment. As we
have seen, dissipative and self-organizing processes far enough from
equilibrium show discontinuous jumps, irreversible bifurcations such as
those phase transitions from independent water molecules to Bénard cell
and from Bénard cell to turbulence, or the sudden appearance of adult-like
stepping. When these dramatic phase changes occur, the whole attractor
regime completely reorganizes as the system undergoes a bifurcation. The
dynamics (their frequency distribution) reset altogether. Topologically,
this is equivalent to a radical alteration of the landscape—a major earthquake. It is not simply a question of existing valleys becoming deeper or
existing ridges steeper: the contour of the entire landscape reconfigures in
a phase-change bifurcation. The metamorphoses of tadpoles into frogs or
caterpillars into butterflies mark such a qualitative transition. The invariant
relations that had characterized the old attractor-separatrix regime dissolve
and a new organization takes their place. The change is qualitative insofar
as it consists in a transformation of the overall dynamic organization, not
merely a quantitative adjustment in the existing organization. The bifurcations that signal the abrupt self-organization of an autocatalytic cycle,
a B-Z wave pattern, or a slime mold slug are also examples of just such a catastrophic phase change. Signaling the appearance of mutual entrainment,
they represent the sudden establishment of new second-order, context-
sensitive constraints: the abrupt alteration in prior probability distributions.

René Thom (1975) developed a mathematical theory called *catastrophe
theory* that illustrates such phase changes and discontinuous transitions to

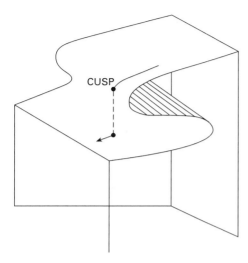

Figure 10.5
The simplest example of a catastrophe or radical discontinuity. A fold point is reached at which the system switches abruptly to a different behavior pattern.

a new dynamical regime. Visually, catastrophic bifurcations can be pictured as the trajectory of a vector abruptly falling off the existing graph onto a new page with different coordinates. As a result of a catastrophe, old probability valleys flatten out or even lift up to become separatrices: a dynamical earthquake. As a result of self-organization, for example, the coordinates of the B-Z reaction are blue and red, unlike before the self-organization. The B-Z graph is a differently organized page as well, on which new attractor valleys appear; it suddenly depicts a limit cycle pattern, not randomly placed dots. As I pointed out, as complex systems move away from equilibrium they can undergo a sequence of such catastrophic phase changes, from point attractor to limit cycle and then to complexity. New context-sensitive constraints appear with each new transition, as do new properties (new coordinates on a new page).

In evolutionary sequences, each bifurcation in a complex adaptive system's phase space marks an irreversible transition paid for by a burst of overall entropy production. Each transition enlarges the available pool of states that the now more complex network of relationships created by the new set of constraints can access. Phase changes in an evolutionary sequence therefore mark the abrupt state space expansion that accompanies hierarchical differentiation. As mentioned earlier, the increased number of cell types produced by differentiation signals an enlarged state space and greater degrees of freedom for the overall system. Once again, this is precisely what happens when the imposition of context-sensitive constraints precipitates the transition from a regime of independent and randomly distributed water molecules to a Bénard cell. Likewise, when blastulas undergo the phase change that marks the onset of cellular differentiation, the sudden appearance of cell types can be represented as a catastrophic bifurcation (figure 10.5).

The first point to be made with respect to action is that dynamical systems theory can therefore explain what traditional information theory could not: why a system's range of possibilities contains at any given moment the alternatives it does. The pool of alternatives currently available to a complex system is given by the coordinates of its present state space. It is also determined by the context-sensitive constraints that give the system its identity. Dynamical systems theory can also explain why state spaces radically alter. The pool of alternatives available to the overall system expands as a result of the sudden appearance of context-sensitive constraints on previously independent and uncorrelated particles.

Summary

Strange attractors are evidence of the existence of highly complex subregions or subvolumes of correlated activity within the organism's state space. Behavior constrained top-down by that self-organized area is channeled into complex pathways through its probability landscape. Attractors constrain behavior by entraining lower-level processes to the attractors' overall dynamical organization. As we saw earlier, one way in which the global dynamics of complex adaptive systems do so—one way in which distributed wholes contextually constrain their parts top-down—is by modifying their prior probability in real time. That is what second-order contextual constraints do—or are. In the laser, to recap, faster, lower-level processes relax and allow themselves to be driven (entrained) by the slower, higher-dimensional attractor (the coherent laser beam), which functions as their virtual governor. Gene regulation works that way too.

In the next chapter I speculate that in the brain, coherent wave patterns embodying the emergent properties of consciousness and meaning emerge as neurons entrain and self-organize. These higher levels of organization impose second-order, context-sensitive constraints on their components by carving out strange attractors that reset the natural, intrinsic firing frequency of the individual neurons, including those controlling motor processes, and in so doing entrain and constrain these to the attractors' dynamics. And that's how all interlevel, top-down causes cause, including conscious states such as intentions. One not insignificant advantage of this claim is that empirical research into brain dynamics will be able to confirm or falsify it. Chapter 11 explores this thesis in detail.

Chapter 11
Embodied Meaning

Both Freeman's and Thelen's research provides strong support for the claim that nonlinear feedback makes human neurological processes self-organize. Brains are extraordinarily redundant, and studies on aphasia have shown that in particular context-sensitive redundancy exists. As research on eye movements and hearing also shows, similar dynamics are at work in visual and auditory—even olfactory—perception as well. But what evidence is there to support the claim that emotional significance and motor skills are not the only emergent properties of the dynamic self-organization of neurological processes: that full-blown semantics might be too? Another type of dynamical system, artificial neural networks, offers tantalizing possibilities.

Evidence from Neural Networks

Compelling evidence from recurrent artificial (connectionist) neural networks suggests that there, too, dynamical self-organization results from the enabling contextual constraints of mutualist feedback. Let us turn to this new form of computation as a model of the way context-sensitive constraints embodying semantics might emerge in the human brain.

Artificial neural networks have layers of units. Minimally there is an input and an output layer and a hidden layer whose units neither receive any direct stimuli from the outside nor directly produce output. Rather, the hidden layer receives output only from the input layer and sends output only to the output layer. A neural network's units are linked by excitatory and inhibitory connections, that vary in strength; the larger the connection weight (excitatory or inhibitory), the stronger the input to the unit to which it is connected. Each unit in the input layer is typically connected to many hidden units, each of which is also connected to many output units. The degree to which each hidden unit is active depends on the total input it receives.

Coarse Coding

Both artificial and biological neural networks share an interesting feature: both are *coarse coded*; that is, each unit receives input from many other units. Moreover, some of the connections to a given unit may be excitatory, others inhibitory. The artificial network as a whole computes all the inputs to all the units and settles into a state that best satisfies the overall set of constraints. The first-order context-sensitive constraint that a particular connection represents is therefore "soft" or "weak": the overall input from the rest of the network can override it. Each layer in a connectionist network in fact integrates information from lower layers by "detecting higher order combinations of activities among the units to which they are connected" (Hinton and Shallice 1991, 79). As a result there is no one-to-one mapping between input and output. Instead, the overall output consists of a blend of the various outputs from the individual units. A significant by-product of this apparent sloppiness is that as a result, neural networks acquire the ability to generalize.

Coarse coding is already known to be the way the human brain processes color. Each cell in the retina responds maximally only to one of three colors (but also minimally to the others). Blending the outputs results in the ability to recognize a broad spectrum of colors (reported in Kosslyn and Koenig 1992). It is plausible to suppose that coarse coding governs many other human skills as well. As Kosslyn and Koenig also note, humans can utter comprehensible statements with their mouth full, while one side of their face is paralyzed, and in many other apparently inhibitive circumstances. This flexibility suggests that some sort of weak constraint satisfaction principle governs meaningful speech, too. Which muscles get activated and how depends on the different conditions—all in the service of uttering the same sentence.

Embodied Meaning

Hinton, Plaut, and Shallice (1993, 78) designed a neural network to "read" words. In that network the input layer is fed information about the visual form of the word. Hinton calls units of this layer "graphemes," for their role in identifying particular letters in specified positions within the word. The output layer, whose units Hinton calls "sememes," represents the correct meaning of the word. For the network to read "cat" as "cat," for example, a precise pattern of connections in the intermediate layer is necessary. Since there is no a priori way to determine which pattern will ensure a correct response, networks must "learn" to produce the right output by being "trained."

One way to train a network is through backward error propagation or "backprop". Before training begins, the connections among the units are assigned random weights. As a result, a random output can be expected in response to the first input (when, say, the word "cat" is presented). That random output is then compared to the desired output and a trainer adjusts the excitatory and inhibitory weights to reduce the differences between the actual and desired output.[50] Many adjustments are commonly necessary:

> One adjustment usually is not enough, and so many presentations of the input are necessary before the weights are fully adjusted. Small steps are necessary because each connection typically is used as part of many different input/output associations, and the right balance must be struck among the connections to preserve all of the stored associations at the same time.... Thus, training usually involves a large set of associations, all of which are learned at the same time. (Kosslyn and Koenig 1992, 25)

People and connectionist networks are different from systems that use traditional, top-down serial computation: the former learn. As even Skinnerian behaviorists knew, people, too, require extensive training. In both, feedback takes each system far from equilibrium, and the system then spontaneously recalibrates. Recalibration thus signals the dynamical entrainment to an incoming signal, the establishment, that is, of context-sensitive constraints between the network and the world. When closure occurs, a network-environment system has self-organized, and that system then imposes second-order, top-down contextual constraints on its components. From a dynamical perspective, then, learning is the recalibration (in both people and neural nets) of their internal dynamics in response to training.

It is important to emphasize that the specific pattern of connection weights that each neural network embodies at any given moment will be different depending on the exact distribution of weights from which it started and the precise sequence of input signals on which it was trained. As a result of such context-dependent coding, the same network can produce a correct output (*bed*) from different patterns of connection weights at different times. It can also produce an incorrect output from the same weight pattern at different times. Also, two different networks can produce different outputs from the same pattern of connection weights, or the same output from different patterns. In short, the network's sensitivity to initial conditions makes each run unique. Both the parallel with the infants Hannah and Gabriel, and the multiple realizability of mental events on neurological ones suggest a similar process at work in the brain.

Whether it is a child or an artificial network, each begins with slightly different inherent dynamics that subsequently recalibrate in response to persistent interactions with and positive feedback from the environment. And the trajectory of each sequence of bifurcations is unique.

Behaviorist attempts to explain action, I claimed earlier, tried to fit action into a covering-law model of explanation in which no unique, creative, or original actions were allowed. As Hinton, Plaut, and Shallice (1993, 80) note, intuitions such as those of behaviorism, which rest on the assumption of a two-dimensional state space, often must be discarded when a multidimensional state space is involved. In networks with enormous state spaces and highly complex attractors, embeddedness in time and space makes unique, novel, and unpredictable behavior possible. And the brain is some multidimensional state space! For Hinton's reader network to identify just 40 words, it had to navigate a sixty-eight-dimensional space, corresponding to the sixty-eight semantic features in its sememe units. If the brain is a complex adaptive system, no covering-law approach, including a behaviorist one, could ever account for human action. If the brain is fundamentally stochastic, as are many other complex adaptive systems, the novelty and unpredictability are in principle so as well.

Recurrent Networks

Some artificial neural networks include connections not only between units within a layer but also from later units back to earlier units. Networks with such feedback loops (which Hinton, Plaut, and Shallice [1993] call "cleanup units") are called recurrent. Networks without such recurrence behave in a static manner: any given input makes the network produce a corresponding output pattern that does not change so long as the input stays constant. The output of recurrent networks, on the other hand, is dynamic: these networks create attractors—they settle gradually into a characteristic pattern. As mentioned in the previous chapter, because they embody constrained pathways within state space, attractors provide evidence of self-organized subregions of that space. In short, as was the case in autocatalytic webs, here, too, feedback takes the network far from equilibrium. In response, the connection weights in a recurrent network's hidden layer can recalibrate and self-organize.

Once trained, artificial neural networks with recurrent feedback display an interesting feature: vector completion. Even if the input is incomplete or fuzzy, feedback from recurrent connections allows the network to function properly; its behavior still converges on the semantically fitting output because feedback from the downstream cleanup units corrects any errors. Cleanup units therefore allow upstream layers (in this case, the level at which the network processes the visual form of the word) to be imprecise. Vector completion due to feedback is a valuable property because it makes neural networks robust to noise: the context-dependence the feedback provides allows them to detect a signal even amid noise. As a result, artificial networks, like people, can make out a faded, blurry text. This robustness seems to characterize all complex systems with homologous dynamics. (I suggest below that this same feature allows people to act intentionally even though the intentions from which the behavior issues are vague and imprecise.)

A Walk through Semantic Space

In Hinton, Plaut, and Shallice's model, damage upstream from the cleanup units causes visual rather than semantic errors. Like a *surface dyslexic*, the network might read "cot" for "cat." Damage either to the cleanup units themselves or to the network downstream from the cleanup units, on the other hand, results in the remarkable errors of *deep dyslexia*: the network might read "bed" for "cot"! Hinton, Plaut, and Shallice claim that postulating the existence of semantic attractors explains deep-dyslexia-type errors. "*We have found it useful to think of the network's output ... as motion through a multidimensional 'semantic space,'* whose coordinates are defined by all the *semantic* features that the network can represent" (Hinton, Plaut, and Shallice, 1993, 79, emphasis mine). The network's attractors describe a self-organized space with emergent properties that can only be characterized as semantic because they embody the word's meaning or sense in the organization of the relationships that constitute the higher-dimensional space. Just as the pattern of processes in the B-Z reaction appears as a colorful wave, so too the pattern of excitatory and inhibitory connection weights in the intermediate layer of the word reading network represents[51] "the semantic features that describe the thing in question: the word *cat* activates such units as 'mammal,' 'has legs,' 'soft,' and 'fierce.' Units representing such semantic features as 'transparent,' 'tastes strong,' 'parts of a limb' or 'made of wood' remain quiescent" (78).

Artificial networks without feedback do not make deep-dyslexic-type mistakes, but those with cleanup units do. This fact suggests that the latter's output originates in a self-organized dynamical space whose second-order context-dependent constraints, as embodying semantics, guide the network's movement within that space. When the network reads the word correctly, the output represents the endpoint of a trajectory through the attractors of this high-dimensional, semantically organized space. The actual path is an unequivocal trajectory on a directed graph, starting at a node (the source) within that semantic space, continuing along a specific trajectory, and terminating at another node (the sink). And it is precisely in virtue of their high-level properties (that is, of the meaning embodied in the relations among their components) that the self-organized dynamics produce the output: the dynamics are causal *as meaningful*. As a result, the behavior is semantically constrained. This is the primary advantage of a dynamic account over an information-theoretic one: the former, unlike the latter, can account for both the emergence of meaning and its causal efficacy.

Separately, Jeffrey Elman (1995) and Jean Petitot (1995) have also constructed connectionist models of linguistic performance whose results support the claim that artificial neural networks construct semantic attractors. Using a simple recurrent network like Hinton's, Elman trained it (using backprop techniques) to predict the next word in a sentence. Instead of thinking of language processing as a static lexicon and a set of rules specifying how words are combined into sentences, Elman proposes that lexicons be viewed

> as consisting of regions of state space within that system; the grammar consists of the dynamics (attractors and repellers) which constrain movement in that space. [This] approach entails representations that are highly context-sensitive, continuously varied and probabilistic (but, of course, 0.0 and 1.0 are also probabilistic), and in which the objects of mental representation are better thought of as trajectories through mental space rather than things constructed. (Elman 199)

Figure 11.1, which could have been depicted as an ontogenetic landscape like that of figure 10.4, shows the clustering pattern of the hidden units in Elman's neural network. *The closeness of the various regions within that state space embodies both semantic similarity and hierarchical self-organization.* According to (Bechtel, 126), connectionist systems identify "the objects or situations with which they are presented as exemplars of semantic categories." On the account presented here, regions of self-organized semantic space embody in their very organization exemplars that, given the inevitable overlap that will occur in a multidimensional space like the brain, are more like family resemblances than universals or Platonic Forms. The basin that embodies e.g., $mouse_{243}$ is differentiable from the basin that embodies $mouse_{241}$. The universal "mouse" is represented only in the sense that other tokens of "mouse" appear nearby in that network's current state space. That closeness carves out a broad region or subvolume that in effect captures the semantic type or exemplar "mouse." Coarse coding makes this generalization possible.

The tree shown in figure 11.1 "was carried out over the mean vector for each word, averaged across contexts" (Elman 1995, 216), but in each case, small but identifiable differences in state space captured differences in context. This particular valley might embody or represent "Herman-in-

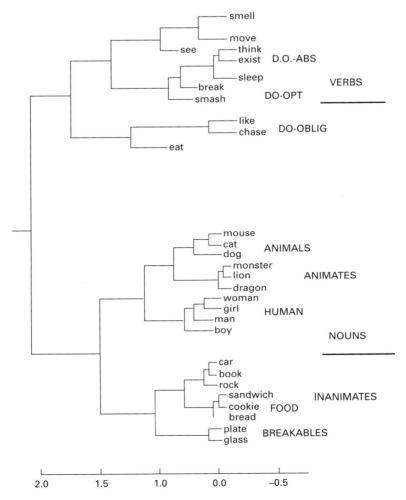

Figure 11.1
Hierarchical clustering diagram of hidden unit activations in the simulation with simple sentences. After training, sentences are passed through the network, and the hidden unit activation pattern for each word is recorded. The clustering diagram indicates the similarity structure inferred from the network's activation patterns.
Source: From Elman 1995, p. 206. Reproduced by permission of MIT Press.

this-context" that valley might embody or mean "Sally-in-that-context." Since there is a discriminable difference between any two valleys, the semantics are built into the topography, making *ad hoc* hypotheses unnecessary. Relative position in semantic space distinguishes one universal from another, even if more fuzzily and idiosyncratically than previously thought. To paraphrase Prigogine (1985, US Naval Academy), these artificial networks' dynamical organization therefore carries its semantics on its back—semantics, moreover, that build in the very circumstances under which those meanings were learned.

If, as appears plausible, people self-organize neurological semantic attractors in similar fashion, eliminativist materialists (Churchland, P. M., 1989; Churchland, P. S., 1986) who claim that concepts and beliefs will prove to be like ether and phlogiston can surrender. Because complex systems are context-dependent, there is every reason to believe that, as in Elman's (1995) artificial network, human neurological dynamics will embody the meanings of those folk-psychological concepts on which the person was trained. Even the tree shown in Elman's cluster diagram reproduces common folk psychological distinctions in its topology: broader, fuzzier basins encompass more general classes of objects; narrower, more precise ones depict more specific objects. But because an indefinitely large number of self-organized spaces can coexist and each run of a complex system is unique, it is also likely that each person will show evidence of idiosyncratic psychological overlaps. These will be the result of the interaction between the person's innate dynamics and the particular training he or she received. For example, although the dictionary shows no conceptual relationship between "goose" and "dangerous," my particular psychological dynamics might—if I was attacked by a goose the first time I saw one.

While the Newtonian framework ruled, discussions about reductionism were usually framed as a strong disjunction: either intentions were reducible to neurophysiology or, if not, they were therefore sui generis. The assumption that neurophysiological structures and their causal relations would be completely describable without reference to semantics has been a central dogma of the philosophy of mind. That assumption was also at the core of a common objection to artificial intelligence (see Searle [1982] on the Chinese room debate): in a syntactically driven machinery, whence the semantics? How do you get from syntax to meaning? The problem dissolves in a dynamical framework: self-organized regions of neural space embody semantics; dynamical attractors (constrained pathways within those regions) embody syntax. In the case of action, I claim below, neurologically self-organized regions that entrain semantic and motor organizations correspond to intentions; the attractors of those dynamics correspond to potential act-types.

Studies of the way infants learn to kick a mobile (reported in Thelen 1995) suggested that we are on the right track, that homologous dynamics can also be postulated for the emergence of cognition in human beings. Learning categories (Thelen and Smith 1994)—the ability to generalize across variations in perceptual stimuli—"may also be depicted as a landscape of potential wells, where the local acts of perceiving and acting come to form wider basins of attraction that represent more general classes of solutions" (95). Commonalities of results are unsurprising in light of the similarity of stimuli across individuals. Radically different environments, on the other hand, will produce differently organized cognitive landscapes. Eskimos recognize many more shades of white than do Floridians. But in any case, the sensitivity to initial conditions of complex systems will produce progressively individuated dynamics and trajectories, even among members of the same community.

Objections

In response to Fodor and Pylshyn's (1988) objection that connectionism is unsatisfactory as an explanation of cognition's compositional nature, van Gelder (1990) argues convincingly that their objection rests on a mistaken notion of the way structured objects can be built up out of parts. Van Gelder shows how Smolensky's (1987) *tensor product framework* can do just that by mapping a structured object onto a vector space. Moreover, as van Gelder notes, these vectors "are unlike standard symbolic constituents in that they are typically context-dependent" (373). As such, they, too, capture a feature of human cognitive structures that traditional syntax could not: the grammar (read "dynamics") has the semantics built in. Explaining the dynamics of intentional behavior in terms of tensors also finds support in the research on the activity in the motor and premotor cortex of monkeys (Georgopoulos 1990). EEGs of monkeys reaching for a target show that cooperating neurons produce a vector field (something like an attractor basin) that constrains the direction of movement. The overall vector field "slaves" the behavior of each cell.[52]

But artificial neural networks are still machines, allopoietically organized, the skeptic might retort, which human brains are emphatically not. Several responses to this objection are possible. First, as discussed in several of the essays compiled in Daniel Gardner's excellent 1993 anthology, *The Neurobiology of Neural Networks,* the more recent artificial neural networks are designed to be increasingly neuromorphic, incorporating many of the features of biological neurons and synapses. Jean Petitot's (1995) computational models, for example, use an algorithm for information processing which retinal ganglion cells are known to employ.

There is no question, however, that researchers in artificial neural networks still face many challenges in their pursuit of biological neuromorphism. Whereas artificial neural networks start out with a random distribution of weights, for example, evolution and heredity have already sculpted a set of connection weights, a basic level of connectivity and organization with which the human infant's brain comes preloaded. At best, therefore, artificial neural networks remain "encapsulated" models of brain function. But insofar as they are "dynamic recurrent networks, with feedback and time-dependent enhancements," artificial neural networks are already "partially consistent with neurobiology" (Gardner 1993, 7). And it is the dynamic, context-dependent features of self-organizing systems that I have emphasized.

I do not wish to get drawn into the debate on consciousness. I am not claiming that artificial neural networks will ever feel pain, or be conscious, much less self-conscious. I suspect that conscious and self-conscious awareness will turn out to be emergent properties of the self-organization of biological neurons, with the level or degree of awareness varying concomitantly with the complexity of the biology involved.[53] My concern in this book is the problem of action, its causes and logic of explanation. My claim thus far has been that the interlevel relationships characteristic of complex adaptive, hierarchical systems provide a way of conceptualizing top-down causality. Doing so allows us to account for the way wholes, as wholes and as embodied in all their attendant, emergent properties, can causally influence their parts: in virtue of those context-sensitive constraints that make them wholes.

Artificial neural networks with recurrent circuits produce behavior that issues from a dynamically self-organized set of connection weights (that is, from internal dynamics that have recalibrated as a result of positive feedback). If Hinton, Plaut, and Shallice (1993) are correct, furthermore, one of the emergent properties of this dynamic organization embodies semantics. If a lesioned network's output can reproduce the errors of deep dyslexia, this can only mean that the network's output issues from the semantic properties of that emergent level of organization. Or to put it differently, it means that emergent semantic properties of this global level of self-organization, as embodied in the organization's invariant relations, can contextually constrain the output top-down. This discovery reinforces the claim that homologous dynamics may be at work in all open systems far from equilibrium, whether artificial or not. It is therefore plausible to suggest that high levels of biological neural organization, implicating those involved in consciousness as well as meaning, can likewise entrain and constrain motor processes top-down to their dynamics, thereby producing behavior that as a result qualifies as action.

Critics of connectionism have also claimed that, unlike artificial networks, people are not trained from the outside. Well, yes and no. Because human beings self-organize, their order parameter is not an externally imposed control as is the heat level of Bénard cells. Attractors describe a system's self-organized internal dynamics, but they are neither pregiven nor externally imposed. As suggested by Thelen and Smith (1994), as well as by Freeman (1991b), they are constructed products of the organism's ongoing interactions with its environment.

The context-embeddedness typical of complex systems does imply, however, that the constraints that govern their behavior run through both the environment and time, as well as through the system's internal dynamics. But, as Thelen and Smith (1994) emphasize, Hannah and Gabriel's "trainers" were not teachers in a classroom, or even parents. Their "trainers" included gravity, body weight, torque, etc. In interaction with such "trainers" as gravity and mechanical tension, an infant's innate dynamics recalibrate (or a fetus's cortex folds up). Similarly, human beings do not learn the meaning of words always and only by consulting a dictionary; we more often figure it out from the context. But that is possible at all because context constrains textual interpretation as much as it does phenotypic appearance and behavior. Researchers on animal behavior learned that lesson far earlier than those studying human beings: ethologists left the lab behind a long time ago to study animals in their natural habitat under normal conditions—that is, in context.

Summary

Instead of representing meaning in a symbol structure, a dynamical neurological organization embodies meaning (Elman 1995; Petitot 1995)—in its very topographical configurations, that is, in the self-organized constraints of its phase space. The more general and abstract a category or concept, the wider the neural valley it describes. Semantic closeness can thus be explained as relative location in this dynamic space, as figure 11.1 illustrates.[54] In networks without cleanup units, the connection weights (the valleys) of the intermediate neurons for "dab and "bed" might be close to one another in self-organized space after only a few training runs. At that point the "closeness" in the organization of their connection weights represents lexicographical relationships. Once feedback is added and the network trained with it, I speculate, constructing a semantic space is the catastrophic reorganization of that space and the reconfiguring of the attractors within it. In the abruptly reconfigured cognitive landscape, the attractors of "bed" and "cot" will now be close to one another in semantic space and those of "bad" and "dab" will not (although they may still be close in a coexisting, lexicographical space). The coordinates of the newly self-organized space of possibilities represent meaningful concepts. Helen Keller's sudden realization that the designs that Annie Sullivan had been tracing on her hand meant something, I think, is a dramatic example of a similar catastrophic phase change: the discontinuous and irreversible transition to a reorganized neurological space embodying meaning.

I speculate that in a complex biological system with feedback such as the brain, context-dependent constraints similarly partition self-organized, uniquely individuated neural spaces that embody emergent semantic properties in their very organization—that is, in their invariant relations. "Every mental and behavioral act is always emergent in context" (Thelen 1995, 72). If so, mental and physical landscapes unique to each individual will be progressively constructed, beginning with the interaction between the child's own dynamics on the one hand and the variation, nature, and sequence of the stimuli presented on the other.

Complex adaptive dynamics thus offer a plausible account of how self-organized patterns of neurophysiological processes can carve out dynamical regimes with semantic properties. The necessity of referring to neurological organization, as meaningful, to describe and explain, for example, some errors of aphasia and deep dyslexia shatters all hope for reductionism. Crucially important for reconceptualizing intentions, more-over, is that it is *as meaningful* that the space's order parameters are caus-ally effective.

Chapter 12
Intentional Action: A Dynamical Account

Recapitulation

Approaching the problem of action through the lenses of information theory allowed us a first pass toward a new way of conceptualizing how intentional meaning flows into action. In chapter 6, I suggested that behavior constitutes an act-token if and only if it is a trajectory that is dependent on a reduction of possibilities at an intentional source. For behavior to qualify as action, the information generated must then be transmitted uninterruptedly into behavior. The technical concepts of noise and equivocation gave us a way of measuring that dependence of outcome on origin; as such they also gave us a way of understanding how information can flow without interruption from source to terminus, which Newtonian causality could not. The problems and objections of wayward chains and act individuation, which earlier theories of action had repeatedly encountered, could thereby be circumvented or resolved. Information theory, however, was unable (a) to account for the set of alternatives from which the selection is made, (b) to provide a plausible account of the method people use to settle on a determinate course of action, or (c) to handle meaning.

Complex dynamical systems theory was able to assist in all tasks. The key to self-organization, as we saw, is the appearance of second-order context-sensitive constraints as a result of the closure of positive feedback. Second-order contextual constraints are sudden changes in the conditional probability distribution of component behavior. By partitioning a system's state space into an ordered subvolume, dynamical self-organization is therefore also analogous to information theory's "reduction of possibilities" at the source. In the case of dynamical systems, the range of alternatives available to a complex structure at any given moment is given by its organization's coordinates and dynamics—its order parameter. Evidence from artificial neural networks also suggests that the very organization of those dynamics can embody a robust sense of semantics. Finally, acting as a system's control parameter, attractors of self-organized dynamics can serve as a causal—but not efficiently causal—mechanism. Those attractors constrain movements within self-organized space such that they preserve the invariant relations that characterize the higher level of organization. By using the information concepts of equivocation and noise it is possible to measure, in terms of conditional probability, the effectiveness of those context-sensitive constraints.

Because research in various fields provides evidence that biological organization displays homologous dynamics, a dynamical perspective can thus offer (1) a neurologically plausible account of the compression of alternatives postulated by information theory; (2) a new way of rethinking meaning: as embodied in dynamical patterns of biological neural space rather than represented in a static lexicon; and (3) an understanding of the type of top-down (self-causal) control at work in intentional action.

A Plausible Scenario for Action

Let us start at the beginning. A fertilized egg does not have an unlimited state space; each generation begins with a characteristic pool of potentialities (Brooks and Wiley 1988) that, no matter how large, is not unlimited—the information carrying capacity of that species. No organism is born with a flat topography either. A particular organism's genotype embodies constraints, according to Brooks and Wiley, that specify a species' primary landscape, the array of basic characteristics typical of that species. Reproduction translates one generation's external structure into the internal structure of the next. That is, a basic set of inherited propensities carves out innate valleys such as a baby's sucking or grasping instincts, phenotypic and behavioral attractors that are more likely than not to occur. These may be as minimal as being attracted by glittery objects or as strong as instincts and innate drives, and are described by conditional probabilities, as explained in an earlier chapter. Brooks and Wiley think of the constraining information of heredity as historical constraints now functioning as initial conditions.

The initial conditions of a particular genetic makeup handed down by the infant's parents also sculpt other dips and hillocks onto the blastula's beginning landscape. The chance encounter of sperm and egg has carved out the phase space of likelihood-weighted tendencies and abilities with which the organism will come preloaded. Thelen and Smith (1994) compare them to tropisms, natural tendencies favoring certain processes over others. They embody an organism's inborn "propensities" (Popper 1990)—that is, the conditional probability distribution of the context-sensitive constraints that give the organism its identity. Unlike behaviorism's stimulus-response patterns, these constraints are embodied in the very dynamics of its biological organization.

The genome's information-carrying capacity limits the degrees of freedom of each fertilized cell. But initial attractor landscapes, as we have seen, are not static, predetermined givens; the fact that organisms are sensitive to context-dependent constraints that channel their development implies that inborn propensities are not determinants. Nor is the preloaded landscape an unchanging one. Initially, that is, almost anything is possible for each cell of the blastula; its landscape is almost, although not quite, flat (see the ontogenetic landscape depicted in figure 10.4). But for differentiation to occur, the near equipotentiality must be harnessed.

Context-sensitive constraints previously established by evolutionary pressures quickly kick in. Top-down contextual constraints from the physical environment in which the blastula is situated and to which it is innately attuned begin to reshape its initial dynamics as the two interact. For example, the structured environment to which the cell that happens to be on top of the blastula resonates reduces that cell's equipotentiality. Although the position of any given cell in the blastula is determined randomly, context-sensitive constraints from its historically established external structure cause the blastula's differentiation by closing off options to some of its cells.

The developmental landscape's coordinates and topography at any given moment represent continually shifting conditional probabilities. The ongoing interaction between the organism's own innate, internal dynamics and its environment establishes and modifies the frequency distribution. As a result of first-order contextual constraints, lower-level processes entrain into higher levels of organization with greater degrees of freedom— and are then constrained (top-down) by them. Over time, as Thelen and Smith's (1994) research shows, structures (both physical and cognitive) as well as competencies (including motor coordination, speech production, and so forth) are dynamically assembled as the organism's interactions with the environment progressively self-organize increasingly complex regions (see essays in Port and van Gelder 1995). These orderly, high-dimensional regions of state space can themselves become correlated with others, and then get entrained into even higher levels of self-organization.

Research in various fields, including those mentioned earlier, suggests that, in similar fashion and as a result of the interaction between its own dynamics and the environment, the brain, too, continuously constructs progressively ordered, complex regions in neural state space. In response to feedback loops with other internal systems and with the environment, previously independent neuron firings—some of them initially random, some of them inherently oscillatory—suddenly entrain, producing a global pattern of distributed, coherent neural activity. Positive feedback for these complex dynamics is provided by phenomena as diverse as gravity, torque, and mechanical tension—as well as classroom teaching, socialization, religious instruction, and the like—all of which take the original system far from equilibrium and precipitate the reorganization.

Motor, visual, olfactory, and similar attractors—constrained pathways within self-organized spaces—are dynamically constructed, dissolved, and reorganized in real time, in a time-dependent manner by and through the interactions between the human infant and its environment. A sequence of increasingly differentiated neural dynamics embodying thoughts, feelings, emotions, and the like also self-organizes. Because each new level's dynamics constrain different pathways through those spaces, novel act-types and regularities also appear with each emergent organization. The more complex the environment, the more complex the organism and its behavioral potential (Artigiani 1995a; Simon 1973), and vice versa: the two coevolve.

As Stuart Kauffman's (1991) research shows, any self-organization requires a critical number of components. In the case of the human brain, a number of lower-level neurological units and layers, recurrently connected, are undoubtedly a prerequisite before self-organized dynamical neural structures with the emergent properties of meaning, consciousness, and even self-consciousness can appear. But it is not unreasonable to speculate that, once those prerequisites are in place, such highly complex levels of neural organization will self-assemble (Swenson 1989). Deliberate purposiveness, self-awareness, and so forth are among the novel properties that will become manifest with that level of emergent neurological organization; they also correspond to an enlarged state space. The attractor regime that gives each of these complex neural organizations its identity is governed by its own dynamics, described by the laws of logic or ethics, for example. Act-types are constrained pathways within those cognitive, semantically organized spaces.

What Might a Dynamical Account of Action Look Like?

Since complex systems possess an indefinite number of attractors whose basins are inextricably intertwined, entrainment likely occurs in other areas of human personality as well. Many if not all human emotions, such as indignation, pride, and even pain, for example, have a cognitive component. Some women report that because they knew it would end, childbirth was not as painful as it would have otherwise been. The placebo effect is well documented. Both of these phenomena can be explained by supposing that in the brain, too, homologous dynamics integrate conscious, meaningful information from the cognitive system with information from the affective system by entraining both into even more complex neural dynamics that embody information as both meaningful and desirable: an evaluative level of organization.

There is evidence of such entrainment. Antonio Damasio's research suggests that the control loop of intentional decision making runs through the neural circuitry that underlies emotions. Or to put it the other way around, intentions coopt emotions to simplify things. Damasio postulates what he calls "somatic markers," neurological patterns that express our overall preferences. On my account, preferences are embodied in conditional probability distributions established by self-organization's context-sensitive constraints. To simplify decisionmaking, these body-based, affectively loaded signals "modify the way the brain handles [different combination of images] and thus operate as a [biasing mechanism]. The bias might allocate attentional enhancement differently to each component, the consequence being the automated assigning of varied degrees of attention to varied contents, which translates into an uneven landscape" (Damasio 1994, 199).

By entraining the brain's emotional circuitry with that dedicated to decision making, the former becomes part of the latter's external structure. Emotions can thereby serve as the context that biases the workings of the decision-making structures; that is, emotions alter potential decisions' prior probability. Context-sensitive biasing, we concluded earlier, establishes conditional probabilities among previously independent processes. Through such context-dependent constraints and interacting with working memory and attention, these somatic states can select and order from the various possibilities available to the cognitive system (Damasio 1994, 198). They stack the odds of these possibilities.

In short, viewed as a complex dynamical landscape organized across various and interrelated dimensions, a person's general state of mind is the high-level, distributed neural organization in place at the moment; its attractors represent available act-types, potential pathways through that dynamical organization. One implication of the previous chapter is that, operating as a top-down constraint, that organization (a dynamical neurological structure of process as conscious and meaningful) can become the agent's virtual governor or order parameter. The resulting act-token is the constrained trajectory through this meaningful, self-organized region of neural space.

Forming a Prior Intention

Self-organized dynamical structures are globally stable despite disorder at the lower levels. However, as illustrated in the example of autocatalysis, complex adaptive systems can be driven far from equilibrium to an instability threshold by the interplay of external conditions and their own internal processes. It is reasonable to suppose that the feedback between external circumstances and internal dynamics can likewise drive neurological dynamics describing a person's current state of mind far from equilibrium. "She worked herself into a frenzy," we say. The disequilibrium and instability that precipitate the restructuring can occur at the cognitive and emotional levels, not just the chemical or biological one. When global systems far from equilibrium can no longer damp perturbations and fluctuations, one of these might become amplified and serve as the nucleation that restructures the overall system's global dynamics and reestablishes equilibrium. Similarly, if taken far from equilibrium, a person's existing mental attractor regime embodying meaning, desire, and similar mental properties might reorganize and thereby recontour the landscape. I propose that settling on a prior intention embodies just such a phase change or bifurcation.

What does self-organizing a prior intention accomplish? If dynamical models are an appropriate theory-constitutive metaphor for people and their actions, the cognitive phase change that takes place when someone formulates a prior intention must dissipate the disequilibrium that had driven the system to an instability threshold. If the disequilibrium that prompted intentional action was cognitive and emotional, so, too, is the reestablished equilibrium. What sort of equilibrium could be restored when someone quits her job as an accountant to become a skydiver? Because of the human brain's astronomical dimensionality, every dynamical structure and attractor regime (emotional, psychological, and so forth) involved in that particular person's decision must be taken into consideration. Choices that appear mad on a two-dimensional scale might not be in a multidimensional manifold. And recall: each run of any complex system is in fact unique.

In addition to restoring dynamic (cognitive, affective, and so on) equilibrium, the new intention's restructured contextual constraints reorganize the earlier state space into a more differentiated and complex set of options. This means that in contrast to the algorithmic procedure described by information theory, but very much like that of Damasio's (1994) biasing mechanisms, once an agent formulates a prior intention, it is no longer necessary for that agent to consider every possible behavioral alternative, only a partitioned subset of those alternatives. The semantic space self-organized by (in) a prior intention automatically reduces the number of logically or physically possible behaviors to a more manageable set of now-meaningful options. Given the overall context established by the prior intention, the prior probability of each of the possible behavioral alternatives has suddenly changed.

By formulating a prior intention, agents avoid having to consider and evaluate explicitly every logical or physical possibility (not only a wasteful utilization of resources but, as we saw, a situation that would effectively paralyze them). By the agent's cognitively reorganizing, only those now-meaningful alternatives described by the new "collective variable" need to be considered. From a dynamical point of view, the multidimensional neurological region that describes the range of allowable variation within an agent's semantic phase space sets the scope of "rather than" alternatives from which that agent selects. Formulating a new prior intention is the self-organizing process that narrows the list of available options by organizing them into meaningful groupings. The new skydiver won't even have to notice advertisements for new spreadsheet software!

Contrast Space

Alan Garfinkel (1981) has argued that questions of the form "Why did X *A*?" are really the compressed query "Why did X *A rather than* B, C, D . . . N?" That is, the first question indirectly refers to a self-organized set of alternatives, a *contrast space* from which a course of action is then selected. Once I form the intention to greet you, that cognitive reorganization circumscribes future behavior to winking rather than waving, saying "Hi!" or shaking your hand. I have just claimed that the current state of mind described by the prior intention is that self-organized partitioned subset; those options serve as the contrast set from which one option will be chosen. By conceptualizing action from a dynamical systems perspective, we can see why agents are spared the need to apply a decision procedure explicitly each time they act: an agent's current frame of mind automatically culls a subset from the indefinitely many other alternatives in principle available to it. It does not even consider those behavioral alternatives excluded from the contrast space. As soon as I form the prior intention to greet you, turning away drops out as a possible act-type: the neural attractor for it flattens out.

Referring to Willy Sutton's notorious reply to a priest's question, "Why do you rob banks?"—"Because that's where the money is"—both Garfinkel (1981) and Michael Bratman (1987) note that, whereas the priest's question partitioned the query space into "rob banks rather than not rob at all," Sutton's reply indicated that *he* had partitioned the contrast space of possibilities along different dimensions: "rob banks rather than, say, movie houses." In dynamical language, prior intentions "structured" the problem at hand by determining the coordinates of the mental framework: in Willy Sutton's case, rob banks rather than movie houses, say. For Sutton, the possibility "not rob at all" is excluded altogether from his self-organized frame of mind. It is therefore not one of Willy's options (from Willy's point of view, that is).

Contrastive Stress

The difference between action and nonaction, therefore, is in part a function of whether the behavior originated in and was constrained by an alternative within the agent's semantically self-organized contrast space. Let us see why. Some years ago Searle (1981) suggested that the distinction between unintentional action and nonaction might be drawn in terms of the "closeness" of the description of the intention's content and that of the action. Oedipus performs the actions of marrying his mother unintentionally and marrying Jocasta intentionally but performs no action at all (in marrying Jocasta/mother) by "moving a lot of molecules" of air, because the description "marrying his mother" is "closer" to the description "marrying Jocasta" (which describes the content of Oedipus's intention) than to "moving a lot of molecules." The "distance" renders the event "moving the molecules of air" nonaction. Conceptualizing self-organization topologically, we saw, gives us a natural way of understanding this "closeness": as relative location in semantic neurological space.

Marcelo Dascal and Ora Gruengard attempted to cash out Searle's (1981) notion of "closeness" in terms of contrastive stress (Dretske 1972). Consider the following three examples:

1. Clyde gave me *the tickets* by mistake.
2. Clyde gave *me* the tickets by mistake.
3. Clyde *gave* me the tickets by mistake.

The scope of the operator "by mistake" is determined by contrastive stress, whose function is to identify one alternative from a set of possibilities, while at the same time excluding other members of this set (Dascal and Gruengard 1981, 108). The intonation with which the sentences are spoken cues the listener to the range of alternatives that the speaker included in the contrast set. In dynamical language, contrastive stress informs the listener of the speaker's state of mind (his or her mental landscape) by suggesting the coordinates and dynamics that identify that mental state. Applying this idea to the problem of action and using Oedipus as a test case yields the following:

4. Oedipus intends to *marry* Jocasta.
5. Oedipus intends to marry *Jocasta*.

Dascal and Gruengard claim that if (5) describes Oedipus's intention, the set of candidates in his contrast set from which Jocasta was selected might have included "Jocasta," "Electra," and "my mother" or "Jackie Kennedy."[55] In (5), alternatives to marriage (befriending, sleeping with but not marrying, and so forth) are not even under review. In (4), other women are not considered; alternatives to marriage are. Dascal and Gruengard's point in example (5) is that, by emphasizing *Jocasta*, Oedipus is "explicitly excluding from his intention the possibilities of marrying either Electra, his mother, or Jackie Kennedy." Those events included in the contrast set but explicitly not selected that nonetheless come to pass are the agent's action, albeit unintentional. Hence Oedipus marries his mother as an act, although unintentionally (Dascal and Gruengard 1981, 109).

Inclusion or exclusion from the agent's mental contrast set can also account for the intensional opacity of action descriptions. If Jocasta/mother happens to be the only woman in Thebes with Rh-negative blood, the two descriptions are extensionally equivalent: they pick out the same person. But since Oedipus did not include in his contrast set "Oedipus married the only Rh negative woman in Thebes"—indeed, Oedipus could not have even considered it—it does not identify an unintentional act. It is a nonact. Because Oedipus is ignorant of the concept "Rh negative blood," his behavior could not have originated in that semantic space, nor could it have been constrained by it. A fortiori, it is indifferent to that description.

Dascal and Gruengard's claim parallels the account of action as the flow of information presented here. I have been claiming that action should be marked off from nonaction in virtue of the behavior's dependence on the information that an intention generates from a range of previously unconstrained behavioral alternatives. The set of alternatives in Dascal and Gruengard's contrast space of possibilities plays the same role as the set of employees in the Herman example: it serves as the pool of alternatives from which the agent chooses. But if action, like information flow, is a trajectory whose pathway is dependent on an earlier selection process, the coordinates that identify and explain the behavior must be those established by the source.

The first point to be made here, then, is that the particular act-token an agent performs depends on the coordinates of his or her contrast space $(B, C, \ldots N)$. A different contrast space, "Why did X A rather than $O, P, Q \ldots Z$?" would be irrelevant to what the agent did. To the extent that an account of the bank robber's behavior addresses the *priest's* query space and not Willy Sutton's, it fails as an explanation of the bank robber's actions.

Awareness of Alternatives in Contrast Space

If people are embedded in time and space, subjective elements defined intrinsically as primary qualities (the way Newtonian atoms are by their mass) cannot be sufficient to fix the content of an agent's intentions. As I noted in my comments on Rawls (1955) and Peters (1958), act-tokens such as signing a check cannot even be intended, much less performed, if the corresponding social practice has not been established. The Martian cannot (on Mars) formulate the prior intention to "sign a check" since that act-type is not available on Mars (so far as we know).

But a course of action can be a meaningful alternative if and only if the agent is (minimally) aware of it. An attractor cannot guide behavior if that behavior is not even in the agent's conscious landscape. If no prior intention is formulated, no corresponding meaningful information can *flow* from *s* to *r*. Information about the behavior that is available to the observer but was not even among the alternatives at the agent's origin is therefore pure noise: nonaction.

But for an agent to be aware of anything, there must be sufficient contrast for the alternative to be noticeable against the background noise. The meaningful contrast space from which actions issue must show sufficient cognitive resolution for the agent to be able to discriminate potential act-types from the background. Thinking of cognitive dynamics as landscapes helps conceptualize this phenomenon. From a dynamical point of view, the "significance" of alternatives in contrast space is given both by the relative depths of their valleys and their location in that multidimensional neurological space, as well as the agent's current orientation. Because self-organized regions in a multidimensional space intertwine, concepts and potential act-types that appear in many dynamical mental regions (emotional, psychological, aesthetic, and so forth) will be more pronounced than those implicated in only a few regions of the neurological system. Low-probability alternatives that merge easily with others, on the other hand, will scarcely be noticeable. These will be, topographically, on the shallower margins. As with interference patterns, one can suppose that when several waves coincide in a dynamical landscape, a hurricane-like focus commanding attention appears.

Still, the hard cases will be those like Oedipus's. Dascal and Gruengard (1981, 109) require that the agent's contrast set "must also take into account the social conditions under which the action is performed, the subject's background knowledge, and other factors of this kind." The reason for this emendation is that, had "my mother" not been included in Oedipus's contrast set, "marrying his mother," which Dascal and Gruengard intuitively wish to classify as unintentional, but very much Oedipus' act-token, would constitute a "nonaction." By requiring that social conditions be taken into account, the contrast set of which Oedipus is minimally aware can be supposed to include "his mother," which makes "marrying his mother" unintentional, but very much an act-token. However, as was the case in the Jewish and Moslem marital cases mentioned earlier, including "mother" in Oedipus's contrast set is plausible only if we assume that Oedipus remembers, even if only faintly, the seer's prediction that he would kill his father and marry his mother. Only on that assumption is it reasonable for Dascal and Gruengard to suppose that "my mother" is included in Oedipus's contrast set.

As the myth is told, however, the Oedipus case is complicated because upon learning of the curse, Oedipus's father, Laius, sends his young son away from Thebes. Oedipus grows up in Corinth with adoptive parents unsuspecting that these are not his real parents. Later, when he learns of the curse, he resolves never to return to Corinth to avoid fulfilling the prediction. Unless we say that, given the Greek belief in the inevitability of all oracular predictions[56] Oedipus should have suspected that in marrying Jocasta he might be marrying his mother, determining whether marrying his mother was an unintentional act or a nonact requires answering the question "Of what possibilities was Oedipus aware (however faintly)?"

Was Oedipus's real fault negligence? If the contrast space of which agents are aware is a self-organized subvolume of mental space, those pronounced foci of greater resolution will be those that are clearly and distinctly discernible. They will strongly influence behavior; motor attractors will more easily entrain to their dynamics. On the other hand, the more shadowy areas at the periphery that cancel out as they interact with other attractors will show less resolution and have a less significant impact on behavior. This overlap occurs because, as we said earlier, in multi-dimensional dynamic space an indefinite number of attractors can coexist, inextricably intertwined with and entrained into each other. Like wave interference patterns, some will reinforce and some will cancel each other.

Negligence, therefore, might be accounted for in terms of those alternatives within the agent's mental contrast space that are not in its focal area: had those possibilities been more centrally located or had superior resolution, they would have constrained a different course of action. The scope and degree of attention will depend on how the agent's conscious awareness and cognitive organization are organized relative both to other internal dynamics and to the environment. We might say of Oedipus, "Sexual attraction clouded his judgment." We will return to the question of why some persons are more attentive than others, or less easily swayed by others, at the end of the book.

Awareness of the Consequences of Alternatives in the Contrast Set

For a behavior to be classified as an action, the agent must also be minimally aware of any significant consequences of the alternatives in the contrast space. This level of cognition also emerges during the course of normal human development. By a certain age a child's mental space has become semantically organized: the child can anticipate and plan ahead.[57] As was the case with Hannah and Gabriel's motor skills, however, the ability to anticipate is probably not simply the result of an unfolding, pre-established program. It too is likely to be a dynamical pattern assembled by the interaction between a particular innate endowment and habituation —from, say, a teacher who constantly drills into her charges, "Plan ahead!" In several Montgomery County, Maryland, public schools, personal agendas are distributed to students, who are later graded on whether they update and check their contents. A mother's admonition or a teacher's homework—both are examples of how additional context-sensitive constraints can recalibrate internal dynamics and thus bias future behavior.

It is reasonable to stipulate, then, that agents who are aware, however faintly, of their behavior's nonbasic ramifications include them among the alternatives of their contrast space and its dynamical pathways, if only by default. Knowingly not preventing something adverse of which one is (however dimly) aware is tantamount to choosing it, in a derivative sense of "choice." We often assume that the degree of awareness is correlated with the significance of those ramifications and accuse those who fail to take appropriate action to prevent their occurrence of being "in denial." As the medievals consistently remind us, acts of omission are acts nonetheless, but only if the agent is aware of the omission! By definition, if the agent logically, cognitively (or emotionally?) could not even have considered an alternative as such, it is not something he or she could have "omitted." The question "Of what was the agent minimally aware, and when?" thus remains central to the question "What did the agent intend?"

Prior intentions and plans of action, Bratman (1987) argues, also channel future deliberation by narrowing the scope of alternatives to be subsequently considered. Reparsing cognitive space in this way helps us act. Let us see how.

In the language of dynamical systems, we said, prior intentions restructure a multidimensional space into a new organization characterized by a new set of coordinates and new dynamics. Since, as mentioned earlier, contextual constraints that partition a prior intention's contrast space embody the emergent property of meaning and the laws of logic, it is plausible to assume that the cognitive level of organization will show semantic and logical consistency. Dynamically, that means that once I form the prior intention to greet you, not every logical or physically possible alternative remains open downstream, and those that do are contoured differently: the probability of waving or saying "Hi!" goes up; the probability of turning away goes down.

Thinking of prior intentions as parsing a self-organized dynamics in this way also explains why settling on one prior intention (say, the intention to rob) precludes settling on a logically conflicting one (not to rob). Once I decide to perform act-token A, non-A is no longer a viable alternative (Bratman 1987): it drops out downstream as one of the coordinates. There is, a fortiori, no attractor that will get me there from here. Once I decide to greet you, the probability of insulting you decreases to the point at which it is virtually eliminated as a possibility.[58] The probability of not greeting you suddenly becomes zero.

Proximate Intention

I just postulated that prior intentions carve out the coordinates and dynamics of the meaningful alternatives that the agent will consider. Prior intentions thus structure the multidimensional graph or landscape that describes the agent's new frame of mind after the intention is formed. Phrased differently, prior intentions are the felt counterpart to dynamical neural reorganizations that take place in response to cognitive, affective, or similar disequilibrium.

Once a prior intention has established a self-organized space of meaningful possibilities, the agent will then settle on one of the options that the new dynamics make available. I now propose that explicitly formulating a proximate intention (do A now) is, in topological terms, the felt counterpart of the positioning of a particular valley or attractor just ahead of the system's immediate position. A dynamical neurological transformation deepens an act-type's pathway and locates it immediately ahead of that self-organized phase space. When an agent formulates a proximate intention, the prior intention's dynamical structure entrains previously constructed motor control attractors to provide what Myles Brand (1984) called, mechanistically, the "pushing component" of proximate volitions. In entraining these attractors, the proximate intention constrains (top-down) established motor control propensities such that, all things being equal, the behavior described by the intention will be carried out. Second-order contextual constraints are responsible for the phenomenon Goldman tried to capture with the phrase "in the characteristic way." They also implement the mechanism of Searle's "intentions-in-action."

The construction of any attractor, once again, results from interactions between the system's current dynamics and its structured environment, whether physical or social. In the case of proximate intentions, the dynamics involved are the meaningfully self-organized regions of the prior intention's belief, desire, and so forth, together with their logic (their dynamical pathways). These dynamics are themselves affected by top-down contextual constraints entering from the environment, and by entraining motor control, explicitly formulating a proximate intention restructures the agent's dynamics even further. An existing valley deepens or a new valley appears where none existed before, but always within the overall qualitative landscape the prior intention has established. By further differentiating a cognitive state space, proximate intentions impose additional context-dependent constraints on that semantic and motor space; they thereby stack the odds that a certain behavior will be performed.

Topologically, the walls of the basin carving out a proximate intention separate that act-type from other potential (but unchosen) behaviors described by the remaining coordinates and attractors of the prior intention's dynamics.[59] Given my prior intention to greet you, the proximate intention to "wink" is an attractor whose walls and sudden location just ahead in phase space separate it from other potential attractors, those for "shaking hands" and "saying 'Hi!'" for example. By visualizing the process as a landscape like fig. 10.4, attractors describing those act-types will appear outside the attractor-chute for winking but still within the semantic coordinates and overall basin of the broader chute that describes the more general act-type "greeting you." Growling is not even a coordinate, so there is no attractor that can take me to that behavior from here.

Semantic Cleanup Units and Action

Because the brain is known to be massively recurrent, we can assume that specific feedback circuits monitor the effectiveness of a proximate intention's contextual constraints (see Edelman 1987 on reentrant pathways). These contextual constraints will regulate the impact of the agent's other self-organized dynamics and those constraints entering from the current environment as well as those set by the agent's past. In constraining the action's trajectory, feedback functions to monitor and ensure that the intention's meaning flows uninterrupted by equivocation to its completion in behavior. In the language of dynamics, cleanup units ensure that the invariant relations that characterize the higher level of organization and embody the intention's content are preserved across coordinate transformations to the motor level. Cleanup units, it will be recalled, are context-sensitive constraints: they modify the degrees of freedom of the system's components.

That is what Hinton, Plaut, and Shallice (1993, 79) mean when they speak of "motion through a multidimensional semantic space." The cleanup units carry out that task and thereby implement the intention by constantly updating and modulating the rate at which lower-level neural processes governing motor control, speech output, and similar things occur.[60] In the case of action, with the assistance of massive feedback pathways (Hinton's cleanup units), proximate intentions constrain motor options so that behavioral output will semantically satisfy the intention's content. Top-down contextual constraints ensure that the behavioral trajectory will remain within the semantic space carved out by the meaning of the proximate intention. Dynamically, the projection from intention to behavior preserves the intention's meaning across coordinate transformations insofar as the motor level retains the dynamic organization that identifies the intention. This approach does away with the atomistic and instantaneous character of volitions and intentions, in effect dissolving the problem of wayward causal chains.

The Problem of Wayward Causal Chains Resolved

From a dynamical point of view, therefore, consequential wayward causal chains are trajectories lesioned below the semantic cleanup units responsible for the basic action: noise and equivocation entered downstream from those units. (In the case of basic actions, the cleanup units are normally a part of the communications channel.) For example, in some consequential chains, like those resulting in the errors of deep dyslexia and of some strokes, an utterance might be generated and constrained by the meaning the agent intends to convey. The agent gets the sense right even though the specific word spoken is incorrect. In consequential chains, that is, the appropriate general basin in semantic space originates and constrains the output, but damage caused by the stroke, say, affects the particular motor trajectory. By preserving the intended meaning but erring in the choice of words, the actual utterance betrays the presence of noise and equivocation, brought on by the stroke. In such cases, the neurological process is no longer serving as the silent communications channel; the lesion is generating its own (noisy) information which, in turn, is producing equivocation. And we know where that is happening: contextual constraints downstream from the semantic cleanup units have malfunctioned.

Antecedential wayward chains, on the other hand—those characteristic of surface dyslexia or the nervous nephew example—can be conceptualized as trajectories lesioned above the semantic cleanup units. When this happens, the resulting behavior is pure noise, even if, as in the case of the nervous nephew, the event happens to satisfy semantically (and can be traced to) an efficient cause. Topologically, the nephew example looks like a directed graph that catastrophically drops off semantic space altogether onto a different, nonsemantic page just after the intention is formulated. As a result, semantics do not constrain the downstream portion of the trajectory at all. It is, to repeat, noise. A dynamical view of action has the advantage that unlike the old causal version, it can handle these distinctions. Multidimensional, intertwined dynamics should even be able to explain Freudian slips in this way!

Multiple Realizability and Equivocation: An Objection

In the chapter on information theory, I said that neurological processes constitute the communications channel for intentions and basic actions. By definition, the communications channel must not generate its own information; if it does it has become a noisy channel. On the other hand, information is generated whenever an option is selected from a set of alternatives. The material presented in that chapter therefore raises the following objection: if different neurological processes can underlie the same intention, isn't information generated as soon as a "reduction of possibilities" takes place when one of those neurological processes is activated? In other words, because intentions and other mental states can be realized in more than one neurological pattern, once one of those alternatives is chosen, is the neurology really silent, as it must be to serve as the communications channel?

In the chapter on information theory I also claimed that to constitute action the trajectory "intention to raise arm → arm rises", must unequivocally identify the intention as the source of the behavior. By "uniquely identify" I mean that the intention's conditional probability *given* the behavior is unity. That is, the conditional probability that the arm went up because someone else lifted it, or as the result of a muscle spasm—or because of anything other than the intention—must be zero. The terms corresponding to "someone lifts my arm" and "muscle spasm" must contribute nothing to equivocation for the trajectory "intention to raise arm → arm rises" to constitute action, that is, for $I_s(r) = 1$.

So far so good. The problem appears one step further back in the process. If, as in figure 12.1, "intention to raise arm" (I_2) can be realized in any one of several neurological processes n_1, n_2, or n_3, isn't the behavior "arm rises" (b_1) equivocal with respect to *those* neurological processes? Doesn't the fact that n_1 realized the intention generate its own information?

Appealing to the dynamics of self-organization can help circumvent this potential objection. Once complex systems self-organize, it will be

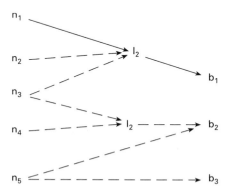

Figure 12.1
Adaptation of figure 6.2 to the problem of action. (n = neurological patterns as neurological; I = neurological patterns self-organized into the emergent global structure that embodies an intention; b = behavior.)

recalled, each level is partly decoupled from the specific components that make it up. The higher level is meta-stable despite multiple realizability at the lower level. As we saw in the case of Bénard cells, it does not matter whether the cells are made of water or other viscous materials. At any given moment, the alternatives that matter to a complex dynamical system, so to speak, are the coordinates of the graph on which the system currently finds itself (blue or red, after the B-Z self-organization, for example). If evolutionary sequences are like a series of catastrophes, the alternatives from which information can be generated are those coordinates of the page the system happens to be on at the moment. Coordinates from an earlier page no longer matter; they have become the process's communications channel.

What is critical is the higher level's "indifference to the particularities of the lower-level realization" (McClamrock 1995, 15). Since that indifference is a defining feature of hierarchical systematization, dynamical self-organization is one way levels become partly sealed off from one another. As explained earlier, under normal conditions the behavior of a complex system's components is at the service of the global level, which, by its very nature, tolerates a certain range of fluctuation at the lower level. The particular embodiment or structure the action takes will depend on its initial conditions. Only when events at the component level compete with the integrity of the systems level organization (as happens biologically in cancer and cognitively with strokes) do the former generate their own information, which can make the output equivocal.

So, too, with respect to the mental. Once the cognitive, intentional level self-organizes, the fact that any one of several neurological processes can implement the same mental event (I_2) becomes irrelevant. Under normal circumstances, my intention and subsequent action are indifferent to whether the former is realized in n_1, n_2, or n_3. The alternatives that matter with respect to whether the behavior "raise my arm" constitutes an act-token are whether I intended to raise it, whether someone else lifted it, and whether it occurred as a result of a muscle spasm, for example. What matters, that is, is whether or not the neural process transmits information as mental. The presence and interference of those possibilities matter because trajectories originating in a spasm, (n_5) for example, would take place entirely outside semantic space. Since the same neurons can be implicated in trajectories inside or outside semantic space, the neurological processes, *as* neurological, don't matter. The role that the intended meaning plays in bringing about the behavior is what counts.

If, as a result of ischemia, say, neurological pattern n_5 abnormally fails to flow reliably into behavior when the agent intends to raise his arm, but instead fires spontaneously half an hour later, the resulting behavior will be the terminus of a nonaction trajectory "Spasm → arm rises" (b_2).

That trajectory is nonaction because the behavior is equivocal with respect to the agent's intention. The behavior therefore occurs outside semantic space. In some cases of strokes and lobotomies, that is, noise either destroys semantic and cognitive organization or prevents it from flowing into behavior; in these cases, but not ordinarily, neurological processes *as* neurological do make a difference to what happens. Under normal conditions, however, neuronal processes do not generate their own information; they merely serve as the communications channel. That is what is meant by "normal conditions."

Summary

Formulating a proximate intention is thus the construction in semantically organized neural space of a new attractor, or the deepening of an existing one, and its placement just ahead of the agent's current state. That is, proximate intentions are quantitative, not qualitative deformations of the topography immediately ahead in the agent's mental phase space. A sharply hewn (and, all things being equal, the deepest) valley appears just in front of the agent's current frame of mind. Again, all things being equal, he or she will be immediately drawn into it. Like Bénard cells, autocatalysis, and laser beams, from a dynamical perspective proximate intentions are dynamical attractors that function as top-down control operators entraining other subsystems, including (in the case of behavior) motor control. These second-order contextual constraints restrict some of the motor subsystems' potential as these become entrained to the intention's organization. Since those attractors design a pathway through conscious semantic space, they embody the meaningful purposiveness of intentional action. The behavior aims at satisfying the constraints of the intention from which it issued. As such it is purposive and teleological.

Earlier I proposed that top-down causality is the operation of second-order contextual constraints. Following that line of reasoning, I now conclude that intentional action should be conceptualized as a trajectory whereby emergent, second-order contextual constraints of dynamical brain organization selectively constrain lower-dimensional motor and speech processes. And these constraints do so in virtue of the meaningful and conative content of the intentions that they embody. Such top-down commands constrain individual motor and speech processes such that the resulting behavior preserves the dynamic organization that embodies the intention's content. As is the case with all structured structuring structures, intentions are causally effective by constraining (entraining) their components in a manner homologous to the way in which the virtual governor of a beam of coherent laser light synchronizes or slaves the random waves of the individual atoms that constitute it: by altering their probability distribution (their rate of firing, for example). Intentions are the changes in the motor neurons' natural firing frequency. Ontologically, behavior that is the top-down projection of self-organized semantic constraints onto lower-level motor or speech processes constitutes an act-token. As such, intentions can function as the action's formal and final cause.[61]

From the perspective of complex dynamics, therefore, proximate intentions (to-do-x now) are not separate blueprints or templates to which the behavior refers; nor are they represented as (by?) a symbol. Much less are intentions external causes operating like Newtonian forces pushing the (rest of the) body into action. Functioning as second-order contextual constraints, proximate intentions are dynamical attractors within a prior intention's self-organized semantic space. They drive behavior in a particular direction because they are changes in the frequency distribution of entrained motor processes. It is therefore more accurate to think of proximate intentions as a dynamical system's operator (Elman 1995), an endogenous control knob that takes the network from one location in state space to another. Both prior and proximate intentions embody top-down, context-sensitive constraints that restrict behavior to within certain regions of semantic space. As such they are structuring, ongoing formal causes.

Because the contextual constraints of attractors within semantic space embody act-types, individual trajectories carrying out proximate intentions constitute act-tokens. One must keep in mind, however, that a particular proximate intention is never the only existing attractor, as we know from studies on *akrasia*. Nor is it always the one that wins out, although, by definition, it usually does. From a dynamical systems perspective, individual act-tokens are unbroken trajectories within an intention's semantic space as it projects and cascades, without equivocation, to lower-level motor and speech levels and terminates in behavior that, ex hypothesi, semantically fits the intention. Once again, that anticipated terminus is the action's goal or purpose: its final cause.

This approach offers a plausible account of the way in which Danto's (1973, 190–92) claim that "action is a matter of making the world fit one's representation" might be physically realized. Dynamical organization's context-dependent constraints make the behavioral output conditional on the intentional source. The action's trajectory thus *embodies* the cognitive content of the intention from which it issues and which, with the help of the cleanup circuits, flows into the behavior to its completion. Using conditional probability as explained in chapter 6, the concepts of equivocation and noise can be used to calculate whether that trajectory is compromised. This reconceptualization of cause in terms of the operations of contextual constraints allows for both the possibility of self-cause and structuring or formal causes that guide and direct as well as initiate behavior, all within a scientifically acceptable framework. It also allows for a rethinking of teleology. The constrained trajectory that implements the intention aims at a behavioral output that reproduces the intention's invariant relations.

Causes of action and their behavioral effects have traditionally been conceptualized as two independent and disconnectable items. Once the volition (intention, and so on) fired, its job was done; the motor units got to do their thing next (separately next). Requiring that action be understood as a trajectory within and constrained by the dynamics of a self-organized semantic space eliminates the atomicity of intentions and volitions. An action's trajectory crosses dynamical coordinates, from the conscious, semantic, and affective levels of neuronal organization to those governing raw motor control. And as mentioned earlier, individual neurons implicated in the motor system for blinks might even be the same ones implicated in winks. The difference between a wink and a blink, however, is that in the former those units have been entrained into the dynamics of a cognitively organized semantic space, whose properties and laws constrain and direct their trajectory.

Chapter 13

Threading an Agent's Control Loop through the Environment

Recapitulation

In chapters 11 and 12, I postulated that dynamical processes homologous to those of self-organizing, far-from-equilibrium abiotic and biological systems are also at work in people and their mental states. In response to disequilibrium either within an agent's own cognitive organization or between the agent's cognitive state and other internal dynamics (psychological, emotional, desiderative, motor, and the like), a person's current frame of mind can undergo a phase change and recalibrate to rectify the disequilibrium.[62]

Formulating a prior intention is just such a catastrophic bifurcation. Since the neurological system can be conceptualized as a multidimensional, dynamic landscape, we can think of this process in terms of plate tectonics and resulting earthquakes. When agents formulate a prior intention, the establishment of second-order contextual constraints dissipates the disequilibrium by reorganizing a more complex region of cognitive and affective space. By imposing new propensities on available pathways, the dynamics of that newly self-organized semantic space constrain (top-down) movements within it. Through the assignation of conditional probabilities, some act-types (some chutes) are eliminated altogether; others are made more likely. Then, and as a result of further interaction among the prior intention, other internal dynamics, and the environment, one option from those weighted alternatives established by the new organization becomes a proximate attractor. By entraining motor dynamics to its own, this pathway directs and constrains action in the immediate future. And so the person acts.

But not all actions are performed as a result of explicit deliberation. If in order to choose among the various alternatives available, agents first needed to implement a decision procedure to determine whether each option was meaningful, any behavior would be indefinitely delayed. If agents first had to consider and evaluate every basic act-type A for its significance, efficiency, parsimony, and other characteristics with respect to the intended nonbasic behavior A', they would never act. We saw in

Freeman's (1991a, 1991b) research on odors, Damasio's (1994) hypotheses about the role of emotions in cognition, and even Hinton's (1992) and Elman's (1995) artificial networks, that the context in which stimuli are experienced or presented plays a primary role in dynamically fixing their identification. Does something similar happen with intention and the way it is implemented in behavior?

Intentions Are Meanings in the Head

How do we decide how to do what we intend to do? We will never answer that question by studying the "toy domains" of classical artificial intelligence (McClamrock 1995). These are too simple; so simple, in fact, that the robot must do everything. It must either rely on brute speed to explore every possible alternative or, as the designers of expert systems have often tried to do, all the information required to reach a decision must have been prebuilt into its database. It is unlikely that this is the way organisms do it (Cherniak 1986): yet another bit of evidence that people are not Cartesian selves.

And yet following the classical epistemological thesis that concepts' meaning is entirely in the cognizer's head, action theorists envisioned the content of intentions or volitions also as onboard pictures wholly in the agent's head. As suggested in part I's excursion through the various theories of action, intentions and volitions were also supposed to function as the trigger-blueprint entirely inside the mind. As we saw in chapters 1 and 2, causal theories of action claimed that behavior qualifies as a basic act-token if initiated by just such an event in the head. For the act-token that the intention causes to be "free," the environment was supposed to contribute nothing either to the way that picture got into the head or to its impact. The difference between unintentional and intentional nonbasic actions also turned on the role the ghostly goings-on played in bringing about the behavior.

We saw the many difficulties this understanding of intention occasioned for action theory. If the picture is a closed and isolated process entirely in the head, it is difficult to understand how it can point to, represent, or mean anything outside itself. Other difficulties that this view of intention brought with it include the following: (1) Not every picture can be imagined. As we pointed out, in societies with no banking system, would-be agents could not conjure up "check signing" to serve as an intention's content. Established social practices are required even for that. (2) Once learned, skills as complex as driving an automobile are ordinarily executed without continuous self-conscious direction. Although we concentrate on and explicitly intend each movement when learning to drive, once we become adept drivers, not only do we not explicitly intend each maneuver, we might not even remember whether the traffic light on our daily commute at the intersection of Elm and Maple was red this morning. Does that imply that driving was not our action? Of course not.

The picture theory of meaning came under fire as a consequence of articles by Quine (1953) and Putnam (1975), who revolutionized epistemology by arguing that "meanings just ain't in the head" (227). What a word means is no longer considered just a picture in the head; it is now thought to be intimately associated with how the word was learned, its causal history, what it is associated with, and similar factors. Empirical evidence from other complex adaptive systems, too, attests to the environment's role in the way they self-organize. Whether the subject is motor coordination, olfaction, or auditory perception, importing history and context into the organism by recalibrating its dynamics is necessary before those complex skills can develop. Even artificial neural networks appear to construct semantic, representational spaces when ongoing feedback embeds them in their environment and their history. Figure 11.1 captured the way the network's pattern of connection weights reset and organized to the stimuli on which it was trained.

Intentions "Ain't Just in the Head" Either

Dynamical systems theory tells us that because they are embedded in history as well as in a structured environment, people are not independent, isolated atoms just plunked into a completely alien environment that affects them through mechanical forces. As we saw earlier, by means of second-order context-dependencies established by persistent interaction with the environment, agents effectively import the environment into their internal dynamics by recalibrating these to incoming signals. Over time, that is, both phylogenetically and developmentally, people establish interdependencies between the environment and their internal dynamics such that the former becomes part of their external structure: their boundary conditions. Context-sensitive constraints established by positive feedback weave both the environment and history into the agent's cognitive and conative states, thereby achieving the embeddedness in space and time that characterizes those complex systems. The way adaptive systems function therefore strongly suggests that, as dynamical structures, intentions "ain't just in the head" either.

Consider flies. A control loop runs directly from their feet and the surface on which they are standing to their wings. As a result, the fly does not need to figure out how to fly; it needs only to decide *what* to do (jump). Once the fly senses the change in the surface under its feet, the wings immediately and automatically flap (reported in McClamrock 1995). So only one decision is required: jump now. The external portion of the fly's control loop (what I have called its external structure) takes care of the rest.

Homologously, we can suppose that once human agents settle on a prior intention, the control loop of the intention's external structure threads through other attractors and self-organized neurological regions such as those embodying psychological and emotional properties. The overall context in which the prior intention is located can therefore be expected to add its own biases to those of the prior intention. As we saw, Damasio (1994) postulates that the cognitive system simplifies its activities by linking up with the affective system. The entrainment provides the biasing that imposes additional context-sensitive constraints on the decision-making and motor systems. As a result, given a particular environment, some behaviors will automatically be assigned a higher probability; others will be ruled out. This spares the cognitive, intentional level the need to do all the work: much of it can be left to the external structure that connects it with the affective and other systems, as well as with the environment. "Just intend to jump; other dynamics will take care of the details."

Like the fly, once Hannah and Gabriel learn to reach, all they need to do is intend to reach. Given the prior intention to reach and previously established contextual constraints, empirical circumstances will elicit the appropriate behavior. In interaction with the constraints the current environment imposes, established motor attractors appropriate to the context in which the infants find themselves will automatically carry out the job. Once the children know how to reach, that is, the context in which they are situated will elicit the appropriate degree or type of motor exertion: the effort required will be different if weights have been attached to the children's arms, or if they are lying down. As a result of its interactions with other dynamics, the intention's attractor thus progressively and automatically narrows over time until in the end only one behavioral alternative is left. And so the agent just acts intentionally without ever having explicitly formed a proximate intention to perform that particular act-token.

Running the Control Loop through the Environment

A framework like this one that can account for the way other desires and beliefs implement a prior intention has a second advantage: as Bratman (1987) convincingly notes, it allows us to say that when I *A*ed intentionally I intended something, even if I did not specifically intend to *A*. Dynamical systems theory can accommodate this point. Let us see how.

Bratman (1987) claims that once a prior intention is in place, the specific behavior that implements that intention can be left to other desires and beliefs. As just described, a dynamical system's external structure can handle this feature of intentional action. Because any intention's control loop also runs through the agent's other self-organized dynamics (such as those responsible for motor control, emotions, and the like), it is plausible to suppose that we can "intend (only vaguely and unspecifically) to something"; other, previously constructed attractors and the environment, as internalized in the agent's external structure, in interaction with the constraints of the vague intention, will then take care of the details. We just formulate the intention and "let the world be its own model."

The degree of specificity or precision of the alternatives in an agent's contrast space will vary considerably; the dynamics of that cognitive space can also be vague and general. A prior intention, for example, might be so vague that it only carves out the contrast space "do something" (rather than nothing). If semantic closeness is analyzed in terms of relative position in dynamic space, some intentions' vagueness or lack of specificity (which Mele [1992] noted) would correspond to the size and character of the area of dynamical space involved. In settling on the vague and unspecific prior intention to "something," the agent topographically organizes an indefinitely broad and fuzzy basin of attraction that, moreover is inextricably intertwined with many other neurological basins. Since attractors embody constrained motions through self-organized regions in state space, the broader an attractor's basin, the more multiply realizable it is. The wider the basin, too, the greater the leeway it can delegate to its external structure. Which neuronal pattern for motor control will carry out the intention can be left to the overall context in which that intention is formulated. Given the brain's multiple realizability, coarse coding, and vector completion, the possibility of such vague and unspecific intentions is unsurprising.

"I intend to something" will be embodied in a more broadly basined attractor than that carved out by "I intend specifically to A." This wider basin embodies the greater latitude in the range of behaviors it allows within its watershed. Act-types A, B, C, D ... N, each with its characteristic probability depth, might be within that broad basin. Any of those lower-level motor process can implement the intention's overall organization. As mentioned earlier, we can utter the same sentence with our mouth full, partly anesthetized, or under numerous other circumstances. In cases where different motor control patterns can carry out the particular action, the "decision" will often be made, as we saw, not by explicit deliberation, but by the interaction between the intention and the particular circumstances in which the agent is embedded. Initial conditions in general, including habits, skills, and other automated attractors already in

place, will implement the vague "intend to something." Whether or not I
A can be "decided" by the combined interaction between the constraints
of the vague and unspecific "intend to something" and other constraints.

How do we go about deciding how to do what we intend to do? The
answer is, "usually we don't have to." Cleanup units, recall, embody
context-sensitive constraints: they are part of a system's external structure, both extending into the environment and incorporating the past.
Context-sensitive constraints embody the connectivity and propensities
that provide the global system with its organization and identity. The
specific structure can be left open. But context-sensitive constraints do not
make contact with the environment or history the way a cue stick pushes
a billiard ball. Cleanup units (that is, context-sensitive feedback) "cause"
actions by altering probability distributions in real time. Throughout an
action's performance, cleanup (recurrent) circuits take care of fine-graining
the details in real time as the behavior proceeds downstream by stacking
the odds against alternative behavior. As a result, context-sensitive constraints sculpt a chute that progressively and automatically narrows until
it terminates in one actual behavior.

The particular trajectory that develops will be the result of the interplay
among the intention, other existing attractors, and the continuous input
from the environment. This is how agents just act (Ginet 1995). Had
Elman's cluster diagram (figure 11.1) been depicted as an ontogenetic
landscape like figure 10.4, the volume spanning the type "mammal"
would be broadly basined; the areas identifying mouse$_{346}$ or mouse$_{343}$
would be narrow canyons. In a corresponding dynamical landscape representing intentions-in-action instead of concepts, the channels might appear funnel-like: more coarsely grained and broadly basined upstream, and
increasingly fine-grained and narrower downstream. The global context in
which the intention is embedded (top-down) culls one alternative from
that set. And so the chute automatically narrows.

For example, suppose, upon noticing a child in distress I form the
vague, unspecific prior intention "do something to help that child": a very
broad and shallow valley self-organizes in my mental landscape. In self-
organizing a region of cognitive space, prior intentions, as we saw, exclude some options from future consideration (Bratman 1987). That is,
forming the prior intention "do something to help that child" eliminates
not doing anything to help that child as a future possibility. The coordinate for that alternative drops out of my phase space, as does a chute that
terminates on that coordinate.

But neither people nor the environment is static; dynamical systems
exist and continually change over time. While holding constant the albeit
vague decision to "do something to help that child," life goes on, so to
speak. As a result, I can just wait until the fuzzy and context-sensitive

constraints that unspecific prior intention carves out encounter an appropriate opportunity. When that occurs, combined constraint satisfaction automatically stacks the probabilities of the attractors in my motor system such that I A. And so I act intentionally, even without specifically formulating a proximate intention. Since more than one behavior could have carried out the intention "do something to help that child," I might have acted differently under different circumstances, given the same prior intention. The particular act-token actually performed (A), therefore, is often the result, not of an explicitly formulated proximate intention to perform a token of that particular act-type, but of the interaction between the vague prior intention and the "lay of the land."[63] That is what context-sensitivity is all about. I Aed intentionally even if I did not intend specifically to A.

Suppose I am walking down the street. I see you, an acquaintance. I form the prior intention to greet you. That intention is embodied, I claimed earlier, in the self-organization of a qualitatively different phase space, whose coordinates include winking, waving, shouting "Hi!", and similar behaviors, all of which together comprise the broad basin "greeting." Opting for one of the alternatives in the contrast space—intending to wink rather than shout, for example—further deforms that landscape: a sharper indentation appears in what was previously a generally broad valley. Given the prior intention to greet you, why wink rather than wave? The answer is that no explicitly formulated decision or proximate intention as such is usually called for. The choice of winking rather than waving can be "decided" by the interaction between my other dynamics and the environment as the process moves downstream. Knowing that you are nearsighted will stack the deck against winking. If I am loaded down with groceries I will probably say "Hi!" If you are thirty feet away I will probably wave. If I am a Christian with my right hand in a cast, I might extend to you my left hand, which I will decidedly refrain from doing if I am a Muslim. None of this, however, needs explicit deliberation or the forming of an explicit proximate intention. I can just decide to greet you and let the world's constraints, as internalized in my other dynamics, take care of the rest. That this is possible at all, once again, is a clear indication that cognitive-affective attractor regimes, including intentions, must be viewed whole cloth as open dynamical systems embedded in a physical, historical, and social fabric.[64]

Explicit Intentions and Basic Actions

In an earlier chapter I claimed that basic actions must be intentional. Does that imply that agents must explicitly intend each basic action? Although on cold winter mornings I almost have to "talk myself into" getting up, most mornings I do not explicitly formulate the proximate intention "get up." I just get up. Does that mean that getting up is not my basic act? Of course not. The prior intention, "carry out your professional obligations in a responsible manner," ordinarily constrains future behavior as required to accomplish that goal. On cold winter mornings, however, that prior intention conflicts with another attractor, "keep warm," and so the first intention requires an extra push to keep on track. Of course, we don't physically push ourselves; instead, we add extra context-sensitive constraints: we buy a programmable thermostat. As Odysseus knew when he lashed himself to the mast to resist the sirens' call, we commonly employ such external devices and rely on them as additional context-sensitive constraints on the circumstances in which we must function. We buy personal organizers, alarm clocks, and the like. Merlin Donald (1991) has argued that the evolution of the modern mind required just such external symbolic memory devices. My claim has been that it depends on context-sensitive constraints generally. These are, of course, similar claims.

Proximate Intentions

On the other hand, if I self-consciously "intend to A now," this specifically formulated proximate intention sculpts a deeper, narrower valley in intentional space, an attractor, furthermore, that is suddenly positioned directly ahead in phase space. The narrower the valley the less latitude in behavior it allows. The deeper the valley, the stronger its attraction (that is, the greater the probability that the behavior it describes will occur). This is especially true to the extent it entrains motor control.

As was the case with prior intentions, once I deliberately intend "to A" I cannot also intend "not to A." The advantage of thinking of these processes topologically explains why: no landscape can simultaneously sculpt a valley and a ridge along the same dimensions. More importantly for present purposes, and as was also the case with prior intentions, once we intend specifically to A, subsequent behavioral options will be more narrowly constrained than they would have been by just the vague, unspecific, and broad attractor of the prior intention, "do something." The external structure of proximate intention "intend to A" allows less latitude in its execution than the intention "do something"; its attractor is less complex. Still, some leeway will exist even in the case of proximate intentions. I might explicitly intend to A now, but not to A quickly now (rather than slowly).

Intend A but not Explicitly A'

With the astronomically dimensioned space that the brain's connectivity affords, that is, it seems reasonable to suppose that even proximate intentions can be coarsely grained. Suppose I self-consciously formulate the proximate intention to "lift an arm." Whether I lift the right or left arm, whether or not I do so slowly, and similar decisions can also be left to that portion of the proximate intention's external structure that runs through the motor dynamics that serve as its communications channel. Even if I do not explicitly intend to "lift *left* arm," if I am left-handed I will probably lift the left arm; if I have arthritis, I will lift the arm gingerly. Despite not having explicitly formulated the intention "lift left arm" or "lift arm gingerly" (A')—only "lift an arm" (A)—lifting the arm gingerly (A') is not nonaction, for the following reason. In cases like these, where an agent explicitly intends to lift an arm but does not explicitly intend to lift the left arm, or to do so gingerly, he or she is implicitly aware of lifting the left arm, gingerly, and makes no effort to change it. Supporting this claim is the fact that if there were severe religious or legal penalties for raising the left arm (and the agent knew of them), he would not raise his left arm, much less automatically. In answer to the question "Why are you raising your left arm?" such an agent would not exclaim, "Oh my, yes, I suppose I am!" That *we* would is evidence that the behavior should be included among our acts.

In ordinary circumstances, therefore, the additional information that the manner of performance carries is about those segments of the intention's control loop that thread through the agent's other dynamics and attractors. Event A' therefore constitutes not nonaction but the outcome of combined constrained satisfaction. If the control loop implementing an agent's intention constrains the agent's behavior, the behavior is (also) among his or her actions. Lifting the left arm slowly is thus the agent's action, even if not explicitly intended. In habitual skills like typing and driving, surprised interruption and retraction betray the presence of an automatic control loop. Although this loop is sensitive to initial conditions, under normal circumstances it remains under the ultimate control of the prior intention's semantic attractor, which, in the case of errors and emergencies, either has malfunctioned or become interrupted.[65]

In other situations, however, events describable as A' might indeed constitute noise and not be attributable to the system's external structure. As mentioned earlier, if the agent intends only (basic act) A, and event A' could not logically or psychologically have been among the coordinates of the self-organized neural space from which basic act A issued, we can agree with Richard Taylor (1970a): event A' is nonaction, "by reason of ignorance," in Aristotle's words. Oedipus could not have married "the only woman in Thebes with Rh blood" *as an action*. In my earlier discussion, I drew the line between action and nonaction in terms of the presence or absence of semantic constraints on behavior and argued that such constraints point to a self-organized region of mental space, one involving consciousness and meaning. Only behavior unequivocally constrained by that organization constitutes action. Because Oedipus's behavior neither originated in nor was constrained by an intention whose coordinates included that variable, the event does not identify a trajectory $I_s(r)$ through semantic space. It is not action.

Intend to (basic act) A and (generated) A' but Do Not Intend to A″

What about a bombardier's attempts to excuse his behavior on the grounds that in moving his hand (A) he intended only to move the appropriate lever on the plane's control panel (A'), or destroy the city (A'), but not to kill the civilians in it ($A″$)?[66] In an earlier chapter I suggested that in such cases $A″$ might be excluded from the agent's actions and classified only as their consequence. Understanding the way in which dynamical systems' control loop threads through other dynamics and the environment now permits a more careful analysis.

I agreed earlier with Bratman (1987) that by partitioning a dynamically organized space, prior intentions filter the range of subsequently available options. Once agents form the prior intention to A, we saw, they are subsequently barred from not Aing.[67] Prior intentions open up and close off downstream alternatives because the laws of logic and meaning governing those intentions close off logically or physically incompatible alternatives later on. The way in which far-from-equilibrium dynamics work supports this interpretation. We said that each level of organization is identified by its own dynamics, as captured in an overall attractor-separatrix regime. In the case of normal, adult human consciousness, the dynamical landscape embodies semantics; its attractors and trajectories represent its grammar (Elman 1995). Topographically, this means that once the system has been captured by semantic attractor for X, the attractor for non-X is no longer dynamically accessible (a separatrix divides the two).

In the case of the bombardier, the walls of the attractor "destroying the city" prevent access to the attractor "not killing civilians." In the cognitive space of normal persons, the former ("destroying the city") flows instead into the attractor "killing civilians." Accordingly, when the bombardier forms the prior intention to destroy the entire city, not killing civilians automatically drops out as a potential coordinate downstream. In effect, therefore, the bombardier's prior intention commits him to killing civilians: doing so is his act. So the bombardier killed civilians intentionally even if he did not (explicitly) intend to kill civilians.

This is so only under ordinary circumstances. Had the bombardier's commanding officers given him every reason to believe that the city would be emptied of civilians, his mental dynamics would structure a very different semantic organization, including—and excluding—very different alternatives, both concurrently and over time. These dynamics would also constrain different behavioral pathways. Once again we see that to constitute action, behavior not only must originate in alternatives that are coordinates of the agent's cognitive space; it must also flow from and be constrained by those self-organized dynamics—without equivocation.

Explicitly Intending Generated Event A'' (but Not A or A')

Suppose instead that the agent had explicitly intended to turn off the light (A''), which she did by flipping the light switch (A'). She did not, however, explicitly intend to flip the light switch. Was it an act-token (when the agent clearly turned off the light *by* flipping the light switch)? In other words: suppose an agent intends the generated event. Must the upstream means or manner by which that intended downstream behavior is carried out (Goldman's [1970] generating event) also be explicitly intended for the upstream behavior to constitute action?

We concluded earlier that a basic act-token (hand movement A, say) must be constrained by at least a prior intention. (That is the point of Chisholm's [1964] nervous nephew example.) If the intention did not even minimally constrain the basic act, the basic behavior would be the output of an antecedential wayward causal chain. If I turned off the light because I accidentally bumped into the light switch, I did not flip the switch, much less turn off the light, as act-tokens, even if I explicitly intended the latter. I must move my hand as a basic act-token for any generated behavior to qualify as action.

Suppose, however, that conditions are normal. I explicitly intend to turn off the light, but I pay no attention to how I accomplish that goal: were there no switch, I would unscrew the bulb or unplug the lamp. (Abnormal conditions requiring that I unscrew the bulb or unplug the lamp would no doubt bubble up to self-consciousness and demand explicit attention.) When conditions are normal, however, we intuitively want to include the means or manner of performance among my act-tokens. We reason that when agents act with a view toward nonbasic events such as turning off the light, they must be aware, however faintly, that some basic means or other are needed to achieve those ends.

The fact that the intention's control loop threads through the context in which it is formulated once again supports our intuitions. As was the case in the earlier examples, once downstream A' is explicitly intended, other attractors previously forged through interactions with the world can be allowed to select the means or manner of performance A. The agent formulates the general intention to A', then lets both the context and other dynamics fine-tune the details. In the language of dynamical systems theory, the intention to A' carves out the purpose's general organization. Which structure carries out that intention can be left to the combined constraints of other internal dynamics and the current environment. When agents intend A', basic act A that carries out A' is among their actions even if not explicitly intended, as long as A is constrained by the prior intention such that there is no semantic equivocation—even if the particular trajectory was left to the external portion of the intention's control loop. This is possible, once again, only insofar as those other dynamics have been entrained to those of the intention.

Consider typing. While learning to type, each letter must be specifically intended, so to speak. Once typing becomes automatic, however, like flies we just intend to type and let automatic pilot take over. (In fact, once we know how to type, specifically intending each letter interferes with performance.) By "automatic pilot," of course, I mean that the typist's finger movements have recalibrated to the contextual constraints of the word to be typed. Automated skill execution falls short, however, when the process either misfires or encounters a serious obstacle—or is attended to! When noise, in other words, compromises the trajectory. When we make a mistake typing, we must self-consciously delete the error and retype the correct letter. The fact that noise and equivocation will often stop us in our tracks is evidence that the movements of our fingers embody normative semantic constraints: they can be felt as having been correctly or incorrectly executed.

That the semantic level of consciousness constrains even automatic portions of the control loop governing action can also be appreciated from the following example.[68] Suppose that while you are driving, a child darts in front of the car. The emergency situation bubbles up to the level of self-conscious awareness, but often only after the appropriate evasive maneuver has been "automatically" executed (reported in Restak 1983).[69] This example, I believe, attests to the fact that a higher level of neural organization, self-organized as a result of training, automatically constrains the right maneuver. Appropriate or correct maneuvers occur, however, only after much practice, clear evidence that continuous feedback is necessary before such self-organization can take place.

What Did the Agent "Mean" to Do?

In those cases in which the agent explicitly intends nonbasic act-token A' but is indifferent to the particular manner of performance, even though she knows that because she cannot A' directly she must select some A, the answer to the question "What did the agent *mean* to do?" or "What is the motive, purpose, reason why the agent did what she did?" is A', not A. In the case of basic acts, on the other hand, the behavior describable as "what the agent meant to do" will correspond only to that behavior constrained by the most specific intention explicitly formulated. Whether referring to basic and nonbasic actions, what the agent means to do, the reason she did what she did, is A'. The connotations of "mean" fit this interpretation.

If, on the other hand, the question is, "What did the agent do as an act-token?" the answer will depend on whether basic or nonbasic acts are involved. The former, as mentioned earlier, are always insensitive to nested information about the communications channel, a characteristic that marks off basic actions from nonaction. We do not activate muscles x, y, and z as act-tokens. What I meant to do was turn off the light, A''. But the manner of performance by which I accomplish that end can also be attributed to me as an act-token if it corresponds to routine, unexceptional means automatically executed by the external structure of the intention's control loop—if, that is, the behavior was within and constrained by the complex attractor that describes "turn off light." I flipped the switch (A') intentionally even though I did not explicitly intend to do so.

Does "I Intend to A" Imply "I Believe I Will A"?

Some mental states with semantic attractors can self-consciously conceive and anticipate the future and constrain behavior accordingly. (See R. Rosen 1985 on whether all self-organized systems, not just some biological ones, are "anticipatory.") At times, however, other dynamics (such as those governing emotions) can override those constraints. Since self-organized systems' basins of attraction are inextricably intertwined, both *akrasia* and autonomy may very well turn out to reflect the degree to which an agent's various dynamical organizations are integrated and the way they are integrated. *Akrasia* indicates that the agent's intentional apparatus lacks such integrity. (It is curious how the ambiguity of "integrity" spans both meanings.) We should have expected this: the global relations among a dynamical system's components give its identity. We also saw that the stringency of a system's internal coupling affects both its stability and resilience. Taking a cue from Hinton (1992), I suspect that many of the philosophical difficulties associated with the concept of *akrasia* (Mele, 1995) are attributable to the mistaken assumption that the brain-mind system has far fewer dimensions and levels of organization than it does, and the corresponding—and equally erroneous—assumption that they are neatly sealed off from each other.[70]

The controversy about whether "I intend to A" implies "I will A" can be traced to just such a simplification. Some theorists (Fishbein and Ajzen

1975) have claimed that "I intend to A" implies "I believe I will A." Others such as Mele (1992) have formulated an objection to this claim that is similar to the wayward causal chain example. Suppose I have never sunk a sixty-foot putt before. It seems odd to say that just because I intend to, I will. Since (given my track record) I believe I won't succeed, can I "intend to sink the putt," or do I only "intend to try" (Mele 1992) or "hope to" (Audi 1995)? Mele suggests that the relationship between "I believe I will A" and "I intend to A" should be thought of as a default condition: if I intend to A, I will A, all things being equal.

A dynamical account of action provides a more satisfactory solution. When I form a prior intention to A, my current, overall dynamics, including other cognitive, physiological, mechanical, conative, and similar attractors, reorganize in such a way as to stack the conditional probability of behavior A differently. The more dramatic the intention, the more radical the change in the landscape. Then by entraining motor control, the dynamics of a proximate intention sculpt an attractor that not only exhibits cognitive and evaluative traits; it now has "executive" or "pushing" ability as well. As a newly hewn valley straight ahead in my motor systems' conditional probability landscape, a proximate intention to A "pushes" by dramatically increasing the likelihood that I will A, given present circumstances. To that extent, Mele is correct.

However, a multidimensional landscape includes many other self-organized phase spaces with their own dynamics that, like waves that cancel each other, can prevent the attractor to A from successfully pulling behavior into its basin. Because the final output of coarsely coded networks blends all the inputs, noise from other attractors and separatrices, as well as from the environment, can interfere with the cascading intentional flow. If I am aware of those factors that can potentially interfere with my putt and, moreover, believe that they not only could (as interfering noise), but in all likelihood will, prevent my intention from successful execution, those beliefs will additionally recontour my other dynamics. The result might even wreak havoc on my self-confidence! If it does, I will describe my intended behavior only as "I will try." In other situations in which, according to my (correct or incorrect) estimate, the likelihood of equivocation is low or nil, I will describe my behavior as "I intend to A" or "I will A." Self-fulfilling prophecies can be understood in this way, as the effect of combined constraint satisfaction operating among the various dynamical regimes. If I believe strongly enough that I will fail (or succeed), those dynamics might pull others into that attractor. Commonsense folk psychology has been more sensitive to connections and interferences among different aspects of a person's personality than the philosophy of action.

Social Skills

Let us return to the prior intention, "do something to help that child." Suppose my first opportunity to do so comes as I am about to catch a plane, but it conflicts with the reason I am traveling, to satisfy another intention, "visit my sick friend soon." Thinking of such social skills as complex, self-organized psychological dynamics constructed through experience and habituation the way Hannah and Gabriel's motor skills were assembled offers several advantages. Conceptualizing the way we navigate the shoals of daily life as a function of the combined constraints of dynamical self-organization allows us to understand how, instead of missing the flight, I ask for (and jot down!) the phone number of the woman I just met in the airport lounge who suggested a feasible way to help the child. I tell her that I'll get back to her when I return. We judge people on their ability to prioritize behavior in this fashion so as to satisfice (Simon 1957) the number and centrality of the prior intentions executed. We judge people, that is, on how (and how well) integrated their various dynamical subsystems are.

Examples

Suppose I intend to get milk on the way home. There are many ways of doing so: I could stop at either this convenience store or that supermarket. I could borrow a quart from my neighbor. Both the fly example and the research on Hannah and Gabriel suggest that all I need to do is formulate the overarching intention: get milk. I can then let the rest of my internal and external structure (the world in which I am embedded and to which my internal dynamics have recalibrated) fine-tune the details. The contextual embeddedness that characterizes dynamical systems (but not Cartesian selves) dissolves any potential frame problem. If I live in Washington, D.C., my interactions with that environment will have recalibrated my dynamics in particular ways. As a result, my external structure or boundary conditions will automatically exclude "getting the milk from the dairy in Wisconsin" as an option. Not so for the Martian who just dropped into the city. Lack of experience with the ways of this planet means that there are no contextual dependencies between the alien's internal dynamics and that environment. As a result, he must consider and evaluate every possible alternative. He might never get around to walking out the door, much less carrying an umbrella!

As the airport example was meant to illustrate, normal, mature adults process many prior intentions simultaneously. If, as embodied in another of my socially constructed attractors (an attractor for values, ethics, morals—a VEM attractor; see Artigiani 1995, 1998), I am also, say, an honest person, that aspect of my character will contribute its own context-sensitive constraints to the indefinite number of physically possible alternatives that could execute the intention, "get milk." As a result, those other dynamics will additionally constrain my behavior: stealing the milk from my neighbor, for example, will not even be in the picture. Because in a multidimensional landscape an indefinite number of attractors intertwine, personality and character are complex landscapes that must be taken whole cloth.

While driving home I decide to signal a left turn. Given the complex environment of driving, I can carry out that intention in any one of several different ways (use the signal lever or extend arm). The complete story, of course, is much more elaborate. The higher-order intention that itself governs the lower-order intention to signal a left turn is, "go home." But I could have walked, driven, or taken the bus home. Because part of my control loop runs through time and space, the fact that it was late at night and I am aware of a mugging in the neighborhood last week means that walking never even occurred to me. "It wasn't even an option," we say. In information-theoretic language, walking home wasn't even in the set of possible alternatives of my contrast set. In dynamical language, walking home wasn't even among the coordinates of my mental state at the time.

In abstraction from everything else, however, walking home would have been one more alternative in an indefinitely large space of logical and physical possibilities including "flying home," "crawling home," and the like. The number of alternatives would have been astronomical, requiring, first, a decision procedure for weighting options as significant or insignificant, and then another for picking one from the first set. McClamrock's (1995) point, which agrees with the empirical evidence from dynamical systems, is that because it is not abstracted from everything else but is instead embedded in the environment, my cognitive system's external structure, together with its initial conditions, can automatically exclude walking home from my space of possibilities. Given the intentional constraints in place and in combination with other dynamics and the environment (as incorporated into my external structure), the alternatives under consideration automatically narrow. Given that I know buses don't run that late at night, and that I need milk (which taking a bus will prevent me from getting), the "decision" becomes a no-brainer. Even if I did not specifically intend to drive home, I drive home intentionally.

I am driving home. I intend to get milk. But I am also a conscientious driver. All three constraints combine automatically to narrow my options such that I signal a left turn now (instead of a block earlier, which would have meant driving the wrong way on a one-way street to reach the convenience store). The car windows are up. Because I know it is cold I never even think of extending my arm out the window to signal the left turn. I flip the turn signal instead. If among my other mental dynamics there is a self-organized region that embodies "frugality," I might drive a few blocks further to a discount store instead of the 7-Eleven, unless the gas gauge reads empty ... and so on. But to repeat, the environment does not function as a trigger the way behaviorism would have it. The agent's own dynamics, albeit continually reset and recalibrated through contextual constraints established as a result of interactions with that environment, partition the space of alternatives and thereby structure and automatically cull the agent's options.

The agent's intentional organization need only "determine the plan of action," as Bratman (1987) would say. This level of organization is the set of semantic constraints whose control loop, once again, threads partly through other dynamics and attractors, as well as through the agent's environment and past. The second-order contextual constraints of that prior intention can therefore allow the rich redundancy of both the environment and experience effectively to reparse the intention's search space as it projects into behavior. Because the environment and other contextual considerations have been internalized as a result of positive feedback loops, my external structure will automatically select from the various alternatives and eliminate the bus as a meaningful option. "I brought my car to work this morning, so if I take the bus I won't have a car at home and buses don't run early enough for me to get back tomorrow morning at 6:00 A.M. ...." and so on.

This way of looking at things does not preclude the possibility of error. As McClamrock (1995) notes, running the control loop through the environment is a fast and efficient but sloppy strategy. But then, nature selects for resilience, not meticulousness. If taking my car to work is something I seldom do, when the bus I usually ride pulls up I might automatically jump on, only to curse myself when it passes by the repair shop at which I service the car (which reminds me that it is badly in need of a tune-up— another contextual cue that reparses my frame of mind), which in turn reminds me, alas, that I brought the car to work, and by jumping on the bus have left it there ... and so on.

Summary

Action theory must be able to explain complex, everyday situations like these. Causal theorists of the Newtonian stripe could not explain how intentions provide actions with ongoing structure and guidance. Even experimental behaviorists knew that dogs must be conditioned to salivate at the sound of the bell. But because they subscribed to a Newtonian model of cause and a Humean one of explanation, behaviorists had no way of threading the agent's control loop through the agent's internal dynamics as well as through the environment.

Most critics of the thesis that minds are machines have identified the problem of meaning as the central impediment to that research program. A second standard objection to cognitive science was that thinking of minds as computers would never capture our contextual embeddedness (Dreyfus 1972). A third was that cognitive science cannot explain the way this background is incorporated in our conscious behavior (Searle 1992). Traditional, serial processing couldn't adequately handle any of these issues, it is true, because it had the wrong dynamics, as did the Newtonian model of cause.

Persistent mutualist interactions that take us far from equilibrium and restructure our internal dynamics are required to do the trick. Because it is concerned with open complex systems that interact with their environment under far-from-equilibrium conditions, a dynamical systems interpretation of mental processes and actions can easily account for the relationship between generating (basic) actions and generated (nonbasic) events. Unlike earlier models of action, and of science, it does so by incorporating their contextual and historical embeddedness—by taking time and context seriously. Dynamical systems theory, I have claimed, makes the problem of action tractable by rethinking both the relationships between parts and wholes and the interlevel causality that these exhibit. Understanding how second-order contextual constraints can recalibrate a system's internal dynamics explains what intentions are and how they are established. Thinking of prior intentions as self-organized dynamics within conscious semantic space, of proximate intentions as control knobs governing that space, and of act-types as attractors through that space allows us to conceptualize act-tokens as individual behavioral trajectories within that semantic space. These trajectories originate in intentional dynamics that both activate and then channel and regulate motor processes top-down such that the latter preserve and execute the invariant relations that embody the intention's meaningful content.

It is nonsense to claim that we end at the contours of our body, or that our individual concepts and intentions exist independently of our experience and surroundings. We have evolved the ability to construct antennae that both extend us into the world and internalize portions of that world. And we carry our history on our backs. In light of our own past and in response to interactions with the world, we continuously restructure our internal dynamics. This embeddedness in time and space allows us to act quickly and efficiently—and intelligently and meaningfully—without requiring that higher levels of self-consciousness be involved at all times in the details that execute conscious, meaningful orders.

Common, everyday examples like the one presented earlier—getting milk on the way home—illustrate the advantages of thinking of intentions and actions as complex systems and trajectories through multidimensional dynamical probability landscapes. The model can explain why disequilibrium is required to dislodge people from an established attractor onto a different one. The framework also emphasizes the coexistence and intertwining (i.e., entraining) of the many dynamics involved and how each imposes its own context-sensitive constraints on others. "Did you deliberately take the bus instead of the car?" "No, not really; I was just tired and not thinking." Spelling out everything packed into "not really" involves telling the whole story, as I have just done.

The need to "tell the whole story" to understand what someone did points to a different model of explanation for action. Part III offers preliminary pointers in that direction.

Part III

Explaining Human Action: Why Dynamics Tell Us That Stories Are Necessary

Chapter 14

Narrative Explanation and the Dynamics of Action

Recapitulation

The ability to predict and control nature that flourished during the sixteenth and seventeenth centuries promised to bring all natural phenomena, including human actions, under its power. We saw in chapters 1 and 2 the relentless influence of Newton's understanding of cause on action theory even in this century. We also saw (in chapters 3 through 5) how Hume's reformulation of cause and, indirectly, of explanation also shaped contemporary ideas on action. Austin's (1961) and Ryle's (1949) logical behaviorism and Skinner's (1953) experimental behaviorism might be considered the academy's last attempt to carry out a Humean agenda.

In part II I implied that, with the discovery of the crucial role that time and context play in the self-organization and behavior of complex adaptive structures (particularly during phase changes), the anomalies plaguing that received logic of explanation have become insurmountable, and its inadequacy as a general model of explanation apparent. Just as turbulent flow in hydraulics and most of biology proved to be recalcitrant to the reductionism that prevailed in modern science, so too have folk psychology and human action. People, their problems, and their behavior have resisted both being shoehorned into a covering-law format and being explained in terms of exogenous forces' impact on primary matter.

However, the philosophical and scientific framework in place at any given period in history influences not only the way even nonscholars approach and understand the problems and situations they confront in their everyday lives. The discomfort of the jurors mentioned at the beginning of the book suggests that even they believe, on the one hand, that they should be able to provide a covering-law kind of explanation but, on the other, find themselves unable to do so. And until recently, theoretical alternatives to the covering-law model seemed to require dismissing any ontological component from explanation. This book's final claim is that only by our referring the explanation of dynamical processes back to their ontology will human beings and their actions become understandable. But that will also require enlarging modern philosophy's views of what counts as a rational explanation. This chapter is devoted to that effort.

Explanation as Unfolding

According to the received model, as we saw, an event is considered fully explained only when its occurrence can be inferred (either deductively or inductively) from a covering law together with initial condition statements. To serve as an ideal *explanans*, the law should be exceptionless or "strict" (see Davidson 1980, 1995). Deduction simply "unpacks" what is already there in the premises, albeit hidden from view. Even in a probabilistic universe, it was thought, increasing the accuracy with which initial conditions are described, together with including fewer ceteris paribus clauses in the premises, would yield a corresponding increase in the argument's predictive accuracy and explanatory adequacy. Even the etymology of "explanation" denotes the spreading out of something convoluted onto a planar surface. "Explication," too, carries the sense of a conceptual unfolding of what is complicated, involuted such that its (eternally true) nature has become hidden. Both terms suggest that the spreading out and unfolding can lay bare and reveal all at once an *explanandum* that is always, already there. Requiring that all phenomena must be ultimately subsumable under a covering law betrays an ontological bias in favor of a deterministic, or at the very least, linear universe devoid of novelty and creativity.

Modern philosophy and science allowed no discontinuities or surprises because a deterministic universe excludes all forms of randomness and nonlinearity. Also, because philosophy's understanding of causal relations and explanation required that the *explanandum* be identified with the generalizable and repeatable, the object or phenomenon in situ to be explained first had to be lifted from its concretely individuated particularity so as to be so always and everywhere. Both of these requirements, in turn, presupposed a static or, at the very least, nonevolving (only developing) *explanandum* that a covering law could capture in all its essential features, always. Indeed, only this assumption makes predictability, the whole point of the covering-law approach, possible at all. As Hempel (1965) once noted, explanation was thought to be related to proof.

"The primacy of seeing is the basis of the deductive-nomological form of explanation" (Gadamer 1985, 420). The philosopher or scientist was supposed to reach understanding by a sort of "surveying" of the other from afar (324). Surveyors stand apart from that which they survey, which stands still or changes minimally so that the surveyors can lay it all out. The object surveyed is not altered by the surveying itself. Analogously, explanation was supposed to be a transparent process that does not interfere with whatever is being explained. Given that what is surveyed is eternal and essentially unchanging, the survey's result should yield answers that are always and everywhere the same. Since no point of view or time is privileged (T. Nagel 1989), contextual features were dismissed as secondary and beyond the scope of scientific explanation. In a theme repeated since the time of Parmenides, the contextual and temporal were considered inexplicable because not fully real. By excluding contingencies and idiosyncracies, science left out the unique and the individual as well.

The aim of modern science, therefore, was

> to so objectify experience that it no longer contains any historical element. The scientific experiment does this by its methodological procedure[s].... [which guarantee], through the objectivity of [their] approach, that these basic experiences can be repeated by anyone.... Hence no place can be left in science or philosophy for the individuating effect of experience. Modern science and philosophy thus [continue] in their methodology what they have always striven after. Experience is valid only if it is confirmed; hence its dignity depends on its fundamental repeatability. But this means that experience, by its very nature, abolishes its history. (Gadamer 1985, 311)

Hempel and Oppenheim's classic article (1948) and Hempel's book (1965) on explanation as inference were explicitly meant to apply to action. In chapters 4 and 5 I showed how. Covering-law explanations were even supposed to apply to reasoning about morals, as Kantian ethics illustrates. Perhaps reflexes such as the patella jerk or reactions like blinks approximate this kind of phenomenon, but the individual trajectories of hurricanes and Bénard cells emphatically do not. Nor does most of biology. Science and philosophy have had no room for individuals in all their novelty and particularity, and no room, as a result, for understanding or explaining individual human act-tokens as uniqe trajectories.

As we saw, explanation was possible at all in the modern, scientific sense only because things were assumed to be in their essential natures atemporal, or, in the case of the phenomena of near-equilibrium thermodynamics, Markovian. Markovian processes are systems whose future behavior is independent of their history; only the future, not the past, is packed into the present. Without the embeddedness in context and history that feedback accomplishes in open systems, there is an arrow of time but no history in the closed structures of classical, near-equilibrium thermodynamics. If mature organisms' distinctive character and behavior embody the sedimentation of the many vicissitudes they have experienced throughout their lives, personality traits and human actions are in consequence truly unfathomable according to the accepted conceptual framework—mere "anthropological considerations," Kant would have insisted.

Although it is clear that causes and effects cannot always be the same in *all* respects, traditional views of causality also assumed that similar causes, under similar conditions, always produce similar results. We have since learned that this is true only for closed, linear systems of independent objects. A specific prediction of the point-by-point trajectory of someone's behavior or its past occurrence is no more deducible from a covering law together with a description of the initial conditions than is the behavior of any complex system (in the sense of "complexity" to which I have been referring). Since contextual dependencies characterize such adaptive systems, two trajectories that issue from origins differing only infinitesimally can diverge dramatically, even when the same (strange) attractor governs them. When explaining such dynamical phenomena, including human action, philosophical theories of explanation should have remembered that the nonlinear differential equations that describe even some chemical systems cannot be analytically solved; they can only be simulated.

As we saw in an earlier chapter, tracking the behavior of dynamical systems over time requires that both their initial conditions and the bifurcations they undergo be infinitely specifiable. Moreover, if the phenomena are stochastic, the endogenous perturbations and fluctuations that play a critical role at bifurcation thresholds are unpredictable even in principle, as is the precise path selected at the phase change. In effect, that is, each run of any complex system is unique. We have long suspected that all of this is true of human beings but, until the elaboration of far-from-equilibrium thermodynamics, it merely left the human sciences in the inferior half of the two cultures. Now complex dynamical systems theory tells us that this is true of all open systems far from equilibrium governed by strange attractors, precisely because of the way the correlations and coupling both among their components and with their environment embed them in time and space. Nonlinear, essentially historical phenomena cannot be explained deductive-nomologically because they are not already there waiting to be rolled out and thereby explained. They are uniquely individuated trajectories embodying irreversible discontinuities that emerge over time.

Behaviorism, as we saw, was a philosophy very much under the influence of modern science. As such, it focused on commonalities across individuals, assuming that the particular subject's uniquely individuated dynamics could be safely ignored. However, we now know that constructing a covering law from commonalities in a series of causal or behavioral events across individuals can be misleading, as the infants described by Thelen and Smith (1994) illustrate. Both infants acquired the skill of reaching successfully within a few weeks of each other. This common result appears to suggest, as Piaget (1975) concluded, that there is a preprogrammed pattern that simply unfolds. Complex dynamical theory, on the other hand, teaches that if you look only at the outside, as behaviorism did, differences both in the way information is generated and in the constrained pathways along which it flows will be overlooked. Focusing on the differences in the two children's starting points and the way these differences interact with the environment, on the other hand, can reveal a dynamical process. Even when the behavioral output (the trajectory's sink) is the same, the pathways taken to get there may be very different.

As a consequence of the modern paradigm, there was no way of explaining how some behaviors can be voluntary and intentional because they flow from an agent's meaning-bearing states, whereas other, empirically indistinguishable behaviors are not. Modern philosophy and science, as we have seen, were unable to account for, say, the difference between an involuntary smile and one commanded, which is now known to be a difference in trajectory (Damasio 1994). Without a way of conceptualizing action as a constrained trajectory across levels of organization, the possibility of wayward causal chains, as we saw, also loomed ever present.

And yet how successful the old modern worldview was! Pretending that everything is a closed, linear system gives the illusion that one can, without penalty, abstract from time and context, starting with the interference of friction. And doing so did indeed make many difficult problems tractable and yielded spectacular results. Who in the fifteenth century would have thought that planetary orbits could be so accurately predicted? But this tidy picture was doomed from the start, because the scientific and philosophical problems posed by the nature and behavior of open systems cannot be ignored. Very few people anticipated the mischief—and benefits—that the nonlinearity of positive feedback unleashes on the modern paradigm.

Because deduction has also failed as a generalized model that can explain complex systems' evolutionary sequence, a different logic of explanation appropriate to action is necessary. I propose that from now on the covering-law model of explanation (including its probabilistic incarnation) should be considered the limit of explanation, adequate for those phenomena that can be idealized as atemporal and acontextual. For isolated, linear systems, the covering-law model often works fine. For those phenomena, the tighter the inference, the better the explanation and the more accurate the prediction. For open, complex dynamical phenomena in which context-dependent constraints (both bottom-up and top-down) create interlevel interactions—that is, for phenomena which that "strange form of causality" progressively individuates and marks as essentially historical and contextual—the deductive model simply won't do.

Understanding human action must begin from the assumption that people are dynamical entities whose behavior reflects their complexity.

One mark of such complexity is that variations in behavior are often not noise at all: irregularities can signal the presence of a strange attractor. When behavior is constrained by a such an attractor, it is the variations that are interesting, for there, lurking behind what at first glance appears to be noise, complex dynamic attractors are in play. The more general and abstract the intention, the more complex the behavior allowed. One significant advantage of a complex dynamical systems perspective, therefore, is that it can account for differences and irregularities in behavior, which covering laws (and a fortiori behaviorism) could not.

So what can we tell our hapless juror? When it comes to the complex dynamics of human action, can anything even approximate the received understanding of explanation as deductive (or even as statistically inductive)? In part II I argued that behavior is meaningful and constitutes action only if it is dependent on the mental, which symbolically organizes and constrains it in such a way that it unequivocally actualizes the intention from which it issued. These interlevel relationships require a logic of explanation appropriate to their strange-loop nature. As Aristotle never failed to remind us, explanations must be appropriate to their subject matter.

Explaining Self-Organizing Systems through Hermeneutics

Within Stable States
Random fluctuations and perturbations are critical to complex dynamical systems only at instability thresholds far from equilibrium. During dynamically stable periods between bifurcation points, even complex systems follow pathways their attractors carve out. Between phase changes, therefore, one can forecast that a complex system will select an alternative from the range described by its attractor's thickness and shape. Far from being a substantive prediction, however, this statement amounts to little more than a tautology. Because complex systems are sensitive to initial conditions, irregularities and fluctuations in behavior will be so significant that any specific prediction of the next move will be practically useless. And the more complex the system, the less the prediction will tell you, even between phase changes. Since the individual trajectories of systems can diverge dramatically even while constrained by a strange attractor (just look again at figure 10.3), explaining why a complex system took the particular path it did will therefore always require interpretation.

When nonlinear interactions result in interlevel relationships like those described in previous chapters, the meaning of individual events can be fully understood only in context: in terms of the higher-level constraints (the dynamics) that govern them. I propose that explaining complex systems, including human beings and their actions, must therefore proceed hermeneutically, not deductively. In textual interpretation "the anticipation of meaning in which the whole is envisaged becomes explicit understanding in that the parts, that are determined by the whole, themselves also determine this whole" (Gadamer 1985, 259). Interpreters must move back and forth: the whole text guides the understanding of individual passages; yet the whole can be understood only by understanding the individual passages. This interlevel recursiveness, characteristic of hermeneutics, is thus "a continuous dialectical tacking between the most local of local detail and the most global of global structure in such a way as to bring both into view simultaneously" (Geertz 1979, 239). The interlevel tacking of the hermeneutic "circle" reproduces the self-organization of complex dynamical processes. By showing the dynamics of complex adaptive systems, hermeneutical narratives are uniquely suited as the logic of explanation of these strange-loop phenomena.

The logic of explanation of hermeneutics is therefore appropriate for *explananda* whose very nature is a product of that strange circle of whole and part. In contrast to covering laws and algorithms and deductions therefrom, that is, interpretation or hermeneutics reproduces the very logic of nature's open, adaptive dynamics. Like intentional actions, interpretations are characterized by strange-loop, interlevel relations and are, in consequence, essentially contextual and historical. Interpretations therefore explain by showing those nonlinear, interlevel processes at work. Reversing Kant's epistemological turn, which privileged epistemology over ontology, Prigogine's followers occasionally make the claim that science operates the way nature does, with parts constituting wholes that in turn provide the contextual framework for those components. My explicit claim here is only that human actions and. their explanations do.[71]

The threat of relativism lurking in the hermeneutic circle has often encouraged philosophers to reject it. By drawing the explainer and the explanation into its strange loop, hermeneutics appears to forestall the possibility of any claim to truth and certainty. If we live in a dynamical universe, the novelty and creativity such complex systems display do indeed signal the end of eternal, unchanging, and universal certainty. Unlike modern science, however, dynamical systems theory provides an understanding of both the construction and integrity of wholes that does not dissolve their unity at that level. According to Gadamer (1985), the resolution to the circularity of hermeneutics is found in Heidegger's recognition that "the circle of the whole and the part is not dissolved in perfect understanding but on the contrary, is most fully realized" (261).

Reconstructing the Origin We make sense of persons and their actions through just such an interpretive dialectic between wholes and parts. Consider the hermeneutical flavor that permeates the following approach, adapted from Rueger and Sharp (1996). From descriptions of the dynamics of a particular instance of behavior it might be possible to reconstruct the agent's character or personality and therefore the intention that constrained the behavior. We can then examine other examples of that person's behavior to see whether the character that these additional examples suggest corresponds to the personality we inferred earlier. If the test is positive, we reasonably conclude that the first behavior was "in character." As a result, we judge it to have been the agent's action and hold him or her responsible.

From empirically available information of a behavioral output $I(r)$, and taking care to note any interference from noise or equivocation, the explainer attempts to reconstruct $I(s)$, the cognitive source from which the behavior issued. The explainer attempts, in other words, to determine the mental dynamics from which a given instance of behavior flowed and the particular intentional attractor that constrained it. The purpose of examining several examples of behavior is to fashion an interpretation of the unknown dynamics (the intention) that constrained the particular behavior in question. The explainer then checks his or her interpretation of the agent's character by examining whether subsequent behaviors fit that initial (always tentative) interpretation.

"How does Rueger and Sharp's procedure differ from any behaviorist's?" someone might object. The answer goes as follows: (1) Between phase changes a complex system's behavior is governed by both the combined constraints of its own internal dynamics and the initial and ongoing conditions in which it finds itself. As a result, in contrast to the covering-law model, the direction of explanatory primacy in interpretation is not the usual downward, reductive direction (Wimsatt 1976). It moves up and down levels, from whole to parts, from inside to outside, and vice versa. This tacking reproduces the interlevel ontological processes that created the *explanandum*. (2) In contrast to behaviorist analyses that attempt to bypass the subject's actual mental state, moreover, the hermeneut-explainer tries to reconstruct the particular internal dynamics from which the actual behavior issued, not bypass those dynamics. (3) Wright (1976) claimed that only the impact of the mental event must be taken into account; this impact, however, could not be determined through commonalities across stimuli-response patterns of behavior over time. Because complex attractors are often implicated in human actions, differences in behavior are sometimes more informative than commonalities. Variations across examples of behavior can reveal a particular intention's complexity in a way that similarities cannot. The back-and-forth tacking of hermeneutics can reveal the convoluted structure of those variations in a way that the covering-law model cannot. (4) By respecting the vectorial nature of the trajectory it is reconstructing, an interpretive narrative does not try to reduce the purposiveness of action to nonpurposive elements. The whole point of hermeneutical interpretation of action is to show how meaningful intentions emerge and then purposively constrain the behavior that flows from them. By recognizing that they are dealing with a unique trajectory, interpretive narratives also take for granted that their account need not apply to other behaviors, even those that appear similar.

It is important, nevertheless, to emphasize that interpretation can discover only whether a particular instance of behavior was "in character." That sometimes—perhaps often—it is possible to judge someone's behavior accurately as being "in character," however, should not lull us into believing that we have achieved certainty in judging a particular instance of behavior. That is, when we are dealing with complex adaptive systems, surprises are unavoidable. Because of their sensitivity to initial conditions—due, in turn, to their contextual and temporal embeddedness—complex adaptive systems are characterized by unusual twists and novel turns. We saw the havoc that equivocation and noise can wreak in interrupting and compromising an intended trajectory. $I(r)$ can semantically satisfy $I(s)$ without being identical to $I_s(r)$. And yet circumstantial evidence often misleads us into supposing that it is. Since we will never be able to specify any dynamical system's initial conditions to the requisite (infinite) degree, a fortiori we will never be able to capture all the details and circumstances of anyone's life and background. Given this limitation, we must always keep in mind that reconstructing specific instances of behavior will always be, at best, an interpretation and not a deduction—a much more fallible type of explanation than we had previously hoped was available. Interpretations of human action are always tentative (Metzger 1995).

Absolute certainty about either what the agent just did, or what he or she will do—specifically—a year from now, is therefore impossible. As the title of Prigogine's latest book (1996) announces, the dynamics of complex systems signal the end of certainty. The exact trajectory of any stochastic entity captured by a complex attractor, even between phase changes, is impossible either to predict or retrodict precisely, even in principle. It cannot be predicted with exactitude in part because of the multiple realizability that self-organized systems support and the mischief that initial conditions wreak, but also because open dynamical systems' control loop runs partly through the environment, as we saw in the last chapter. The dramatic fluctuations in behavior that strange attractors allow make any hope of predicting a dynamical system's specific future trajectory a futile wish. Knowing someone is ambitious will not tell you what specific path his or her behavior will take.

Since it is equally impossible to retrodict with absolute precision, what would a hermeneutic explanation of chapter 5's maverick psychotherapist look like? Explaining the therapist's behavior as an act-token will require doing what I did when I presented the proposed counterexample: it will be necessary to identify and describe the many details and connections that illustrate how the unusual behavior flowed from and was constrained by the psychiatrist's intuition that the moment represented a unique intersection of events and circumstances. The psychiatrist must describe in rich and vivid detail her interpretation of the patient's situation at that moment, how it had reached that crisis, the history of the relations between therapist and patient, the unique events that precipitated the crisis, and so forth. Providing a robust and detailed historical narrative of all the background and context surrounding the unique moment can suggest the mental dynamics from which the psychotherapist's unorthodox behavior flowed. Describing such concrete details of the entire historical, contextually grounded situation allows the explainer to situate the unorthodox intervention in context (both internal and external) such that the behavior reveals itself as an act-token, that is, as behavior constrained by meaning and purpose.

Hermeneutical explanations must begin, that is, by describing the mental dynamics from which the action flowed into behavior. Recall the earlier discussion on contrastive stress: "It is the presence or absence of an alternative in the contrast set taken into account by the agent that draws the line between his unintentional actions and his non-actions" (Dascal and Gruengard 1981, 110). This claim has the following implications for the way actions must be explained: a correct explanation of why X Aed must first of all reconstruct the set of choices available to the agent. They must be the agent's choice points.[72] Explaining actions therefore requires, first and foremost, that the explainer correctly reconstruct the agent's contrast space, the self-organized mental state of the agent's prior intention from which the behavior issued. The better the explainer knows the agent, the circumstances surrounding the behavior, and how the two interacted, the more smoothly this reconstruction will proceed. If the pertinent act-type is not even included among the dynamical attractors of the agent's cognitive state, the behavior will not be an act-token of that type. If a narrative, interpretive explanation fails to identify correctly those alternatives of the agent's contrast space on which the behavior was dependent, the explanation offered will describe a plausible trajectory that terminates in the empirically observed behavior, but one that began at an origin other than the agent's. That alleged explanation will not therefore explain the agent's actual behavior at all.

As the Willy Sutton case also illustrated, we depend pragmatically on the contrastive stress of oral explanations to do just that. For example: assume the explainer is also the agent. The explainer verbally implies that he or she chose A rather than $B, C, \ldots N$ (the remaining options in the contrast set). By using contrastive stress, the explainer informs the listener that, rather than evaluate every possible alternative, he or she considered a more restricted set of alternatives. Intonation, moreover, supplies the context-sensitive cues (the explanatory context) that inform the listener of the coordinates in that contrast space: the list of alternatives in the agent's cognitively partitioned contrast space. Intonation also informs the listener of the remaining logically or physically possible alternatives that are outside that space and that the agent never even considered. Finally, contrastive stress also tells the listener which particular option the agent in fact selected from the choices available within the contrast set. Contrastive stress thus assists in the pragmatics of explanation by providing context-sensitive cues that allow the listener to reconstruct the goings-on at the intentional source correctly.

Even though agents are usually in a privileged position to determine the alternatives present in their conscious contrast space and the degree of their awareness of each, extensive reflection and probing may be necessary before they can articulate all the relevant content of that awareness. In the end, therefore, as we saw in our objections both to behaviorism in chapter 4 and to attempted reductions of teleology in chapter 5, the subject's own overall mental state (whose coordinates and dynamics identify the contrast space) parses potential behavioral alternatives from others not even contemplated.

Reconstructing the Behavior's Trajectory   I have claimed that a given instance of behavior constitutes an act-token (as opposed to a nonact) if and only if the information available at the behavioral end was *constrained by* (not merely contingently connected to) the intention's dynamical attractor. Even after the contrast space of alternatives that the agent had in mind has been established, however, the explanatory narrative must still historically reconstruct the behavior's actual trajectory and show that the intentional source constrained it unequivocally. For it to do so, the explainer must describe at each choice point why the agent took this fork rather than that one: what were the available options, and which was chosen.

Explaining why the agent took this path rather than that after forming the prior intention will require reconstructing the agent's background, circumstances, particular frame of mind, and reasoning, whether self-conscious or not. Once the explainer establishes, for example, that Willy Sutton's contrast space spanned the alternatives "rob banks"—rather than, say, people, movie theaters, or supermarkets—it will be necessary to explain why *banks* were the proximate attractor: "because that's where the money is." Reconstructing the mental attractor that constrained Sutton's behavior requires accounting for the particular behavioral trajectory by situating it in its full historical, social, physical, and psychological context and showing how interaction with that context changed that particular alternative's prior probability.

In the previous chapter I claimed that the organism's external structure "runs part of the agent's control loop [both] through the physical and social environment" (McClamrock 1995) as well as the agent's other dynamical structures. The tacking required to describe all these interconnections is most obvious at this point: the explainer must account for each fork selected in terms of both the constraints established by the dynamics of the origin and the way those interacted with the lay of the land: "I decided to greet her but since she was so far away I could only wave." This is the only way of taking seriously the claim that agents are embedded in time and space (both physical and social). Determining whether specific aspects of the behavior were constrained by an intention but were being carried out by the external portions of its control loop or, to the contrary, whether the details of the behavior are more accurately attributed to noise, can be very difficult, as we saw from the examples presented in the previous chapter: "Did you really mean to do that or did you just get lucky?" The explainer must also account for the possibility of noise and equivocation and, if necessary, describe why these were not a factor.

We saw earlier that the degree of specificity of the prior and proximate intentions on which the behavior depends sets the stringency of the intention's constraints. When the agent intends only "to something," almost any behavior can satisfy that intention. Intentions that vague and unspecific support a wide range of behavior; in dynamical terms, they describe a more complex attractor than, for example, the attractor for the more specific intention to A. The more vague and general an intention, the fewer the act-types that can logically "err" in carrying out that intention.

When the agent intends only "to something," it will therefore be difficult to tell whether the behavior was constrained by the external portion of the intention's complex control loop or was entirely attributable to external forces. In some cases noise could make the behavior equivocal with respect to the intention; to that extent the behavior's status as action would be compromised. But given that vague intentions "to something" must nevertheless be concretely and particularly carried out, the person will likely be held accountable if the intention is realized in an illegal or unethical manner. Because the control loop of any self-organized system threads through other dynamics, when the intention's contextual constraints are so fuzzy and "thick" that almost any behavior can implement the intention, we often attribute the behavior to the agent as action and hold him or her responsible if that behavior is unacceptable. Camus's "stranger" was taught just that lesson.

On the other hand, if an agent intends specifically to *A*, the attractor governing that behavior will be much less complex (its path will be more narrowly circumscribed and will fluctuate less). Any departure or deviation from that more precisely delineated path will require an explanation. For example, suppose at 1:50 P.M. I explicitly and specifically intend to walk the dog at 2:00 P.M., but then I don't. Either something must have physically prevented me, or I changed my mind, or I failed to follow through, or some similar explanation. Whatever it was must be mentioned in the explanation. As suggested earlier, *akrasia* can be conceptualized as the result of equivocation arising from other dynamics within the agent himself. The constraints from those other dynamics waylay the proximate intention's execution. The narrative explanation must include all of these dynamics and constraints. As well as any noise and equivocation.

As we have seen, their embeddedness in time and space makes dynamical systems inordinately sensitive to initial conditions. Two trajectories with infinitesimally close starting points will diverge dramatically, often within a few iterations. Whether the agent changes his mind or simply fails to follow through might therefore just be a matter of timing or circumstances. Explaining which of several alternatives happened and why therefore requires describing background and context in sufficiently vivid and concrete detail to reconstruct retrospectively both the internal dynamics and the external circumstances as well as the way they interacted.

The more influential initial or ongoing conditions are in someone's behavior, the more likely a complex attractor is in play. "It all depends on when you ask her" implies the operation of a strange attractor. "You just can never tell with her; she's so moody" might in fact be the best explanation available. When we know someone well we intuit that his or her behavior is neither random nor mad. We know complex dynamics are involved, even if we cannot describe them any more precisely than as "moodiness." This imprecision becomes an in-principle unpredictability in the case of natural (as opposed to mathematical) complex systems, which are stochastic. When we are aware that the requisite level of precision is impossible to articulate, we often finesse the explanation of our own behavior by saying: "I was just playing it by ear."

These considerations show that things are not as easy as even Aristotle —much less modern thinkers—believed: things are not clearly and neatly inside or outside the agent's awareness and control. It is more a matter of what and how much is inside and what and how much is outside: how much the agent attended to and how much was peripheral background.

One point at which we might decide to call the person mentally unbalanced is if we conclude that the dynamics themselves are abnormal. We might also call the person mad if we cannot imagine any attractor, however complex, at work at all, just randomness. The cautionary tale of complex dynamics is that we can never be absolutely certain that there is no complex attractor constraining the behavior: we just might not have found it yet. It took a long time for science to discover that chaotic behavior is not chaotic at all. Even worse, what looks like behavior constrained by an intention may in fact have been noise all along, as Chisholm's nervous nephew would no doubt protest.

Explaining the agent's convoluted path from one point to the next therefore will often require identifying many other internal dynamics and external circumstances involved in bringing about the behavior. As chapter 13's commonplace example of explaining the act of getting milk on the way home illustrated, other internal dynamics might prevent the agent from taking the most direct path from here to there. When all the intertwined attractors (all the entrained emotional, sociological, psychological, and other attractors) that make up a mature person are taken into account, those labyrinthine explanations we often launch on do not seem so preposterous after all.

The ever-present fallibility of historical narrative interpretation is unavoidable: despite taking every precaution, our reconstruction of what the agent did might still be mistaken. Hermeneutics is emphatically not *episteme*. No wonder jurors are troubled. But instead of trying to force judgments about human actions into an argument-like mold to which they do not belong, the solution must come from improved skills in *phronesis*: practical wisdom. Interpretation, however, can be taught only through example and practice. Children must be educated so that they develop a nurtured sensibility to context and circumstances. Only through habituation can the requisite interaction and dependencies between children and their environment be established. These context-sensitive couplings will provide them as adults with a better sense of or "feel for" people, their intentions, and the circumstances under which they can and do carry out those intentions. And this practical judgment can be taught only through selected and persistent interaction with others.

Summary   Behavior that occurs between phase changes must be explained by a hermeneutical, interpretive reconstruction. First, the agent's mental state that initiated the behavior must be identified. To do this, the explainer must describe both the contrast space of alternatives that embodies the agent's frame of mind and the attractor-separatrix dynamics that govern those coordinates. Unlike that of Newtonian particles, dynamical systems' behavior depends crucially on their history and experience and on the environment they are currently in. Whether the *explanandum* is a snowflake or a person, explaining any dynamical system's behavior requires that we fill in all that relevant background. Explanations of actions must therefore provide a narrative that interprets and recounts what those cognitive and affective dynamics were like at the time they initiated the action.

Next, because the agent opted for one of the alternatives in the contrast space, the historical and interpretive narrative must describe the specific path the behavior took, mentioning at each step along the way how much was specifically constrained by the intention and how much by the lay of the land or the external structure of the intention's control loop, as well as by the agent's other dynamics. The explainer must also determine how much equivocation, if any, compromised the flow of the intention's content into behavior, as well as how much information available at the behavioral end is extraneous noise unconstrained by intentional attractors.

Narrative hermeneutical explanations, I emphasize, are not simple temporal listings of discrete events; that is mere chronology, a linear sequence of independent frames on a film. In a true interpretive narrative the telling of the tale explains by knitting together sequential but interconnected threads such that it describes a temporal and contextual pattern, the meaningful organization that flows through the singular sequence of events and binds them into a whole. Just as first-order contextual constraints bind individual molecules into an integrated autocatalytic network, hermeneutic explanations of actions must construct a narrative that hangs together as a story. Unlike covering-law explanations of behavior, which abstract away time and space in favor of universalities, hermeneutics explains by highlighting and showing the concrete and temporal, context-dependent dynamical interrelationships that give the action its unique character.

Across Phase Changes

But, once again, this can be done only during "stable" periods. Between phase changes, while a system is in a particular dynamical regime, naturally occurring fluctuations and perturbations are damped, and explanation can proceed in the manner just described. Explanation will consist in the back-and-forth interpretive reconstruction of the established dynamics that originated and constrained the behavior, and then in the tracking of the actual trajectory to its terminus in actual behavior. But a phase change itself cannot be explained that way. What needs explaining there is the change itself in the established attractors, the system's transformation into an entirely different dynamical regime. An alcoholic's turnaround cannot be explained in terms of his earlier state of mind. The radical mental transformation itself needs explaining.

A phase change is the qualitative reconfiguration of the constraints governing the previous attractor regime. The shift creates new relationships among the system's components as well as between the system and its environment. Phase changes signal a reorganization of the old dynamics into a new system with renewed relationships among the parts. These new relationships embody new properties and are governed by new laws. How do we explain changes in a dynamical system's equilibrium points?

Within an established dynamical regime, the components' meaning is given by their contextual setting (which, it is true, in part they constituted). There the meaning of individual actions depends on the agent's overall psychological dynamics, in combination with the circumstances in which these are embedded and from which they issued, as outlined in the previous section. But Paul is not "in character" with Saul. We will never be able to explain (in the old sense of deduce and predict) the abrupt, discontinuous change of Saul into Paul. Despite the physical continuity between the two, in a very important sense Paul is not Saul precisely because the former's character describes a phase space—a psychological dynamics —organized quite differently from the latter's. These dynamics structure and constrain very different types of behavior. And we want an account of this change in the dynamics themselves when we ask for an explanation of the events that took place on the road to Damascus.

Determining when or even whether a system will undergo a phase change and switch attractors is even more difficult than reconstructing either the dynamics of an established state or a trajectory through that established regime. Close inspection, however, can at times reveal that a phase change is imminent. As mentioned earlier, when dynamical systems are taken far from equilibrium to a critical threshold, the pull of the established attractor begins to weaken. The landscape begins to flatten out, so to speak. The system accesses states it would not ordinarily have visited. In human terms, when a person's behavior begins to fluctuate widely such that previously uncharacteristic behavior becomes commonplace, watch out: a psychological crisis is in the offing.

Far enough from equilibrium, that is, we all have physical or psychological breaking points homologous to a Bénard cell's instability threshold or a faucet's sudden switch to turbulence. If we are lucky and things go well, we may come out of these breaking points a more complex person with renewed potential. We sometimes grow from a crisis and are the better for it. But there is no guarantee that any complex system will reorganize. As psychiatric wards show, it—or we—might fall apart. And as Aristotle never failed to remind us and the study of dynamical systems confirms, which of the two happens can be a matter of *tuchê* (luck). It is impossible to predict with certainty whether an established attractor regime will be able to damp a naturally occurring fluctuation and stabilize or, to the contrary, whether the system will reorganize or disintegrate. Which critical fluctuation happens to be the one around which the system will reorganize or which perturbation is the one that will destroy the system is often a chance matter. And not just which: when is just as important. Timing is crucial: the perturbation that would have taken us over the edge as a child might have only minimal impact today. A full narrative explanation must include all these details. Interpretive explanations of individual actions are therefore always historical and concrete; as such they mark a return to the casuistry and case studies of medieval times.

Phase changes cannot be explained in terms of the dynamics from which they issued. The reason, to repeat, is that phase changes mark a qualitative, catastrophic transformation in the dynamics themselves. Across phase changes, therefore, what requires explanation is how the meaning that governed one stable state is transformed into qualitatively different dynamics governing a different space of possibilities with a different frequency distribution. As a result, a narrative reconstruction of the genealogical, evolutionary process must explain the "neogenesis" enabled by this strange form of causality operating far from equilibrium. Because, as mentioned, each run of a complex system is unique, this can only be done retrospectively, after the bifurcation.

Within stable periods, as we saw, the system's dynamics do much of the causal and explanatory work; the initial conditions account for the particular twists and turns within the behavior's attractor. The less complex the system, the more explanatory work the dynamics do; the more complex the system, the more the initial conditions do. Between phase changes, on the other hand, it is first necessary to reconstruct the process that drove the system far from equilibrium. Did the agent's own internal dynamics drive him or her to a threshold point? Or was it more a case of external perturbations driving (the agent's) weak internal dynamics to an instability?

There is no one-to-one relationship between the dynamics in place before the phase change and those that appear after. The direction that a stochastic dynamical system's bifurcation will take cannot in principle be predicted even by ideal, omniscient observers. The precise path that the phase change takes—the addict's sudden resolve to "go clean" rather than, say, go on methadone—can be explained only after the fact. Such explanation must take the form of a genealogical narrative that reconstructs the bifurcation by painstakingly describing (1) the interlevel and contextual interactions that took the system far from equilibrium in the first place, (2) the particular fluctuation or perturbation that drove it over the edge, and (3) the specific pathway that the bifurcation took (as opposed to other possible alternatives).

Because storytelling, narrative, and drama can reproduce the creative, temporal process of nature in a way that the deductive-nomological model cannot, Gadamer (1985, 420) states that "the primacy of hearing is the basis of the hermeneutical phenomenon." When we listen to a melody, the notes we hear derive their aesthetic quality from their relationship to and dependence on the earlier notes. Similarly, a counselor's appearance will be meaningful to the addict only in a particular historical context. Stories retell these temporal, concrete, and particular interactions in a way that deductive-nomological explanations do not.

In the transformation across stable states, serendipitous events carry the explanatory load. In contrast to covering-law accounts, hermeneutic explanations of phase change transformations must therefore make note of and emphasize the particular case's concrete and temporal details even more than when they explain behavior issuing from established dynamics. The narrative or dramatic reconstruction of those transformations must describe the role random, unique events and coincidences play. Recovering addicts often explain their turnaround by pointing to such events: "I had hit bottom and the counselor just happened by at the right moment." As historians and novelists have long known, those singularities are often responsible for the turning points in people's lives. They serve as the chance fluctuations that can take a system already far from equilibrium over the edge and cause it to disintegrate. They can also be the focus around which the new system will nucleate, if it reorganizes at all.

Singularities are thus crucial to the phase changes of historical processes constrained by positive feedback and context-dependence. Across phases, that is, unique events play a pivotal role, thereby complicating the explainer's task even more. In short, to explain not only the everyday genesis of prior intentions but also dramatic personal transformations, it is often necessary to provide a retrospective and interpretive narrative that makes ample references to the particular physical, cultural, social, and personal circumstances that took the individual far from equilibrium. Special attention must then be given to the unique and chance events that precipitated the change. Why did the alcoholic quit just now? Any explanation must identify and interpret these dramatic turning points. "His daughter, whom he adores, ran into him, dead drunk, at a bar. She had never seen him like that before and he was devastated."

Genealogical narratives reconstruct the leap that the *explanandum* undergoes at a bifurcation point. If I am correct and forming a prior intention is just such a phase change, a historical interpretation recounting both the background conditions and dynamics that led to disequilibrium, as well as the singular circumstances that precipitated a particular course of action, is required to explain both the genesis of the intention and its execution. "Why did I decide to greet you? Well, I was walking along Wisconsin Avenue when I saw you walking ahead of me. [Disequilibrium set in.] Should I acknowledge you? After all, you were not very pleasant to me the last time we met; on the other hand.... And suddenly, you turned around and saw me. What could I do? I couldn't very well be rude.... So I decided to greet you."

Phase changes embody essentially incompressible information. That is, there exists no law or algorithm more concise than the process itself that can capture and describe what happened. That is why fiction and drama, Bible stories, fairy tales, epics, novels, and plays will always be better than deductions or formulas for explaining personal transformations of this sort. The rich, vivid descriptions and reenactments that these genres provide represent meaningfully for the reader and spectator the processes that precipitate such personal transformations. They do so by paying special attention to the role played by both the agent's internal dynamics and the particular environmental perturbations that drive a system far from equilibrium. Stories and dramas also show the reader and viewer how random, unrepeatable events and circumstances can be responsible for either destroying people or renewing them at a different level. Often insignificant in themselves, these unique events can be the proverbial straw that breaks the camel's back. Had the characters in those novels and dramas not been near a crisis point, of course, those unique events would not have had an impact. By interacting with background conditions far from equilibrium, unique events provide the turning points along a singular trajectory. Reenactment, which is what both simulations and theatrical performances offer, is even more explanatory than narrative because we get to see how the tensions of living with Torvald Helmer, George Tiesman, and Charles Bovary drive Nora, Hedda, and Emma to the edge.

David Lewis's Logic of Explanation

Hermeneutic interpretation, within a narrative framework, thus comes closest to the logic of explanation advocated by David Lewis (1973a). Twenty-five years or so ago, Lewis argued that causes should be analyzed in terms of counterfactuals: if x had not occurred, y would not have. Despite the potential objection, "What underwrites the counterfactual itself if not causality?" thinking of y in terms of its dependence on x can be helpful, as we saw with the concepts of equivocation and noise, in capturing the way meaning flows from intention into action. Remarkably, however, neither Lewis's ideas on cause nor Wesley Salmon's (1977) claim that a cause is whatever transmits a mark has found its way into mainstream philosophy's literature on action.

If causes are conceptualized in terms of counterfactuals—if x hadn't been, y would not have, determining that y depended on, x, which in turn depended on w, and so forth—an explanation will explain by retracing the phenomenon's entire historical trajectory. Providing a genealogical or historical narrative tracks all those dependencies. But if the dependencies are due, not to external forces impacting on objects, but to those contextual constraints that weave the phenomena and processes together into systematic wholes and then take those very wholes far from equilibrium and over the edge into a new regime, tracing that genealogy will not proceed in a simple straight line. A full-bodied historical and interpretive explanation will require a concrete and detailed narrative that describes all of those interrelationships. A complete and correct explanation must reconstruct the entire historical and contextual bramble bush, which it will do by taking full advantage of the polysemy of narrative or reenactment to describe the many temporal and spatial interconnections involved. When it comes to explaining the details of the paths we take, uncharacteristic behavior, or especially those dramatic turning points in our lives, Proust and Ibsen will therefore always trump Hume and Hempel.

The Explainer

In the nineteenth century, hermeneutics attempted to emulate the method of the natural sciences of the period, "the conquest of mythos by logos" (Gadamer 1985, 242). As was true of the natural sciences and philosophy of the time, experimenters and thinkers claimed to be able to detach themselves from the object of experimentation or analysis. In Schleiermacher's words, the goal of textual interpretation was "to understand a writer better than he understood himself" (quoted in Gadamer, 160), a result purportedly achievable through the application of a "canon of grammatical and psychological rules of interpretation" (163). Hence the desire to formulate accurate methodological principles that, when applied to the obscure object, would render it transparent. Correct hermeneutical interpretation, in other words, would approach the deductive-nomological limit.

Complete understanding would be achieved by effectively detaching the interpreter from the object, text, or behavior under scrutiny. Hence the claim of nineteenth-century hermeneutics to objective knowledge: interpreters do not interpret; like a clear mirror they simply reflect what is all there, always and objectively, in the text. Nineteenth-century hermeneutics thus shared with Newtonian science and modern philosophy the goal of achieving objective, certain, universal knowledge by escaping the constraints of time and other "anthropological considerations." As unwitting heirs to this conceptual framework, Andrew Hacker's (1995) puzzled jurors mentioned at the beginning of the book are convinced that they too, not only are expected but should be able to do something like this in determining whether the behavior of the accused was first- or second-degree murder or manslaughter. Impossible.

Nineteenth-century hermeneutics failed to take into account that the explainer, as much as the phenomenon explained, is embedded in time and space. Twentieth-century students of hermeneutics, in contrast, have finally come to appreciate that interpretation is doubly historical. The phenomenon being explained has a history, and so must be understood within that history; but interpreters, too, are situated within history, within a tradition, which their interpretation both reflects and influences. This double historicity affects the pragmatics of explanation. When the subject is planetary orbits and billiard balls, that is, when interactions can be ignored, the role of interpreter recedes in importance; not so when the subject is either quantum processes or human actions. Dynamical systems have therefore brought the interpreter back into the pragmatics of explaining action (if not into the metaphysics of explanation, as quantum processes have).

In dynamical terms, the tradition in which interpreters are situated is itself an attractor. As social beings, interpreters are embedded in its dynamics. As Gadamer (1985, 216) notes, "[t]he anticipation of meaning that governs our understanding of a text is not an act of subjectivity, but proceeds from the communality that binds us to the tradition." Jurors as well as the rest of us are located within a tradition, which frames our interpretation. This fact, which even the popular media harp on, need not lead either to paralysis or to the deconstructionist's conclusion that any interpretation is as good as any other. As Umberto Eco (1990, 21) insists and our discussion of top-down constraints has shown, context constrains the range of plausible interpretations. "A text is a place where the irreducible polysemy of symbols is in fact reduced because in a text symbols are anchored in their context."

Following Eco's lead, I submit that two contexts provide an action's "literal" meaning: the historical background and contextual setting in which the action was performed, and the context established by the "small world" of the action itself. Two contexts likewise frame the meaning of a hermeneutical explanation: the historical background and contextual setting in which the interpretation is offered, and the context established by the "small world" of the interpretation itself. When both the explainer and the agent whose action is being explained share the same historical background and contextual setting, interpretation usually proceeds smoothly. Not so in a society whose members bring with them radically different backgrounds and perspectives. If explainers are as much situated in a context (a tradition) as the phenomenon they are trying to explain, bringing this background-that-goes-without-saying to the foreground is a valuable contribution to the pragmatics of explanation: it helps determine how much the explanatory context itself has contributed to the explanation. Hermeneutics's emphasis on the concrete, individual, and temporal is also particularly well suited to this task.

Implications for Jurisprudence

The atomistic conceptual map, as I pointed out earlier, held that an object's essential traits were those it displays always and everywhere—when it is isolated from history and context, in other words. In a legal context, the practice of forbidding jurors from learning the defendant's prior history is symptomatic of this snapshot ontology. Jurors clearly cannot be expected, however, to decide whether the defendant is guilty of first- or second-degree murder, manslaughter, or negligence on the basis of just a single-frame description of the accused's behavior described in terms of raw movements. From the perspective of the approach presented in this book, jurors need as much concrete details of the context and dynamics of the defendant's life and circumstances as possible to be able to understand the particular behavior by reconstructing the frame of mind from which it issued. That is, the accused's behavior must be situated in its overall context. Ample details also help jurors judge whether that mental state unequivocally constrained the behavior or whether, to the contrary, noise might have compromised its flow into action.[73]

Given the importance in legal circles of determining whether a piece of behavior constitutes action, it is unsurprising that elements of hermeneutics have found their way into the law reviews. No thanks to academic philosophy, the legal community's rediscovery of context and time has been the driving force behind the so-called narrative turn in legal theory. For example, Cover (1983) argues that legal prescriptions are situated in a narrative discourse that gives them meaning. "For every constitution there is an epic, for every decalogue a scripture" (4). Not quite accepting Cover's claim that jurisgenesis takes place primarily through narrative, Stephen Winter (1990) disagrees, insisting that only shared social experience can carry the persuasive force that creates meaning. The sedimented meaning that characterizes a tradition reflects that shared social experience. That said, however, Winter acknowledges that even in a legal setting the significance of narrative lies in its transformative potential, which inheres in the empathetic potential of concrete imagery (1486–88) and the ambiguity and indeterminacy of narrative's natural language (1989, 2276).

As both Toulmin (1990) and Kuhn (1970) have noted, the abstract reasoning of *episteme* lacks the potential to make someone look at an issue from a different perspective and be able to decode it from within a different context. (See also Nussbaum 1990.) Martha Minow (1987) has persuasively argued this point with respect to the law. Minow quotes Audre Lord in support of her claim that we can change perspective only if we are made to "[s]ee whose face [difference] wears" (79). To encourage this change in perspective, for example, Minow advocates that "the [Supreme] Court can, and should, seek out alternative views in friends of the court briefs such as the autobiographical accounts of the men and women who believed their lives had been changed by the availability of legalized abortion" (80). She also espouses "the use of vivid, factual detail," like that used in the famous Brandeis brief in Muller v. Oregon, as a way to break out of formalist categories. She cites Grimshaw's claim that "[c]oncreteness requires that one experience or vividly imagine such consequences, either to oneself or to others, and judge on the basis of that awareness" (89).

Fresh analogies allow all of us, not just jurors and judges, to understand, if not quite sympathize with, different contexts and experiences. If grounded in the particular and concrete, unfamiliar analogies also allow us to see connections among things ordinarily conceived as different. Unexpected analogies, especially those making connections across contexts, "scrape off barnacles of thought" and "challenge views so settled that they are not thought to be views" (Minow 1987, 87). Metaphors can make an obvious contribution to this process because metaphors are like compasses: one leg is anchored in the familiar, the other free to float and connect with the unfamiliar (Hayles 1990). I have relied heavily on metaphors in this book: thinking of people as landscapes, and of their actions as constrained pathways through that topography, has been, I hope, heuristically useful.

In each of these cases the purpose of using concrete imagery and metaphors is to induce the explainer or interpreter to "see it fresh" by recognizing that criteria used to identify "similar" and "different" reflect the particular shared experience from which they are formulated. Metaphors and analogies become specially necessary when explainer and explained do not share a common tradition. Far from abstracting from context, the aim of vivid, detailed narrative is precisely to bring the background of a forum—its context—to the fore and make it the issue being explored. Once we recognize the astronomical multidimensionality of human experience and the context-dependence of dynamical self-organization, we can use vivid detail and fresh analogies to explain action. Doing so highlights the complexity of human behavior instead of abstracting it away to simplicity.

The Explanation's Own "Small World"

We can now understand why Melden (1961) and Peters (1958) reached the right conclusions for the wrong reasons. According to these authors, human action as opposed to "mere behavior" involves a "redescription" of the behavior in terms of the reasons, rules, and standards informing the behavior. Actions cannot be explained causally, they claimed, because in human actions cause and effect are not contingently related and cannot be generalized into a covering law, as they must be if actions are to be causally explicable. This is not so. Explanations in terms of reasons conflict with causal explanations only if we assume a Newtonian model of cause and a Humean model of explanation. Those earlier theories of action relied on the wrong models and the wrong dynamics. According to a dynamical point of view, on the other hand, explanations in terms of reasons are part-whole and whole-part interpretations of actions. They interpret by fully embedding behavior in context, thereby reproducing the nonlinear, interlevel interactions between the agent's internal dynamics (both mental and motor) and the physical, social, and temporal environments in which the agent lives and in which the behavior is performed.

Interlevel hermeneutical narratives track and reproduce those historical or genealogical processes that characterize and cause self-organization. The explanation they offer must be judged in terms of the explanatory context that these narratives create. Does the narrative make sense of the phenomenon? Does the story hang together as a story? Does it ring true? Refusing to call these interlevel relations "causal" begs the question in favor of the Newtonian model. Refusing to call hermeneutical, genealogical interpretations "explanation" begs the question in favor of the Humean model.

I have claimed that when it comes to dynamical processes, including action, the genealogical, historical narratives of hermeneutics are more suitable than any other as a logic of explanation. Hermeneutics requires, however, an enlarged understanding of what counts as "explanation." In this chapter I have claimed that hermeneutics explains, not by enabling us to deduce and thereby predict, but by providing insight into and understanding of how something happened, that is, into its dynamics, background, and context. Hermeneutical narratives explain by showing all the messy interactions and how they operate within and between different levels. Such explanations explain and make sense of behavior by supplying rich, vivid descriptions of the precise, detailed whole-part and part-whole trajectory that an agent's behavior took, including the temporal, physical, social, and cultural context in which the agent was embedded and in which the action occurred. We understand why Nora slams the door, even if we could not have predicted it.

We don't just accept that Nora slammed the door as an exercise in civility and tact. We understand why she did it. Richard Rorty (1979) sells hermeneutics short as merely therapeutic, not cognitive (much less onto-logically grounded). There would be no need for hermeneutical explana-tion in a closed, linear, deterministic universe. But in an open, complex, dynamical world, a more expansive form of reasoning than the narrow, straightjacket rules and formulas of *episteme* allows us to understand why Nora suddenly behaved the way she did. When we are asked to explain human action, there is often no universal or lawful regularity from which to strictly deduce its parts and predict an agent's future course of behav-ior. Because the dynamics are complex, induction won't do either; that logical technique searches for commonalities across individuals to formu-late a lawful regularity from which future individual cases can then be inferred. But because complex systems, whether hurricanes or people, are embedded in time and space, unique circumstances and individual experi-ence play a crucial role in their identity, their behavior, and in the way in which they must be explained. In the case of complex systems, as we saw, the devil is in the way differences and variations, not commonalities, hang together in a particular context, given a particular background. As infor-mation theory has always insisted, the differences make a difference. As Salthe has pointed out, that's why hurricanes are given proper names!

Once, Embedded in Time and Space

I am unconcerned with theories that claim that explanations are good explanations to the extent that they provide intellectual satisfaction (Braithwaite 1953) or are appropriate to the listeners' interests and knowledge (Achinstein 1983). In general, antirealist accounts of explana-tion (van Fraassen 1980) do not interest me. That said, however, I suspect that the current revival of interest in myth, the tales of Genesis, and storytelling in general is not unrelated to the perceived inadequacies of the received logic of explanation that modern philosophy and science have offered the public at large. But it is not, as some have suspected (Rorty 1979), that we find in myths and conversations a mechanism for coping. In this chapter I have claimed that by relying on concrete, con-textual, and temporally grounded narratives and reenactments, myths and tales explain because they recreate the open, nonlinear dynamics of the real processes they purport to explain. By reconstructing a storyline that hangs together despite and because of many twists and turns, myths and stories respect time and origins; by emphasizing concrete, particular details, they respect connectivity and correlations, that is, contextual embeddedness. They respect, in other words, the human being's sense of place, the importance of a particular temporal and spatial point of view in human life and behavior. In contrast to the approach taken by science, human beings and their actions do not adopt "the view from nowhere" (T. Nagel 1996).

We have therefore come full circle, it seems, to a much earlier understanding of what counts as explanation: to explanation as genealogical, story-like, and richly contextual. In Greek mythology, explanation and justification of phenomena were always genetic or genealogical: to legitimate was to trace temporally the connection between the *explanandum* and its origin. Herodotus says of the Egyptians that they didn't know until recently the origins of things, a disparaging comment because in the language of myth, authority and legitimacy are established temporally and historically. The ubiquitous genealogies in classical Greek literature as well as in the Pentateuch are explanations.

The idea that all reasoning must be prooflike is a fairly recent one, as we have seen: only a few hundred years old. What changed between the mythic framework and that of philosophy and science? The earlier poets referred to time in three ways to explain and justify.

First, because the bards were inspired and taught to sing by the Muses, their songs and tales themselves had authority because of their origin: divine inspiration. "What I'm singing is so because the Muse speaks through me." After the first philosopher, Thales, suggested that water was the originary source of all reality, where the explanatory song or story came from became unimportant. Having replaced inspiration with reasoning, Thales no longer thought it necessary to provide an account of the origin or source of his own explanation.

Second, in mythology all things, the *explananda* (such as natural phenomena) as well as the *explanantia* (such as chaos and the gods), exist equally in time. Thales retained this temporal aspect of explanation; water, the originary source, was itself thought to have a beginning, as did Chronos, Zeus, and Oceanus in earlier accounts. With Anaximander this second element of time dropped out of explanation. If the *apeiron* is conceived as eternal, the principle in which explanation of temporal events is ultimately grounded must itself be timeless.

Third, in the mythic world the very form or logic of the explanatory tale was itself genealogical. Why do the Achaians win the Trojan War? They "can show of all the longest lineage." Explanations consisted in an explicit retelling (through a series of begats) of the path the *explanandum* traveled. Historiography was explanation.

When Socrates/Plato insisted that explanation must be formulated as definition, not history, this third temporal element was discarded. By answering the question "how can the many be one?" with an appeal to eternal unchanging Forms, Plato completed philosophy and science's debasement both of time and of the lush texture of the contingent world. Henceforth the complex and changing world of daily life would be judged unreal; the details of experience and change were just "stories," and stories were untrue illusions, poets the "mothers of lies." Philosophers and scientists thus usurped the bard's divine authority by substituting for the concretely and messily real the absolutely and abstractly Real. Despite his respect for the individual and the embodied, even Aristotle gave pride of place to the eternal and universal. Through philosophical and scientific reflection, thinkers were expected to dismiss the here and now, discard all indexical references, and tap into Universal Truth, which exists only in eternity. Parmenides had won.

In contrast, the logical form of mythic narrative, "In the beginning ...," was both temporal and contextual. Not only did mythic narrative regard change and place as ontologically real. Myth also recognized the epistemological role of such connections: in all stories, time and context are the crucially necessary cues for decoding the narrative's meaning (Eco 1990). As Proust's descriptions of madeleines and Flaubert's of dinner parties also vividly illustrate, stories explain in virtue of their rich descriptions, which trace the multiple temporal and contextual connections woven into the very being of a particular event.

Definition, on the other hand, with its eternal unchanging *definiens*, aligned itself with the universal and general, with the eternal and absolutely true "one," which can only be so in abstraction from the profuse variation of contingent detail exhibited by the "many." Symbolic logic and mathematics advanced this trend away from time and context as their abstract notations put more and more distance between formal systems and the messy here and now. Newtonian science and covering-law theories of explanation followed in this tradition. And so for 2,000 years, the search continued for a perfect, that is, a universal, language (Eco).

But neither the universal nor the abstract explains the particular as such when that particular is an open, dynamical system far from equilibrium. Discarding the unique characteristics that time and context impress on natural phenomena in favor of universal and eternal essences, therefore, had an additional consequence: the very contingent details exhibited by the "many"—those idiosyncratic characteristics and vicissitudes that make each individual unlike any other—disappeared from ontology and epistemology as well. When time and context are banished, in other words, individuality is banished as well. Despite his claim that individuals are the only true substance, as we saw, even Aristotle was unable to break entirely with this approach and carve out a scientific role for the idiosyncracies of time and place, or for the peculiar—and creative—circularity of self-cause. Philosophy in general, and action theory in particular, have been living with the consequences ever since.

Rehabilitating a narrative logic of explanation as I have attempted in this chapter will be necessary if we are ever going to pay more than lip service to the individual. For centuries philosophers have spoken with a forked tongue: one the one hand they have praised and admired the free, unique individual; on the other the universal and repeatable were considered the only grounds for scientific respectability. Dynamical systems theory's value is that it does not zero in solely on the individual at the expense of the context or larger whole in which the individual is embedded. Nor does it dismiss the individual and unique in favor of the general and the repeatable. Both are given equal billing. Many implications follow from this position. The book's last chapter will offer a cursory survey of some of the social and political consequences that flow from this theory-constitutive metaphor.

Chapter 15

Agency, Freedom, and Individuality

Free Will

It is beyond the scope of this book to examine in detail the implications with respect to free will suggested by the claim that homologous dynamics may be at work in all complex dynamical systems, whether autocatalytic webs, slime molds, or people. However, I wish to note a few salient points.

Despite the numerous attempts to "derive" free will from quantum uncertainty, the consensus—correct, in my judgment—is that quantum randomness provides little support for belief in free will; chance is as chancy a foundation for grounding moral and legal responsibility as is determinism. We are no more morally responsible for behavior produced by a random event than for behavior that results from mechanical, forceful causes operating deterministically. It is just as unwise to attempt to derive free will from the stochastic nature of some complex adaptive processes. The macroscopic fluctuation around which a phase change nucleates is as iffy a basis for imputing agency or moral responsibility as a quantum one.

John Dupré (1993, 216) notes that "[w]hat is problematic about humans is ... that they are extraordinarily dense concentrations of causal capacity." In light of this fact, therefore, he proposes that we think of free will not as the absence of external determining (Newtonian) causes, but as the human capacity to impose order on a progressively disordered world. The dynamics of complex dissipative structures support Dupré's proposal. Let us see why.

Whether a system will reorganize at a new level of complexity or, to the contrary, will disintegrate, is in principle unpredictable. And if it does reorganize, the particular form it will take is also in principle unpredictable. Even if the phase change is fundamentally stochastic, however, whenever adaptive systems bifurcate, the newly reorganized regime into which the structure settles (if one is found) will lower the system's rate of internal entropy production even as it increases total entropy production. So if the system does leap to a more differentiated organization, there will have been a method to its madness: reorganization always increases complexity and renews both internal order and overall disorder.

On the view I have been presenting here, imposing order is what all top-down constraints of dynamical systems do (Pols 1975, 1982). Whether in autocatalytic cycles or human beings, significance is a result of the interplay between the system's own top-down inhibiting constraints and the alternatives available to its components. In linguistics, constraints supplied by a sentence's context narrow the potential meaning of individual words. In genetics, the overall context in which a particular DNA codon is located affects its phenotypic manifestation. There is no understanding meaning independently of those interlevel relationships.

Recall the concept of ascendence: Ulanowicz (1997) labeled an organized entity "ascendent" insofar as it develops as a focus of influence that grows in cohesion and integrity and thereby withstands the environment's destabilizing influence. The in-house pruning and streamlining of autocatalytic webs are carried out in the service of the higher level's focus of influence. While the system is ascendent, its overarching dynamics function as its formal cause, constraining the lower levels that make it up. In that way they ensure the continuity and enhancement of the global level. In self-organizing, that is, a complex system partly decouples from the environment, from which it wrests a measure of autonomy. As discussed in chapters 8 and 9, the difference between the behavior of objects while they are independent entities and their behavior once correlated and interdependent provides a measure of the contextual constraints in effect at the global level (see Brooks and Wiley 1988). The greater the difference between random and systematic behavior, the more stringent the constraints reducing potential variation must be. That difference measures the system's degree of organization and its autonomy vis-à-vis the environment. Dynamical systems are also partly independent of their parts, which, in self-organizing, have become replaceable components. Once organized, a system's attractors serve as its formal and final cause, both preserving its identity and drawing behavior into its overall organization.

Consider one last time the initial, almost random flailing of Thelen's (1995) infants. Before learning to reach successfully, each child flailed around according to its own innate dynamics, and every so often, accidentally made contact with the object. As a result of these persistent interactions, however, a motor attractor was eventually constructed. Once this occurred, reaching behavior issued from the organized dynamics of the attractor; for that very reason, the action of reaching is less random or subject to the environment's influences than flailing was. Divergence from randomness, in other words, is a measure of any dynamical system's integrity or cohesion relative to the environment's disintegrating effects, that is, of the system's independence from its environment. That ontology, we said, underwrites a particular epistemological stance: behavior constrained top-down is always amenable to purposive and intentional characterization (Dennett 1987). This is why behaviorists described their pigeons teleologically, as "seeking food," and why news agencies phrase their reports as "In an attempt to stave off a takeover, GM today took measures to. . . ." The more robust a system's higher levels of organization, the more *they* and not external mechanical forces control the output. The more robust a system's higher levels of organization, therefore, the freer the resulting behavior. The system is autonomous; it behaves "from its own point of view." That is one sense in which any behavior constrained top-down can be considered free.

Insofar as all self-organizing structures, from hurricanes to ecosystems, act to preserve and enhance the overall global level, even at the expense of the particular components, complex systems are goal-directed, if not fully goal-intended (Dretske 1988). By curtailing the potential variation in component behavior, however, context-dependent constraints paradoxically also create new freedoms for the overall system. As we saw, each emergent level of self-organization is nearly decomposable from the one below, and each new order possesses emergent properties absent at lower levels. That ontological feature allows scientists to identify and study chemical processes without having to refer to physical processes.

I claimed earlier that emergent, high-level psychological properties correspond to complex neurological dynamics constructed as a result of the coevolution of human beings and the complex social organization that they both structure and are structured by (Artigiani 1995). Once the neuronal processes self-organize into a conscious and meaningful space, behavior constrained by that organization can express and carry out an agent's intent. And just as the constraints of syntax allow meaning to be expressed, constraints on behavior thus make meaningful *actions* possible. At the same time as the intention's meaning and values limit behavioral alternatives, a renewed variety of possible behaviors also opens up. In humans, there emerges both the remarkable capacity for self-awareness and the sophisticated ability to think of, describe, judge, and act in terms of the meaningfulness of our choices—even in terms of ethical and aesthetic values (Artigiani 1996). The greater the phase space, the greater the number of alternatives available to the organism. To the extent that higher-level semantic considerations constrain behavior, it has more and different alternatives open to it than before. The enlarged phase space is the novel, emergent capacity to act: in the infants' case, for example, to reach. The increased complexity that phase changes bring with them is obvious: Hannah and Gabriel have more ways of acting meaningfully, foolishly, and so on than they had of just flailing. They can *reach* (but not *flail*) carefully, playfully, and so forth. The astounding number of dimensions (which dynamical self-organization has made available to human beings) provides a second sense in which human beings are free.[74]

We find here, once again, a curious parallel with Kant, this time with his distinction between acting in accordance with duty and acting for the sake of duty. This distinction is somewhat like the one mentioned earlier between following a rule and merely conforming to a rule. Did a particular behavior issue from and was it constrained by cognitive neurological dynamics embodying the meaningful concept of duty, or did the behavior just happen to fit such a description? A trajectory through semantic space captures the former, $I_s(r)$, not the latter, $I(r)$. The paradox of context-dependent constraints is most clearly in evidence here. Once an attractor embodying meaning and values self-organizes and is effectively originating and constraining the agent's actions, some behavioral alternatives previously available to the person will be excluded. Just as the sonnet's constraints restrict the poet's choices while they simultaneously open up new possibilities for meaningful and beautiful expression, so too with action. Acting consciously from a meaningful level limits the range of potential behavior: if you're going to behave ethically, there are some things you just can't do. At the same time, however, together with the decision to be ethical, other new possibilities appear, thus making the agent freer within that context.

What dynamical systems theory implies for the philosophy of mind and the philosophy of action is that once a semantic state space self-organizes, the trajectories within that higher dimensional, neurological space embody new rules: the constraints of logic, meaning, value, and the like. The difference between the variation in behavior before and after that semantic space self-organizes measures the degree to which those rules constrain its range of motion. The free person, in yet a third sense, is therefore the person whose behavior those higher levels of meaning and value constrain. "Freedom is choosing meaningfully, not spontaneously" (Artigiani 1996b, 13).

Aristotle speaks of action as behavior that is up to the agent: winks as opposed to blinks. Rather than attempting to cash out that distinction exclusively in terms of whether the source of the behavior is inside the agent or whether the behavior had no forceful cause at all, as Augustine suggested, I have proposed that action is behavior constrained, top-down, by the meaningful alternatives that the agent considers and from which he or she chooses. That action is also free in the sense that it originates in and is constrained by meaningful and value-laden considerations. Furthermore, the more robust and well-integrated those higher-level attractors constraining meaningful, ethical behavior, the freer the person. People who act as they think they should except when fearful of retaliation by others are less free than those with the courage of their convictions, so to speak. And the higher the level of meaning and value from which the person acts, the freer he or she is as well. Just as the act of reaching is freer than flailing, acting ethically is freer than just acting.

Dupré (1993) is therefore correct in proposing that we think of free will as human ability to project meaningful distinctions into behavior. To act top-down from the intentional level in which meaning is embodied is thus to exercise free will, in the following senses: (1) Because all self-organizing systems select the stimuli to which they respond, behavior constrained top-down is to that extent increasingly autonomous of force-ful impacts from the environment. Self-organized systems act from their own point of view. The more structured the entity, the more complex its organization and its behavior, and the more decoupled from and independent of its environment: the more autonomous and authentic, in short. (2) In a second sense of "free," the more complex an organism the freer it is because it simultaneously has new and different states to access. Even more importantly, however, (3) intentional human action is free to the degree that contextual constraints put the most complex levels of its neurological organization, those governing meaning, values, and morals, in control. Even as these levels regulate and close off options, they simultaneously free up qualitatively new possibilities for the expression of those values and morals (Artigiani 1997).

Robustness and Akrasia

Theory-constitutive metaphors are as fruitful as the new avenues for research they suggest. The central lesson of complex adaptive systems is that when everything is ultimately connected to everything else, expecting to isolate one aspect of a problem and, by dealing with it, solve the entire problem is a senseless endeavor. Taking the web metaphor seriously means that just as movements on one end of a trampoline affect the other end, modifications to one portion of a probability landscape automatically alter the rest: a particular contextual setting that increases the probability of x on this end of the net will automatically alter the probability of y on the other, often unpredictably. A different time or place might not alter the probability that x will happen, yet another time or place might even lower it. That is what taking dynamics and context-dependence seriously is all about.

Thinking of people and their actions as complex systems therefore implies that attention must be directed to the organizational settings in which they grow up and are educated. "Mary is of strong character," we say, "but John is not." More than once I have posed the questions, Why are some dynamical regimes but not others robust? Why and how do the psychological dynamics of adults get to be the way they are? Why are some people's intentions more vulnerable to the environment's perturbing influence than those of others?

Bratman (1987) notes that plans of action and intentions may be stable in some respects but not others. "I do not normally decide how stable my plan is to be.... Rather, the stability of my plan is largely determined by general, underlying dispositions of mine" (65). These insights resonate with a dynamical perspective. Any system's contextual constraints, I emphasized, must possess sufficient cohesiveness to buffer the system from disintegrating influences, whether from subsystems attempting to compete with the higher level (as in cancer) or from perturbations entering from the environment. Cultural constraints, we also saw, must provide enough flexibility for the system to be resilient. Both sensitivity to context and robustness to perturbations and noise are characteristic of dynamic organizations.

One cause of robustness, I also suggested, is historical: both robustness and its absence are the sedimented result of the interplay between an agent's original internal dynamics and the environment. Following the suggestions offered in the chapter on information theory, therefore, robustness can be measured in terms of the probability that an intention will be carried out without equivocation, given the agent's other dynamics and the current environment in which it is formulated (social and cultural, as well as physical). The intention's overall robustness is the weighted sum of its robustness under each of those conditions. In other words, whether or not an intention is robust will be a function of the historical and contingent sedimentation of ongoing, unique interactions between the agent's dynamics and his or her environment: how vulnerable it is to noise and equivocation, in short. The degree of robustness of individual attractors, therefore, is not a feature intrinsic to them but is dependent rather on the overall system's "general, underlying" nature. So is *akrasia*, or weakness of will.

So the depth of a prior intention's valleys (that is, how robust the resolve) or the steepness of its separatrices (that is, how vulnerable to outside influences) is a function of many factors, including the agent's original internal dynamics, the past history of his or her interactions with the environment in which that history unfolded, and the current dynamics and environment. Individual attractors cannot be isolated from others that characterize the system in which they are embedded: they are like the warp and woof of a fabric. So no matter how firm someone's resolve about a particular course of action, if other features of the person's character and personality are stronger, these will override the agent's intention. The firmness of a particular intention will depend less on its intrinsic features than on the general context of which it is but one component. Whether someone follows through on a particular resolution may depend more on the overall stability of the person's character than on any feature of the resolve itself. Once again, the ambiguity of the term "integrity," with which we describe both people's character and a system's stability, spans both these meanings.

In some persons, for reasons having to do with the interplay over time between their inherent dynamics and the environment with which those interacted, those self-organized regimes and their attractors are less robust than normal. That is, the conditional probability is low that their intentions will unequivocally constrain behavior given the context in which they are situated. Equivocation inevitably sets in; the neuronal self-organization governing intentionality is not sufficiently cohesive to resist the disintegrating influences of environmental noise or competition from other internally constructed dynamics such as, for example, those governing instant gratification. Such persons are easily swayed and vulnerable to buffeting by the prevailing winds; they are "weak willed," we say.

Similarly, accusations of negligence are judgments that the accused did not measure up to expected standards of attentiveness and foresight. Why are some people unfocused and distracted while others seem always alert and able to concentrate? From a dynamical systems perspective the likely answer repeats the earlier one: it depends on the sedimented resolution of the overall attractor regime that characterizes the person. Does it have many fuzzy, broad and shallow valleys, or are these crisply delineated and contoured?

Resetting Dynamics

One advantage of dynamical systems theory is that it can handle self-cause. It is for future research, however, to determine whether and to what extent we can teach children to focus and channel their internal dynamics. Habituation is probably one way; deliberately imposing contextual constraints on the environment to alter future behavior is probably another. As mentioned earlier, Odysseus did just that by tying himself to the mast; we do it by buying alarm clocks and personal organizers. Group therapy probably serves the same purpose. Ruth Benedict (1989) is well known for having categorized cultures as either "guilt-based" or "shame-based." It would be interesting to study whether the fact that humans are contextually embedded in social organizations makes shame and embarrassment a more natural basis for personal restraint than guilt.

If many of the ideas borrowed from complex dynamical systems are applicable to human development and education, their implications are indeed sobering. We are far from understanding the dynamics that govern cognition, psychology, and emotion at any given stage in our lives, much less the processes that precipitate fundamental transformations from one

stage to another. We still cannot identify those thresholds of psychological or emotional disequilibrium when intervention would be most effective. Making matters worse is the fact that since in practical terms, each
run of a complex adaptive system is unique, educational and child-rearing
techniques that might work for a Hannah may not work for a Gabriel.
And techniques that might have worked for Hannah yesterday may not
today.

Complex dynamical systems theory suggests that many psychological
and emotional problems may be due to dynamical malfunction. Only in
recent years have psychologists entertained the possibility that schizo-
phrenia and manic-depression might have a dynamical origin. If we knew
how to reset mental dynamics we could also fix these illnesses. Rom
Harré and Grant Gillett (1994) have called for the adoption of what they
label a "discursive psychology." In and through discourse (by which they
mean not just language but something closer to Wittgenstein's forms of
life) we construct our psychological dynamics. When something goes
wrong with that organization, it might be possible to reset it by reproducing that discourse, they claim. However, if the paths that psychological dynamics take are as sensitive to initial conditions as those of all
complex systems, reproducing the original discourse might be impossible.
It is a task for clinical psychology, in any case, to determine whether it is
possible to reset psychological dynamics that have gone awry.

Lock-In

One thing we do know is that dynamic systems exhibit a curious duality. Because they are fundamentally rooted in their environment and history through context-dependent constraints, complex adaptive systems,
including people and their actions, are not isolated atoms. Nor do they
start out from scratch. We are always already networked in both time and
space. Complex dynamical systems, as we have seen, at all times carry
both their phylogenetic and their developmental histories on their backs.
Information is stored, "not in a stable, inert structure ... but in the self-
consistent web of transformations. But the particular web accessed is a
function of the history of the environments to which the autocatalysis has
adapted" (Kauffman 1993, 333). If so, and if human beings, including their
psychology, are complex adaptive systems, as I have been claiming,
we cannot start afresh, halfway through our lives, as if the previous years
had never happened. On the other hand we are not, for the same reason,
condemned to a predetermined future. Yesterday's choices affect today's
options, but choices made today will also bias those options available
tomorrow. The environment coevolves with us; niches change in response
to the organisms that occupy those niches every bit as much as adaptive

organisms are selected by existing niches. Day to day, changes may be undetectable, but they add up, for better or worse. Partly in response to our own earlier steps, the ground shifts constantly under our feet, constructing valleys and hillocks as we go along. In a process of continuous landscape reconfiguration, each step enhances or diminishes the downstream options available to the organism. That is, each choice alters both the availability and probability of future steps.

We are not passive products of either the environment or external forces. In a very real sense we contribute to the circumstances that will constrain us later on. "Being your own worst enemy" means that your own earlier behavior in part created the new ragged peak that suddenly appeared just ahead and that you now face scaling. Some aspects of the environment coevolve with the agent, so mature agents aware of these dynamics are responsible for putting themselves in situations that virtually guarantee that they will behave in a certain way in the future.

The more we let things drift, the harder they are to change. Stuart Kauffman (1993, 76) notes that the Cambrian explosion 550 million years ago established "essentially all the major animal body forms ... and hence all the major phyla which would exist thereafter." Following the Permian extinction 200 million years ago, when approximately 96 percent of all species became extinct, "there [was] a rapid increase in species abundance and taxa up to the family level, but no new phyla or classes were created." Kauffman concludes that as evolution becomes increasingly canalized or constrained (as it moves down a landscape such as the one depicted in figure 10.4), fewer new alternatives are available. Because young adaptive systems are malleable—they are more potential than actual—a very different fundamental regime of traits might have been fairly easy to establish early on given the same initial dynamics had the system interacted with different environmental conditions. Over time, however, development and experience produce an increasingly furrowed, differentiated landscape with more and different states than the initial and nearly equiprobable plain that only had a few slight dips in it. In time, that is, each of us develops into a more complex, individuated person, but one more set in our ways as well. And once locked in, a particular regime is increasingly resistant to change. In other words, the lesson that dynamical systems teach is that the consequences of choices sediment.

Implications

Explaining voluntary behavior by postulating an external object that activates the agent's desire and thereby serves as final cause, Aristotle's account had the advantage of embedding the agent in the environment. Because the chain of activation routes through the agent's psyche, he or she could be held responsible for his or her actions. How do agents go about deciding whether or not to act on their desires? According to Aristotle it works like this: a child's social behavior is, initially, for the most part heteronomous: that is, it is to a significant degree the effect of external efficient causes. Mom literally sits Johnny down to write his grandmother a note thanking her for the birthday present she sent him. In the language of dynamics, the cumulative effect of such persistent training or habituation—call it "moral education"—is the establishment of contextual dependencies. The youth's character is thereby slowly shaped in a particular direction, molding certain desires and character traits that the presence of external objects will activate in the appropriate context.

Given its initial malleability, that character may have been easy to mold early in life. But self-organizing dynamics also suggest that the psychological results of development and experience progressively sediment as well. The potential for fundamental change diminishes over time. Although dynamical landscapes are never fixed and static, once established, the fundamental traits of a person's character become increasingly locked in. Changing something as basic as an adult's character and personality is enormously difficult, requiring major restructuring of the physical and social environment in which the person is situated. Absent such major restructuring, interventions to an established system, whether an adult's or that of any other dissipative structure, usually produce only minor, superficial changes. The robustness increasingly resists change.

Even though desire is activated by objects in the environment operating as final cause, the agent's desire itself is neither an entirely inborn phenomenon nor the passive product of external forceful causes. Like autocatalytic webs, even very young children can and will select the stimulus to which they will respond; all self-organizing systems behave from their own "point of view." This becomes even more obvious when self-consciousness appears and entrains the level of semantics. But even the internal cause of voluntary motion—the choice of desire—is not entirely unrelated to the environment. Very early in life, it is itself the downstream product of even earlier interactions between the system's innate dynamics and the environment.[75] The desire that, in context, the external object automatically activates is part of the agent's character, which has been (and continues to be) shaped over a lifetime.

Philosophers and scientists were wrong: it is not an exclusive disjunction—nature *versus* nurture—it is both, and fortunately, if dynamical systems are an appropriate metaphor, nature appears to be very generous in the flexibility that it confers on its initial endowment. But that malleability narrows quickly as interactions lead to self-organized structures that lock in, and the dependencies children establish early on become increasingly, if not completely, resistant to future modification. The social and educational implications of this discovery are truly sobering. It might be wiser, for example, to redirect those resources devoted to remedial instruction at the college level to head start programs.

Stability

Contexts supply the closures that create the more or less settled meanings that constitute "a world." Within a stable frame of reference, as Eco (1990) insists, the process of interpretation is limited. So, too, with people. Within a stable framework, as we saw, contextual dependencies established through persistent interactions with that environment limit our need to constantly interpret the world. Under stable conditions, we simply order ourselves to "drive home" and let the world be its own model. No need to analyze and evaluate every stimulus; the stable context, as embodied in our external structure's contextual constraints, will automatically reparse the environment for us. Higher-level monitoring can continue in place while the constraints of the internalized environment fine-tune the details. That is how organisms solve the frame problem. But this efficiently slack attitude can be successful only while the contextual frame of reference is not undergoing radical transformation. When the context alters so radically that the earlier interdependencies no longer apply, organisms must be on constant "alert" or risk extinction.

As mentioned earlier, complex systems don't wander out of a deep basin of attraction, nor do they fall off a page with high ridges around the edge, so to speak. For bifurcations and phase changes to occur, the current landscape must show signs of flattening out: it must first become unstable. When top-down constraints begin to weaken, fluctuations in the system's behavior indicate a disintegrating system. As Alvin Toffler (1991) worried in *Future Shock*, how much radical social change can the average agent tolerate without becoming unstable?

Ortega y Gassett (1960), one of the few contemporary thinkers to insist that, despite the tenets of modernity, we are not Newtonian atoms, is well known for the slogan "I am I and my circumstances." Less well-known is his claim that we never ponder and deliberate about problems in the abstract; problems are addressed only in their full situatedness. Only when there is a difference between where we are and where we want to be, he says, do we bother to do something about it. According to nonlinear dynamics, too, systems reorganize only when driven far from equilibrium to an instability threshold. Deciding on a radical change of lifestyle such as the alcoholic's prior intention to stop drinking, for example, requires just such a dramatic phase change, a catastrophic drop onto a radically rearranged mental page. "Going to the neighborhood pub" suddenly drops out of the newly reformed alcoholic's list of possible behaviors. Dynamical systems theory explains why such transformations truly require a radical change in lifestyle: one attractor cannot be changed while the rest remain in place. We are seamless wholes.

Do other features of complex dynamical structures such as ecosystems also apply to human psychology, in particular, to the shaping of character and action? I mentioned that the Great Lakes ecosystem is stable but not resilient. Is it also true that very stable personalities with predictable, minimally fluctuating behavior tend not to be psychologically resilient? Does cognitive and/or emotional stability tend toward rigidity and stasis? I noted earlier that resilience is usually correlated with flexible coupling among the components of a system's internal structure. Is this also true of people? Is psychological and emotional stability inversely correlated to the stringency of coupling within those subsystems? That is, do persons whose various personality traits are flexibly coupled tend to be more psychologically and emotionally resilient than those whose traits are tightly linked? The damage wrought by inflexible, rigid coupling between specific thoughts and behavior patterns might provide valuable insight into obsessive-compulsive disorders. In particular, a dynamical perspective might provide a way of understanding the circular causality whereby obsessive-compulsive behavior results in anxiety, which in turn exacerbates the obsessive-compulsive behavior. The relation between character and/or emotional stability on the one hand and the stringency and variability of coupling of internal components, on the other, is a topic for any future clinical psychology grounded in a dynamical systems perspective.

If evolution selects for resilience, not stability, whereas development and experience locks individuals into a progressively set landscape, the implications for educational psychology and sociology are also daunting. Salthe (1993a) characterizes the end of biological development as the onset of *senescence*, the condition in which the organism is no longer able to adapt and change. How do we promote psychological resilience and retard senescence? How do we teach people to prefer adaptation instead of "the evil you know over the evil you don't know"? Answers to these questions are indispensable to those counseling and retraining workers who have already lost or are about to lose their jobs to automation, downsizing, or other forms of "creative destruction."

Dynamical systems theory also tells us that variety among subsystem coupling is correlated with increased resilience at the global level. How do we teach persons to be flexible enough to risk connecting A to B and C, instead of only to B, with which A has always been associated? Novel connections can be dangerous: they might not work. They might even increase the chances of extinction. On the other hand, traits that have become maladaptive because of altered circumstances (however adaptive those traits might have been originally) will surely lead to extinction. Plato is skeptical: the prisoner in the *Cave* is released by another, not by his natural inquisitiveness or thirst for knowledge. Moreover, the released prisoner tends to persist in his earlier views even when a superior alternative is offered. Plato, that is, does not seem to hold out much hope for widespread resilience. What kind of retraining encourages and promotes that kind of adaptability? More importantly, how do we educate young people so as to promote flexibility and resilience from the outset?

Socrates taught that "the unexamined life is not worth living." However, the lack of psychological cohesiveness and emotional fragility of some adults, not to mention many teenagers, can be severe enough to make self-examination and risk taking impossible. The last 700 years of Western history have witnessed the change from feudal organization, through capitalism, to today's American culture of entrepreneurship— from social, political, and economic heteronomy to greater autonomy, in other words. Social and economic survival in the next millennium might very well require more than ever before that agents be self-confident risk takers. Do a robust character and psyche provide the space for such reflection and self-motivation? If so, what contextual setting facilitates their organization? Considering the differing innate dynamics we saw in Hannah and Gabriel, the answer will likely not come in a one-size-fits-all solution.

Fail-Safe versus Safe-Fail

Elsewhere (Juarrero-Roqué 1991) I have argued that if the lessons of complex dynamical systems apply to human beings, attempting to design fail-safe social systems (whether legal, educational, penal, or other type) that never go wrong is a hopeless task, for several reasons. First, since we carry our history on our backs we can never begin from scratch, either personally or as societies. Second, perfection allows no room for improvement. Plato was one of the few thinkers who understood that if a freshly minted utopia were ever to be successfully established, the only direction in which it could change would be downhill. Stasis and isolation are therefore essential to maintaining the alleged perfection, not only of Plato's *Republic*, but of most other utopias as well. The noumenal self that Kant postulates as the seat of moral choice and free will is likewise not part of this world. The possibility of perfection requires isolation and has nowhere to go but downward.

Because of their interaction with the environment and their embeddedness in history, on the other hand, open dynamical systems far from equilibrium can ratchet upwards and evolve into even more complex structures better adapted to a new environment. Because we desire not just to make do but to improve what we have, our only choice, evolution-like, is to cobble together safe-fail family and social organizations, structures flexible and resilient enough to minimize damage when things go wrong, as they inevitably will.

New, emergent potentials and capacities appear in some processes of creative destruction. Learning to embrace that promise of novelty and creativity must be the twenty-first century's rallying cry. Newton has been called the "god of the gaps" (Hausheer 1980) for trying to close the conceptual potholes that continually open up at our feet so as to produce a certain, fail-safe world. Can we learn instead to spot—on the spot—the chance fluctuation around which a system (be it a personal relationship, a business, or a social or political organization) could advantageously reorganize, and then embrace and "amplify" it, to use dissipative structure language? Or will we continue to hang on to persons, theories, and institutions that promise certainty and predictability? Is it possible, that is, to learn to embrace uncertainty? Because the price we pay for the potential of true novelty and creativity *is* uncertainty.

"What we need, then, is an ethics appropriate to a universe of uncertainty" (Rubino 1990, 210). And yet, as Carl Rubino notes, "uncertainty in its very form is a negative word." It should not be. A universe in which certainty is possible must exclude novelty and individuation. Complex dynamical systems, in contrast, teach us that "change, novelty, creativity and spontaneity are the real laws of nature, which makes up the rules as it goes along. This is good news, cause for rejoicing; we should lift up our voices, as the prophet says, and not be afraid." In any case, in a world of rapid change such as ours, we may have no other choice.

The Payoff: Novelty, Creativity—and Individuality

Dynamical psychological landscapes are essentially historical and contextual. They are progressively constructed by the persistent interactions between the system's structure and its environment. The overall attractor patterns thereby sculpted and resculpted capture a time-lapse portrait of the larger organism-environment system and cannot be understood through snapshot models. The context-sensitive constraints established through persistent interaction with a structured environment can ratchet up the system to increasingly varied and complex levels of organization. The price paid for this global differentiation and heterogeneity is that the individual components lose some of their earlier equipotentiality: adults are unable to regenerate a limb if lesioned, for example. The downside of our paradoxical duality is that as members of a community we lose some of our freedom. Living in society can and often does "cramp our style."

On the other hand, components in a system acquire characteristics and an identity they previously lacked (and could never acquire on their own): they become nodes in a network of relationships that permits forms of life and act-types unavailable to the hermit. Only as members of a complex social system can we be citizens and senators, teachers and wives, scientists and philosophers. The more complex the entity, the larger the number of choices. Only as members of a complex social system can we perform actions that identify us as such. The more complex the entity, the more meaningful the choices as well: as citizens and teachers, senators and wives, whatever roles we have or choose, we can be responsible or irresponsible, conscientious or careless, virtuous or not.

A second advantage of being embedded in time and context is revealed only through time-lapse photography: in the progressive construction of a landscape unlike any other. In contrast to the science of both Aristotle and Newton, open, far-from-equilibrium systems theory incorporates individuality and concreteness into its very conceptual framework, thereby explaining those dynamics that make precise prediction impossible. Exact prediction and determination are possible only in a world of robots. In constrast, and as is true of all living and even some nonliving things, human beings progressively self-organize over time into uniquely individuated, multifaceted and complex persons. The person's hierarchical dynamics become increasingly specified (Salthe 1997)—his or her own self.

But in a world with room for unique individuals and the creativity and novelty they promote, precise prediction is impossible—thankfully. And this is the point the unhappy jurors must not forget. Too often we long for Newton's simple, clockwork universe, whose unambiguous, tidy formulas can resolve once and for all our uncertainty. The answer to the question, "When will the eclipse occur?" can be determined with astounding precision: "At 3:45 P.M. on December 11, 4022." We yearn for a metaphysics and an epistemology that will provide similar certitude when answering the question, "Was it first- or second-degree murder, or manslaughter?" For centuries, the theories of philosophers and scientists encouraged such yearnings. They are blameless, however (by reason of ignorance!), for not having understood that such a wish can be granted only to closed, linear systems, that is, to a determinist universe of cookie-cutter automata: "answered prayers," indeed.

In a complex world of astronomical dimensionality, the amount of variation even within regularities is astounding. There may be ethical problems involved in cloning, but producing identical copies is not one of them. Not even monozygotic twins are identical, either in appearance or behavior. It would be a much impoverished world it they were. However, living in a universe so richly creative as to have produced complex societies and unique individuals comes at a price. The very dynamics that allowed us to evolve the capacity to wink, and even to deliberate about whether we should wink, also prevent us from establishing with absolute certainty whether someone's past behavior was a wink or a blink, or from definitively predicting whether he or she will wink in the next few minutes.

We are enmeshed in a fabric of time and space, which we unravel at our peril. In part, we are the product of a complex dance between our innate endowments and an already structured physical and social environment. We are never passive in this entire process, however. Even the environment in which we are situated is itself, in part, the downstream consequence of our own upstream doings, both phylogenetically and ontogenetically. As such both culturally and individually, we bear a measure of responsibility for that environment. Once we are mature and aware, we can self-consciously select the stimuli to which we will respond and that will affect what and who we are in the future. At that point we are as responsible for who we will become as is the environment. And once again, this is true for each of us both as members of a community and as individuals.

Complex dynamical systems suggest, in other words, that although there is an ontological difference between a wink and a blink, and my vote as a juror will be based on my judgment as to which it was, it may be impossible to tell definitively and once and for all which was which. But the alternative is not total ignorance and impotence. We have the ability both to impart through example and to acquire as an exercise in personal responsibility the sensitivity to contextual nuances (spatial, historical, and cultural) in others and in ourselves that will enable us to better understand the dynamics and behavior of both. With that ability comes the obligation to nurture the practical wisdom with which we can make reasoned, reflective judgments about ourselves and the messy, complex world in which we live—and to act from that wisdom.

With any luck, we might be more often right than wrong.

Notes

1. Formal cause is often erroneously identified with shape. Although in the case of a vase, it is the vase's shape that makes it a vase, what is the formal cause that makes a particular eye movement a "wink"?
2. Even Newton, however, was aware of the so-called three-body problem: calculations that are simple for two planets go very badly when a third planet is brought in. The impossibility of idealizing every system as isolated would not be squarely faced until the twentieth century.
3. Chisholm (1995) has since reneged on this claim, maintaining instead that agent causation is a subspecies of event causation. Doing so permits him to retain the view of cause as constant conjunction.
4. Aristotle would have enjoyed the congressional questioning concerning the Watergate burglary: "What did President Nixon know and when did he know it?" In Aristotle's mind, a definitive answer to that question would have decided the issue of moral responsibility. Requiring awareness as a necessary condition of moral responsibility also plays a part in the McNaughton judicial ruling on "not guilty by reason of insanity" pleas.
5. We will see below how important it is for Aristotle that the possibility of self-cause be disallowed. Causes must always be other than the effects they bring about. I am indebted to Mary Louise Gill and James J. Lennox's (1994) anthology *Self-Motion: From Aristotle to Newton* for excellent essays on Aristotle's understanding of self-motion and self-cause.
6. Moreover, by setting up the problem in the way it did, philosophy thereby created another problem for itself, the problem of personal identity.
7. A curious sidebar of this entire subject matter is that as a result, Plato and Augustine won: voluntary behavior came to be considered free, not in Aristotle's sense of being partly routed through the agent, but in the sense of being totally unrelated to anything in the external world!
8. We sometimes do speak that way. "She killed her mother," we say, referring to something the daughter did ten years before the mother even became ill. So vague a concept of agency is useless.
9. Here Melden uses the word "motive" where others would use "intent." In part because "Why did you do that?" can be answered by describing either motive or intent, action theorists have not been as consistent as one would wish either in distinguishing these two mental states or in specifying the role that each plays in bringing about action. The "reason why the agent behaved the way (s)he did" is also ambiguous between motive and intent. See chapter 14 for legal implications of this distinction.
10. Because it has been used to mean many different things, I avoid the term "supervenience."
11. We will return to the subject of constant conjunction in the next two chapters.
12. By "mechanism" I mean Newtonian mechanics, and in particular the second law of mechanics, which states that a body tends to remain in its state of rest or motion unless acted upon by an external force.

13. Material causes have been taken for granted. Perhaps the controversy surrounding cognitive science will revive this topic.

14. Someone whose identity I have forgotten offered a wonderful objection: once my neighbor drops one of his shoes, I expect the other shoe to drop. These two constantly conjoined experiences lead me to expect the second after the first. But it would never occur to me that the first one caused the second!

15. Not until the middle of the twentieth century would the precise specification of initial conditions pose a problem for the ideal of explanation as prediction.

16. The tacit, un-Humean hope was that the regularity's lawfulness is underwritten by causal relations of the Newtonian, forceful sort.

17. More recent work in explanation theory (by van Fraasen [1980], Achinstein [1983], and others) has concentrated on the erotetics and pragmatics of explanation, its instrumental value, and so forth, not on its metaphysical aspects.

18. Reference to the agent's mental life makes Melden an unorthodox behaviorist. He remains a behaviorist, nonetheless, because he analyzes the contents of mental life in terms of stimulus-response patterns.

19. In the past fifteen years or so publications on the concept of design have focused by and large on biological functions, not on intentional human action.

20. Notice both the shift from metaphysics to epistemology, and the emphasis on intrinsic characterizations.

21. I have no quarrel with Wright's analysis insofar as it refers to biological functions (see Godfrey-Smith 1993). The issue at hand, however, is whether intentional action can be assimilated into the same analysis. My objections to Wright's analysis apply also to those by Nagel (1953), Braithwaite (1946), and Rosenblueth, Wiener, and Bigelow (1943)—indeed, to any other behaviorist reductions of purposive behavior, such as Sommerhof's.

22. Even in someone insisting on a behavioral analysis of teleology, the determinist universe begins to loosen into a probabilistic one, with the law in the major premise of the explanatory argument softening into a probabilistic one.

23. In this citation Nowell Smith does not distinguish between motives and intentions, perhaps because both have a "for the sake of" clause. In the example, Nowell Smith does not question whether the agent intended to run for office. The difference between the two cases would be a difference in trajectory: political ambition—run for office—gain fame in one case; patriotism—run for office—help one's country in the other. Part II proposes a way of tracking such trajectories. See also chapter 14 for legal implications of the differences between motive and intent.

24. Recall that for behaviorists, dispositions are not internal states of affairs. The term is merely a shorthand for the regular stimulus-response pattern itself.

25. In recent decades, the continuing inability of traditional artificial intelligence to preload computers with all the information necessary for intelligent action forced researchers to acknowledge the so-called frame problem: if all the information required for a computer to act must be on board for algorithmic processing to start, there is no reason to suppose that a decision will ever be reached in real time (Cherniak 1986).

26. Sometimes, the crackling of static noise on a phone line occurs only during the silent intervals between the spoken words. In cases like these, no message is lost; when the crackle occurs during the spoken words, on the other hand, the noise can occasion equivocation if information is lost in transmission.

27. So far I have employed an eviscerated notion of information: amount of information, not meaningful information. Had Susie been chosen instead of Herman, the amount of information transmitted would still have been 3 bits; that it was Herman and not Susie is irrelevant. We will return to the need for semantics and meaning later.

28. To anticipate: insofar as explanations of action tell us why the agent did A *rather than* B, the distinction between cause and information shows why those explanations will be informational, not mechanically causal explanations.

29. See Juarrero-Roqué, "Dispositions, Teleology, and Reductionism," *Philosophical Topics* 12 (1983a).

30. For a fascinating true account of a similar case, see Oliver Sacks's *A Leg To Stand On* (1987).

31. I will modify this claim somewhat in chapter 13.

32. In part II, I will argue that only a dynamical systems account can handle a multidimensional state space such as this multiplicity requires.

33. See Juarrero-Roqué (1983b), "Does Level Generation Always Generate Act-Tokens?"

34. This definition of structure comes out of biology, not structuralism.

35. Complex open systems that change over time as a result of interactions with their environment are often called "complex adaptive systems." More on this particular type of system below.

36. Here is an example where the word "structure" is being used to mean "organization."

37. A distinction must be made between ordinary feedback and adaptive control. In a thermostat, which is an example of ordinary feedback, the process by which it makes corrections is unchanging. An adaptive control mechanism, on the other hand, is a higher level of control in that it "modifies the process by which a lower level control device makes its 'corrections.' In adaptive control, in other words, a feedback device modifies a feedback device." If several of these adaptive control systems were mutually entrained, Dewan postulates that a "(super) adaptive optimum control system" would emerge that would adjust not only the performance index but also its method of correction. Hypercycles provide the means for the emergence of just such a superadaptive system.

38. Written before the elaboration of complex dynamical systems theory, Edward Pols's (1982) work on mental causation anticipates a hierarchical account of interlevel constraints.

39. Technically, "bifurcations" are features of mathematical models. The term, however, is often used to refer to the actual process.

40. Numerous terms have been used for variants of this phenomenon: *autopoiesis*, Francisco Varela's (1980) term, is often used even though Varela meant it to refer strictly to synchronic, homeostatic models. George Kampis (1991) prefers *autogenesis*, to include development; and Rod Swenson (1989) uses *autocatakinesis*, to connect it with thermodynamics.

41. Jeremy Campbell's *Grammatical Man* (1982) was the first to see the applicability of Lila Gatlin to philosophy of mind.

42. This is an important point since the term "information" *tout court* is often equated with randomness, suggesting that at equilibrium, actual information is at a maximum. It is information-carrying capacity (or information capacity, or informational entropy) that is maximal at equilibrium, not information content.

43. As we also saw, however, "Susie" or "Jack" or "Mary" would have carried the same 3 bits of information as "Herman." We still need to account for a robust sense of meaning.

44. Freud compared human psychology to a near-equilibrium dynamical system, with primitive forces and instincts serving as the piston that creates a pressure that must be released, thereby causing neuroses and spurring action.

45. It can, of course, cause a landslide, as Per Bak's (1988) famous example of self-organized criticality shows.

46. Does a cell's location on a blastula alter the probability that a particular gene will be expressed *there*, beginning the process of differentiation? The answer there, too, is yes, but let us stick to language for the moment.

47. The important point, of course, is that this kind of constraint also operates in chemistry and biology.

48. This is in this respect a poor example (deliberately chosen because of its link to the prior chapters): the existence of different types of molecules presupposes some form of organization. Without context-sensitive constraints already in place, different types of molecules would not exist.

49. According to Rod Swenson (1989), the second law of thermodynamics should be extended: processes do not just show an increase in entropy production; they tend toward maximum entropy production. Self-organizing processes satisfy that principle.

50. All different forms of network training share this "gradient descent" feature to minimize differences between input and output. It will be recalled that self-organization, too, dissipates the nonequilibrium.

51. For stylistic reasons I sometimes use "represents" and "representation" even when "embodies" or "realizes" might be more accurate.

52. Whether monkeys reach for a target as target is another matter. For this to be possible, the behavior must originate in an even higher-level semantic attractor. Thinking of dynamical systems as hierarchically organized can handle these subtle differences. Hierarchical levels, however, share homologous dynamics.

53. I use the term "conscious" and its cognates to refer to that property zombies and today's robots lack. Even if the cutoff point between zombies and robots on the one hand, and persons on the other is unclear, it seems undeniable that degrees of human consciousness exist. I reserve the term "self-consciousness" for either the property (1) being conscious of being conscious, or (2) being conscious of self. Whether (1) is necessary for (2)—or vice versa—is open to question. That toilet training, whether in dogs or humans, is effective even during sleep is evidence that organisms can learn to inhibit certain natural behavior even when self-consciousness is absent, which is why we punish dogs for soiling the carpet! It would be unreasonable for philosophers of mind to restrict the label "action" to those behaviors that issue only from self-conscious mental states. Could the agent have inhibited (otherwise natural) behavior? is probably the crucial issue in action theory. Could the agent's conscious—if not self-conscious—awareness of the behavior (of its significance, its consequences, etc.) have constrained it? will be pivotal in determining whether we hold the agent morally responsible and legally liable. See chapters 14 and 15 for more discussion on this subject.

54. In a multidimensional space, however, valleys intertwine, so that they would be impossible to pry apart epistemologically.

55. Jackie Kennedy is in some respects a poor example. For the same reason that Dascal and Gruengard (1981) exclude "marrying the only woman in Thebes with Rh negative blood"—that Oedipus could not be expected to know anything about blood composition—Jackie Kennedy should also be excluded from Oedipus's contrast set.

56. I am well aware of those who claim that Oedipus represents the appearance of the "modern" man, a person more confident of what he can accomplish through reasoning than someone who believes himself to be a puppet of moira. This interpretation just reinforces my claim that we must give priority to what is going on in the agent's mind when determining whether some instance of behavior constitutes an act-proper or not. This point does not entirely obviate Dascal and Gruengard's (1981) claim that social circumstances must be taken into account; it only involves determining to what extent the agent is or can be expected both to be aware of (and, in Oedipus's case, believe in) those circumstances.

57. Some religions used to refer to the "age of reason" (around age seven) as the minimal age at which a child can be assumed to understand right from wrong and similar concepts. Is it reasonable to identify this age as normally achieving a certain degree of semantic organization?

58. As befits a complex dynamical system, this will be true only in certain contexts. Teenage boys, for example, might consider it "cool" and the epitome of friendship to greet each other with insults.

59. This occurs, as described in the previous chapter, by the sudden alteration in the frequency distribution of behavioral alternatives.

60. It has been suggested that this regulation might be carried out either by a tensor transform (Pribram 1991; Pietsch 1981; Smolensky 1987) or by a "forcing function" (Kauffman 1993, 204).

61. Thinking of mental causes in this way not only naturalizes them, it also shows that the process is homologous to that exhibited by other "anticipative" systems. (See Salthe 1997, brought to my attention after this manuscript was completed.)

62. There is no guarantee that reorganization will occur. In all complex dynamical systems, the possibility of disintegration is ever present, as psychiatric wards show.

63. By "lay of the land," I mean all my other dynamics, in interaction with the environment.

64. A recent article in the *Washington Post* reported that no one winks anymore! Our understanding of the potential minefield of sexual politics has virtually eliminated that alternative from our universe of possibilities.

65. I am skeptical of the oft-mentioned significance (e.g., Restak 1983) of objections based on experiments (first conducted by Libet and Feinstein in 1969 and since replicated with variations) that show that conscious awareness often appears after the brain has begun motor activity. Dynamical systems illustrate that carving out the boundaries of various and intertwined neural organizations will be extremely difficult and always somewhat arbitrary. It will be very difficult, therefore, to determine at what particular moment a particular action began.

66. I was surprised at the similarity between this objection, formulated long ago, and Bratman's (1987) terrorist example.

67. The topological illustrations described earlier are useful: nothing can be simultaneously a ridge and a valley.

68. There is evidence that sensory perception is under cognitive control even during some phases of sleep. Whereas loud but familiar sounds will not wake us up, soft sounds that signal a potentially dangerous condition will.

69. This has negative implications for free will only if this concept is envisioned as a Newtonian cause that itself must have no earlier causes.

70. More on *akrasia* in part III.

71. This book's implicit claim, of course, is that so does philosophy in general. For example, the substantive pronouncements of action theory can be understood, evaluated, and corrected only by situating them in the overall context of the history of philosophy and science. In turn, the flaws of this history are best exposed by noting the difficulties they occasion for action theory. Hence the strange-loop tacking that has characterized this book.

72. A correct explanation must reconstruct the agent's contrast space, not the explainer's.

73. Federal Rule of Evidence 404 states that evidence of previous crimes is not admissible to establish that the defendant has a generalized propensity toward bad character or criminal activity. However, such evidence is admissible to prove facts at issue in the particular case. These can include motive, opportunity, or intent.

74. The involuntary coprolalia uttered by sufferers of Tourette's syndrome might be an example of weak semantic constraints.

75. I am not suggesting that an autocatalytic web acts intentionally or teleologically; it takes the degree of complexity of the human brain to construct the incredibly high-dimensional attractor that describes a full-blown intention. I am suggesting only that homologous dynamics are likely to be at work in both cases.

References

Abraham, R. 1987. Dynamics and self-organization. In *Self-Organizing Systems: The Emergence of Order*. ed. E. Yates. New York: Plenum.

Achinstein, P. 1983. *The Nature of Explanation*. New York: Oxford University Press.

Allen, P., and M. Sanglier. 1980. Order by fluctuation and the urban system. In *Autopoiesis, Dissipative Stuctures, and Spontaneous Social Orders*, ed. M. Zeleny. Boulder, CO: Westview.

Alvarez de Lorenzana, J. 1993. The constructive universe and the evolutionary systems framework. Appendix to S. N. Salthe, *Development and Evolution: Complexity and Change in Biology*. Cambridge, MA: MIT Press.

Aristotle. 1968. *The Basic Works of Aristotle*, ed. R. McKeon. New York: Random House.

Armstrong, D. 1980a. Acting and trying. In *The Nature of Mind and Other Essays*. Ithaca, NY: Cornell University Press.

Armstrong, D. 1980b. The causal theory of the mind. In *The Nature of Mind and Other Essays*. Ithaca, NY: Cornell University Press.

Artigiani, R. 1992. Chaos and constitutionalism: Toward a post-modern theory of social evolution. *World Futures* 34: 131–56.

Artigiani, R. 1995a. Self, system and emergent complexity. *Evolution and Cognition* 1(2): 137–47.

Artigiani, R. 1995b. Toward a science of meaning. *Technological Forecasting and Social Change* 48: 111–28.

Artigiani, R. 1996a. Contemporary science and the search for symmetry in nature and society. *Symmetry: Culture and Science* 7(3): 231–46.

Artigiani, R. 1996b. Societal computation and the emergence of mind. *Evolution and Cognition* 2(1): 2–15.

Artigiani, R. 1997. Interaction, information, and meaning. *World Futures* 50: 703–14.

Artigiani, R. 1998. Social information: The person is the message. *Biosystems* 46: 137–44.

Audi, R. 1995. Mental causation: Sustaining and dynamic. In *Mental Causation*, ed. J. Heil and A. Mele. Oxford: Oxford University Press.

Austin, J. 1961. Performative utterances. In *Philosophical Papers*. Oxford: Oxford University Press.

Baier, K. 1965. *The Moral Point of View*. New York: Random House.

Bak, P., C. Tang, and K. Wiesenfeld. 1988. Self-organized criticality. *Physical Review A* 38: 364–374.

Bakhtin, M. M. 1993. *Toward a Philosophy of the Act*. Austin, TX: University of Texas Press.

Bechtel, W., and A. Abrahamsen. 1991. *Connectionism and the Mind: An Introduction to Parallel Processing in Networks*. Cambridge, MA: Basil Blackwell.

Benedict, R. 1989. *Chrysanthemum and the Sword: Patterns of Japanese Culture*. Boston: Houghton Mifflin.

Bertalanffy, L. von. 1981. *A Systems View of Man*. Boulder, CO: Westview Press.

Blakeslee, S. 1997. Solution offered to old puzzle: how the cortex got its folds. *The New York Times* (January 28): C3.

Bohm, D. 1971. *Causality and Chance in Modern Physics*. Philadelphia: University of Pennsylvania Press.

Boltzmann, L. 1877. Uber die Beziehung eines allgemeine mechanischen Satzes zum zweiten Hauptsatzes der Warmetheorie. *Sitzungsber. Akad. Wiss. Wien, Math.-Naturwiss. Kl.* 75: 67–73.

Boyd, R. 1979. Metaphor and theory change: What is "metaphor" a metaphor for? In *Metaphor and Thought*, ed. A. Ortony. Cambridge: Cambridge University Press.

Braithwaite, R. 1946. Teleological explanations. *Proceedings of the Aristotelian Society* 47: i–xx.

Braithwaite, R. 1953. *Scientific Explanation*. Cambridge: Cambridge University Press.

Brand, M., ed. 1970. *The Nature of Human Action*. Glenview, IL: Scott, Foresman.

Brand, M. 1980. Philosophical action theory and the foundation of motivational psychology. In *Action and Responsibility*, ed. M. Bradie and M. Brand. Bowling Green Studies in Applied Philosophy.

Brand, M. 1984. *Intending and Acting*. Cambridge, MA: MIT Press.

Brand, M., and D. Walton, eds. 1976. *Action Theory*. Dordrecht: D. Reidel.

Bratman, M. 1987. *Intentions, Plans and Practical Reason*. Cambridge, MA: Harvard University Press.

Brooks, D., and E. Wiley. 1988. *Evolution as Entropy*. 2nd ed. Chicago: University of Chicago Press.

Bunge, M. 1979. *Ontology II: A World of Systems*. Dordrecht: D. Reidel.

Campbell, J. 1982. *Grammatical Man*. New York: Simon and Schuster.

Casti, J. 1994. *Complexification*. New York: Harper Collins.

Champlin, T. 1988. *Reflexive Paradoxes*. London: Routledge.

Cherniak, C. 1986. *Minimal Rationality*. Cambridge, MA: MIT Press.

Chiel, H., and R. Beer. 1993. Neural and peripheral dynamics as determinants of patterned motor behavior. In *The Neurobiology of Neural Networks*, ed. D. Gardner. Cambridge, MA: MIT Press.

Chisholm, R. 1964. The descriptive element in the concept of action. *Journal of Philosophy* 61: 613–25.

Chisholm, R. 1995. Agents, causes & events: The problem of free will. In *Agents, Causes, Events: Essays on Indeterminism and Free Will*, ed. T. O'Connor. Oxford: Oxford University Press.

Churchland, P. M. 1989. *A Neurocomputational Perspective: The Nature of Mind and the Structure of Science*. Cambridge, MA: MIT Press.

Churchland, P. S. 1986. *Neurophilosophy: Toward a Unified Science of the Mind*. Cambridge, MA: MIT Press.

Cohen, J. 1950. Teleological explanation. *Proceedings of the Aristotelian Society* 51: 225–92.

Collier, J. 1986. Entropy in evolution. *Biology and Philosophy* 1: 5–24.

Collier, J. 1988. The dynamics of biological order. In *Entropy, Information and Evolution*, ed. B. Weber, D. Depew, and J. Smith. Cambridge, MA: MIT Press.

Compton, J. 1979. Human science, human action, and human nature. *Tulane Studies in Philosophy* 18: 39–62.

Copleston, F. 1962. *A History of Philosophy*. Vol 1, part II. Garden City, NJ: Doubleday.

Cover, R. 1983. The Supreme Court, 1982 term. Foreword: Nomos and narrative. *Harvard Law Review* 97: 4–68.

Damasio, A. 1989. Time-locked multiregional retroactivation. *Cognition* 33: 25–62.

Damasio, A. 1994. *Descartes' Error*. New York: Grosset/Putnam.

Danto, A. 1973. *Analytic Philosophy of Action*. Cambridge: Cambridge University Press.

Danto, A. 1976. Action, knowledge and representation. In *Action Theory*, eds. M. Brand and D. Walton. Dordrecht: D. Reidel.

Danto, A. 1979a. Basic actions and basic concepts. *Review of Metaphysics* 32: 471–85.

Danto, A. 1979b. Causality, representations, and the explanation of actions. *Tulane Studies in Philosophy* 28: 1–19.

Dascal, M., and O. Gruengard. 1981. Unintentional action and non-action. *Manuscrito* 4: 103–13.

Davidson, D. 1963. Actions, reasons and causes. *Journal of Philosophy* 60: 685–700. (Reprinted in Davidson 1980.)

Davidson, D. 1967. The logical form of action sentences. (Reprinted in Davidson 1980.)

Davidson, D. 1970. Mental events. In *Experience and Theory*, ed. L. Foster and J. Swanson. Amherst: University of Massachusetts Press. (Reprinted in Davidson 1980.)

Davidson, D. 1971. Agency. In *The Nature of Human Action*, ed. R. Binkley. Toronto: University of Toronto Press.

Davidson, D. 1980. *Essays on Actions and Events*. Oxford: Oxford University Press.

Davidson, D. 1995. Thinking causes. In *Mental Causation*, ed. J. Heil and A. Mele. Oxford: Oxford University Press.

Davis, L. 1970. Individuation of actions. *Journal of Philosophy* 67: 520–30.

Davis, L. 1979. *Theory of Action*. Englewood Cliffs, NJ: Prentice-Hall.

Dennett, D. 1987. *The Intentional Stance*. Cambridge, MA: MIT Press.

Depew, D. 1997. Etiological approaches to biological aptness in Aristotle and Darwin. In *Aristotelische Biologie: Intentionen, Methoden, Ergebniss*, ed. W. Kullmann and S. Follinger. Franz Steiner.

Depew, D. 1998. Darwinism and developmentalism: Prospects for convergence. In *Evolutionary Systems: Biological and Epistemological Perspectives on Selection and Self-Organization*, ed. G. van de Vijver, et al. Dordrecht: Kluwer.

Depew, D., and Weber, B. 1995. *Darwinism Evolving*. Cambridge, MA: MIT Press.

Dewan, E. 1976. Consciousness as an emergent causal agent in the context of control system theory. In *Consciousness and the Brain*, ed. Globus et al. New York: Plenum.

Donald. M. 1991. *Origins of the Modern Mind*. Cambridge, MA: Harvard University Press.

Dretske, F. 1972. Contrastive statements. *Philosophical Review* 81: 411–37.

Dretske, F. 1981. *Knowledge and the Flow of Information*. Cambridge, MA: MIT Press.

Dretske, F. 1983. Mental events as structuring causes of behavior. In *Mental Causation*, ed. J. Heil and A. Mele. Oxford University Press.

Dretske, F. 1988. *Explaining Behavior: Reasons in a World of Causes*. Cambridge, MA: MIT Press.

Dreyfus, H. 1972. *What Computers Can't Do: The Limits of Artificial Intelligence*. New York: Harper and Row.

Dupré, J. 1993. *The Disorder of Things*. Cambridge, MA: Harvard University Press.

Dyke, C. 1988. *The Evolutionary Dynamics of Complex Systems*. Oxford: Oxford University Press.

Earley, J. 1981. Self-organization and agency: In chemistry and process philosophy. *Process Studies* 11: 242–58.

Eco, U. 1976. *A Theory of Semiotics*. Bloomington, IN: Indiana University Press.

Eco, U. 1990. *The Limits of Interpretation*. Bloomington, IN: Indiana University Press.

Edelman, G. 1987. *Neural Darwinism: The Theory of Neuronal Group Selection*. New York: Basic Books.

Elman, J. 1995. Language as a dynamical system. In *Mind as Motion*, ed. R. Port and T. van Gelder. Cambridge, MA: MIT Press.

Ermarth, E. 1992. *Sequel to History*. Princeton, NJ: Princeton University Press.

Fetz, E. 1993. Dynamic neural network models of sensorimotor behavior. In *The Neurobiology of Neural Networks*, ed. D. Gardner. Cambridge, MA: MIT Press.

Fischer, R. 1990. Why the mind is not in the head but in the society's connectionist network. *Diogenes* 151: 1–28.

Fishbein, M., and Ajzen, I. 1975. *Belief, Attitude, Intention, and Behavior*. Reading, MA: Addison-Wesley.

Fodor, J., and Pylshyn, Z. 1988. Connectionism and cognitive architecture: A critical analysis. *Cognition* 28: 3–71.

Foster, L., and Swanson, J. eds. 1970. *Experience and Theory*. Amherst: University of Massachusetts Press.

Frankfurt, H. 1978. The problem of action. *American Philosophical Quarterly* 15: 157–62.

Freeland, C. A. 1994. "Aristotle on perception, appetition, and self-motion." In *Self-Motion: From Aristotle to Newton*, ed. Gill and Lennox. Princeton, NJ: Princeton University Press.

Freeman, W. 1991a. Nonlinear dynamics in olfactory information processing. In *Olfaction*, ed. J. Davis and H. Eichenbaum. Cambridge, MA: MIT Press.

Freeman, W. 1991b. The physiology of perception. *Scientific American* (February): 78–85.

Freeman, W. 1995. *Societies of Brains: A Study in the Neuroscience of Love and Hate*. Hillsdale, NJ: Erlbaum.

Furley, D. 1978. "Self-Movers." In *Aristotle on Mind and the Senses*, ed. G. E. R. Lloyd and G. E. L. Owen. Proceedings of the Seventh Symposium Aristotelicum. Cambridge, 165–79. Reprinted in Gill and Lennox.

Gadamer, H. G. 1985. *Truth and Method*. New York: Crossroad.

Gardner, D., ed. 1993. *The Neurobiology of Neural Networks*. Cambridge, MA: MIT Press.

Garfinkel, A. 1981. *Forms of Explanation*. New Haven, CT: Yale University Press.

Garfinkel, A. 1987. The slime mold dictyostelium as a model of self-organization in social systems. In *Self-Organizing Systems*, ed. E. Yates, et al. New York: Plenum.

Gatlin, L. 1972. *Information and the Living System*. New York: Columbia University Press.

Geertz, C. 1979. From a native's point of view: On the nature of anthropological understanding. In *Interpretive Social Science: A Reader*, ed. P. Rabinow and W. M. Sullivan. Berkeley and Los Angeles: University of California Press.

Georgopoulos, A. 1990. Neurophysiology of reaching. In *Attention and Performance*, ed. M. Jeannerod. Hillsdale, NJ: Erlbaum.

Gill, M., and J. Lennox, eds. 1994. *Self-Motion: From Aristotle to Newton*. Princeton, NJ: Princeton University Press.

Ginet, C. 1990. *On Action*. Cambridge: Cambridge University Press.

Ginet, C. 1995. Reasons explanation of action: An incompatibilist account. In *Agents, Causes, and Events: Essays on Indeterminism and Free Will*, ed. T. O'Connor. New York: Oxford University Press.

Glass, L., and M. Mackey 1988. *From Clocks to Chaos*. Princeton, NJ: Princeton University Press.

Gleick, J. 1987. *Chaos*. New York: Viking.

Globus, G., G. Maxwell, and I. Savodnik, eds. 1976. *Consciousness and the Brain*. New York: Plenum.

Godfrey-Smith, P. 1993. Functions: Consensus without unity. *Pacific Philosophical Quarterly* 74: 196–208.

Goldman, A. 1970. *A Theory of Human Action*. Englewood Cliffs, NJ: Prentice-Hall. (Reprinted as a Princeton Paperback, 1976.)

Goodwin, B. 1987. Developing organisms as self-organizing fields. In *Self-Organizing Systems*, ed. E. Yates. New York: Plenum.

Grobstein, C. 1973. The organization of complex systems. In *Hierarchy Theory*, ed. H. Pattee. New York: George Braziller.

Hacker, A. 1995. Twelve angry persons. *The New York Review of Books*. September 21: 44–49.

Haken, H. 1983. *Synergetics: An Introduction*. Berlin: Springer-Verlag.

Haken, H. 1987. Synergetics. An approach to self-organization. In *Self-Organizing Systems*, ed. E. Yates. New York: Plenum.

Harman, G. 1976. Practical reasoning. *Review of Metaphysics* 79: 431–63.

Harré, R., and G. Gillett. 1994. *The Discursive Mind*. Thousand Oaks, CA: Sage Publications, Inc.

Hausheer, R. 1980. Introduction to Isaiah Berlin. In *Against the Current: Essays in the History of Ideas*, ed. H. Hardy. New York: Viking.

Hayles, N. K. 1990. *Chaos Bound*. Ithaca, NY: Cornell University Press.

Heckhausen, H., and J. Beckmann. 1990. Intentional action and action slips. *Psychological Review* 97: 36–48.

Heil, J., and A. Mele, eds. 1995. *Mental Causation*. Oxford: Oxford University Press.

Hempel, C. 1965. *Aspects of Scientific Explanation and Other Essays in the Philosophy of Science*. New York: Free Press.

Hempel, C., and P. Oppenheim. 1948. Studies in the logic of explanation. *Philosophy of Science* 15: 135–75.

Hinton, G. E. 1992. How neural networks learn from experience. *Scientific American* 267 (September): 145–51.

Hinton, G., and T. Shallice. 1991. Lesioning an attractor network: investigations of acquired dyslexia. *Psychological Review* 98 (January): 74–95.

Hinton, G. E. D., C. Plaut, and T. Shallice. 1993. Simulating brain damage. *Scientific American* 269 (October): 76–82.

Hofstadter, D. 1979. *Gödel, Escher and Bach*. New York: Basic Books.

Holling, E. 1976. Resilience and stability in ecosystems. In *Evolution and Consciousness*, ed. E. Jantsch and C. Waddington. Reading, MA: Addison-Wesley.

Holyoak, K., and P. Thagard. 1995. *Mental Leaps*. Cambridge, MA: MIT Press.

Hume, D. 1977 [1748]. *An Enquiry Concerning Human Understanding*. Indianapolis: Hackett.

Hume, D. 1964 [1739–40]. *A Treatise of Human Nature*. Oxford: Oxford University Press.

Jantsch, E. 1980. *The Self-Organizing Universe*. Oxford: Pergamon.

Jantsch, E., ed. 1981. *The Evolutionary Vision*. Boulder, CO: Westview.

Jantsch, E., and C. Waddington, eds. 1976. *Evolution and Consciousness: Human Systems in Transition*. Reading, MA: Addison-Wesley.

Juarrero, A. 1998. Causality as constraint. In *Evolutionary Systems: Biological and Epistemological Perspectives on Selection and Self-Organization*, ed. G. van de Vijver, et al. Dordrecht: Kluwer.

Juarrero-Roqué, A. 1983a. Dispositions, teleology, and reductionism. *Philosophical Topics* 12: 153–65.

Juarrero-Roqué, A. 1983b. Does level-generation always generate act-tokens? *Philosophy Research Archives* 9: 177–92.

Juarrero-Roqué, A. 1985. Kant's concept of teleology and modern chemistry. *Review of Metaphysics* 39: 107–35.

Juarrero-Roqué, A. 1987–88. Does action theory rest on a mistake? *Philosophy Research Archives* 13: 587–612.

Juarrero-Roqué, A. 1988a. Non-linear phenomena, explanation and action. *International Philosophical Quarterly* 28: 247–55.

Juarrero-Roqué, A. 1988b. "What did the agent know?" *Manuscrito* 11: 108–13.

Juarrero-Roqué, A. 1991. Fail-safe versus safe-fail: Suggestions toward an evolutionary model of justice. *Texas Law Review* 69(7): 1745–77.

Juarrero-Roqué, A. Language competence and tradition-constituted rationality. *Philosophy and Phenomenological Research* 51: 611–17.

Kampis, G. 1991. *Self-Modifying Systems in Biology and Cognitive Science: a New Framework for Dynamics, Information, and Complexity*. Oxford: Pergamon.

Kant, I. 1980. The critique of teleological judgement. In *The Critique of Judgement*, trans. J. C. Meredith. Oxford: Oxford University Press.

Kauffman, S. 1991. Antichaos and adaptation. *Scientific American* 265 (August): 78–84.

Kauffman, S. 1993. *The Origins of Order*. Oxford: Oxford University Press.

Kim, J. 1984. Epiphenomenal and supervenient causation. *Midwest Studies in Philosophy* 9: 257–70.

Kim, J. 1995. Can supervenience and "non-strict laws" save anomalous monism? In *Mental Causation*, ed. J. Heil and A. Mele. Oxford: Oxford University Press.

Kosslyn, S., and O. Koenig. 1992. *Wet Mind*. New York: Free Press.

Kuhn, T. 1970. The *Structure of Scientific Revolutions*. 2nd ed. Chicago: University of Chicago Press.

Lawson, H. 1985. *Reflexivity*. La Salle, ILL: Open Court.

Lewin, R. 1992. *Complexity: Life at the Edge of Chaos*. New York: Macmillan.

Lewis, D. 1973a. Causation. *Journal of Philosophy* 70: 556–67. (Reprinted in Sosa and Tooley 1993.)

Lewis, D. 1973b. *Counterfactuals*. Cambridge: Cambridge University Press.

Lewis, D. 1986. Causal explanation. In *Philosophical Papers II*. Oxford: Oxford University Press.

Lindsay, R. 1961. *Physical Mechanics*. Princeton, NJ: Van Nostrand.

Lockery, S., and T. Sejnowski. 1993. Realistic network models of distributed processing in the leech. In *The Neurobiology of Neural Networks*, ed. D. Gardner. Cambridge, MA: MIT Press.

MacIntyre, A. 1981. *After Virtue*. Notre Dame, IN: Notre Dame University Press.

Marchal, J. 1975. On the concept of a system. *Philosophy of Science* 42: 448–468.

Malcolm, N. 1968. The conceivability of mechanism. *Philosophical Review* 77: 45–72.

Maturana, H. 1980. Autopoiesis: Reproduction, heredity and evolution. In *Autopoiesis, Dissipative Structures, and Spontaneous Social Orders*, ed. M. Zeleny. Boulder, CO: Westview.

McCann, H. 1986. Intrinsic intentionality. *Theory and Decision* 20: 247–73.

McClamrock, R. 1995. *Existential Cognition: Computational Minds in the World*. Chicago: University of Chicago Press.

Melden, A. 1961. *Free Action*. New York: Humanities Press.

Mele, A. 1992. *Springs of Action*. New York: Oxford University Press.

Mele, A. 1995. *Autonomous Agents*. New York: Oxford University Press.

Merzenich, M., T. Allard, and W. Jenkins. 1990. Neural ontogeny of higher brain function: Implications of some recent neurophysiological findings. In *Information Processing in the Somatosensory System*, ed. O. Franzn and P. Westman. New York: Macmillan.

Metzger, M. 1995. Multiprocess models applied to cognitive and behavioral dynamics. In *Mind as Motion*, ed. R. Port and T. van Gelder. Cambridge, MA: MIT Press.

Minow, M. 1987. The Supreme Court, 1986 term. Foreword: Justice engendered. *Harvard Law Review* 101: 10–95.

Nagel, E. 1953. Teleological explanation and teleological systems. In *Vision and Action*, ed. S. Ratner. New Brunswick, N.J.: Rutgers University Press.

Nagel, E. 1961. *The Structure of Science: Problems in the Logic of Scientific Explanation*. New York: Harcourt, Brace and World.

Nagel, T. 1989. *The View from Nowhere*. Oxford: Oxford University Press.

Nowell Smith, P. 1954. *Ethics*. Harmondsworth: Penguin Books.

Nussbaum, M. 1990. *Love's Knowledge*. New York: Oxford University Press.

O'Connor, T., ed. 1995. *Agents, Causes, and Events: Essays on Indeterminism and Free Will*. New York: Oxford University Press.

Ortega y Gassett, J. 1960. *What Is Philosophy?* New York: W.W. Norton.

Pattee, H. 1973. The physical basis and origin of hierarchical control. In *Hierarchy Theory*, ed. H. Pattee. New York: George Braziller.

Penfield, W. 1975. *The Mystery of the Mind*. Princeton, NJ: Princeton University Press.

Peters, R. 1958. *The Concept of Motivation*. New York: Humanities Press.

Petitot, J. 1995. Morphodynamics and attractor syntax: Constituency in visual perception and cognitive grammar. In *Mind as Motion*, ed. R. Port and T. van Gelder. Cambridge, MA: MIT Press.

Piaget, J. 1975. *The Development of Thought: Equilibration of Cognitive Structures*. New York: Viking.

Pietsch, P. 1981. *Shufflebrain*. Boston: Houghton Mifflin.

Pols, E. 1975. *Meditation on a Prisoner: Towards Understanding Action and Mind*. Carbondale, IL: Southern Illinois University Press.

Pols, E. 1982. *The Acts of Our Being: A Reflection on Agency and Responsibility*. Amherst: University of Massachusetts Press.

Popper, K. 1990. *A World of Propensities*. Bristol: Thoemmes.

Port, R., F. Cummins, and J. McAuley. 1995. Naive time, temporal patterns, and human audition. In *Mind as Motion*, ed. R. Port and T. van Gelder. Cambridge, MA: MIT Press.

Port, R., and T. van Gelder, eds. 1995. *Mind as Motion*. Cambridge, MA: MIT Press.

Pribram, K. H. 1991. *Brain and Perception: Holonomy and Structure in Figural Processing*. Hillsdale, NJ: Erlbaum.

Prichard, H. A. 1949. Action, willing, desiring. In *Moral Obligation*. Oxford: Clarendon.

Prigogine, I. 1976. Order through fluctuation: Self-organization and social system. In *Evolution and Consciousness: Human Systems in Transition*, ed. E. Jantsch and C. Waddington. Reading, MA: Addison-Wesley.

Prigogine, I. 1996. *The End of Certainty: Time, Chaos, and the New Laws of Nature*. New York: Free Press.

Prigogine, I., and I. Stengers. 1984. *Order out of Chaos: Man's New Dialogue with Nature*. New York: Bantam.

Putnam, H. 1975. The meaning of meaning. In *Mind, Language and Reality: Philosophical Papers*. Vol. 2. Cambridge: Cambridge University Press.

Quine, W. 1953. Two dogmas of empiricism. In *From a Logical Point of View*. Cambridge, MA: Harvard University Press.

Rawls, J. 1955. Two concepts of rules. *Philosophical Review* 64: 3–32.

Rescher, N. 1970. *Scientific Explanation*. New York: Free Press.

Rescher, N. 1979. *Cognitive Systematization: A Systems-Theoretic Approach to a Coherentist Theory of Knowledge*. Totowa, NJ: Rowan and Littlefield.

Restak, R. 1983. Is free will a fraud? *Science Digest* (October): 53–55.

Rorty, R. 1979. *Philosophy and the Mirror of Nature*. Princeton, NJ: Princeton University Press.

Rosen, R. 1985. *Anticipatory Systems*. Oxford: Pergamon.

Rosen, S. 1980. *The Limits of Analysis*. New York: Basic Books.

Rosenblueth, A. 1970. *Mind and Brain*. Cambridge, MA: MIT Press.

Rosenblueth, A., N. Wiener, and J. Bigelow. 1943. Behavior, purpose and teleology. *Philosophy of Science* 10: 18–24.

Rubino, C. 1990. The evolution of our choices: Notes toward an ethics of uncertainty. In *Toward a Just Society for Future Generations*, ed. B. H. Banathy and B. A. Banathy. *Proceedings of the 34th Annual Meeting of the International Society for the System Sciences* 1: 205–12.

Rubino, C. 1993. Managing the future: Science, the humanities, and the myth of omniscience. *World Futures* 38: 157–164.

Rueger, A. and W. D. Sharp. 1996. Simple theories in a messy world: truth and explanatory power in nonlinear dynamics. *British Journal for Philosophy of Science* 47: 93–112.

Ryle, G. 1949. *The Concept of Mind*. New York: Barnes and Noble.

Sacks, O. 1987. *A Leg to Stand On*. New York: Harper & Row.

Salmon, W. 1965. The status of prior probabilities in statistical explanation. *Philosophy of Science* 32: 137–46.

Salmon, W. 1977. A third dogma of empiricism. In *Basic Problems in Methodology and Linguistics*, ed. R. Butts and J. Hintikka. Dordrecht: D. Reidel.

Salmon, W. 1990. *Four Decades of Scientific Explanation*. Minneapolis, MN: University of Minnesota Press.

Salthe, S. 1985. *Evolving Hierarchical Systems*. New York: Columbia University Press.

Salthe, S. 1993a. Development and evolution as aspects of self-organization. In *Theory of Evolution—In Need of a New Synthesis?* ed. M. Sintonen and S. Siren. *Philosophical Studies from the University of Tampere* 50: 5–19.

Salthe, S. 1993b. *Development and Evolution*. Cambridge, MA: MIT Press.

Salthe, S. 1997. Modeling anticipative systems. In *Advances in Modeling of Anticipative Systems*, ed. G. E. Lasker, D. Dubois and B. Teiling. International Institute for Advanced Studies in Systems Research and Cybernetics.

Searle, J. 1981. The intentionality of intention and action. *Manuscrito* 4: 77–101.

Searle, J. 1982. The Chinese room revisited: response to further commentaries on 'Minds, brains, and programs.' *Behavioral and Brain Sciences* 5: 345–48.

Searle, J. 1983. *Intentionality*. Cambridge: Cambridge University Press.

Searle, J. 1984. *Minds, Brains and Science*. Cambridge, MA: Harvard University Press.

Searle, J. 1992. *The Rediscovery of the Mind*. Cambridge, MA: MIT Press.

Shannon, C. 1948. The mathematical theory of communication. *Bell System Technical Journal* (July and October). Reprinted with the same title, and an introductory essay by Warren Weaver, by the University of Illinois Press, 1949.

Shannon, C., and W. Weaver. 1949. *The Mathematical Theory of Communication*. Urbana, ILL: University of Illinois Press.

Simon, H. 1957. *Models of Man*. New York: John Wiley.

Simon, H. 1973. The organization of complex systems. In *Hierarchy Theory*, ed. H. Pattee. New York: George Braziller.

Skinner, B. F. 1953. *Science and Human Behavior*. New York. Macmillan.

Smolensky, P. 1987. The constituent structure of connectionist mental states: A reply to Fodor and Pylshyn. *Southern Journal of Philosophy* 26 (Supplement): 137–63.

Snow, C. P. 1964. *Two Cultures and a Second Look*. Cambridge: Cambridge University Press.

Sommerhof, G. 1989. *Analytical Biology*. Oxford: Oxford University Press.

Sosa, E. 1980. Varieties of causation. *Grazer Philosophische Studien* 11: 93–103. (Reprinted in Sosa and Tooley 1993.)

Sosa, E. 1984. "Mind-body interaction and supervenient causation." *Midwest Studies in Philosophy* 9: 271–81.

Sosa, E., and M. Tooley, eds. 1993. *Causation*. Oxford: Oxford University Press.

Stent, G., W. Kristan, W. Friesen, C. Ort, M. Poon, and R. Calabrese. 1978. Neuronal generation of the leech swimming movement. *Science* 200: 1348–57.

Strawson, P. 1959. *Individuals: An Essay in Descriptive Metaphysics*. London: Methuen.

Swenson, R. 1989. Emergent attractors and the law of maximum entropy production. *Systems Research* 6: 187–97.

Taylor, C. 1964. *Explanation of Behavior*. London: Routledge and Kegan Paul.

Taylor, R. 1966. *Action and Purpose*. Atlantic Highlands, NJ: Humanities Press.

Taylor, R. 1970a. Simple action and volition. In *The Nature of Human Action*, ed. M. Brand. Glenview, IL: Scott Foresman.

Taylor, R. 1970b. Thought and purpose. In *The Nature of Human Action*, ed. M. Brand. Glenview, IL: Scott Foresman.

Thelen, E. 1986. Treadmill-elicited stepping in seven-month-old infants. *Child Development* 57: 1498–1506.

Thelen, E. 1995. Time-scale dynamics and the development of an embodied cognition. In *Mind as Motion*, ed. R. Port and T. van Gelder. Cambridge, MA: MIT Press.

Thelen, E., and D. M. Fisher. 1983. The organization of spontaneous leg movements in new-born infants. *Journal of Motor Behavior* 15: 353–377.

Thelen, E., and L. B. Smith. 1994. *A Dynamic Systems Approach to the Development of Cognition and Action*. Cambridge, MA: MIT Press.

Thom, R. 1975. *Structural Stability and Morphogenesis*. Reading, MA: Addison-Wesley.

Thomson, J. J. 1971. The time of a killing. *Journal of Philosophy* 68: 115–32.

Thomson, J. J. 1977. *Acts and Other Events*. Ithaca, NY: Cornell University Press.

Toffler, A. 1991. *Future Shock*. New York: Bantam.

Tooley, M. 1987. *Causation: A Realist Approach*. Oxford: Clarendon Press.

Toulmin, S. 1990. *Cosmopolis*: The Hidden Agenda of Modernity: New York: Free Press.

Ulanowicz, R. 1986. *Growth and Development*. Berlin: Springer-Verlag.

Ulanowicz, R. 1990. Aristotelean causalities in ecosystem development. *Oikos* 57: 42–48.

Ulanowicz, R. 1995. The propensities of evolving systems. In *Social and Natural Complexity*, ed. E. Khalil and K. Boulding. London: Routledge.

Ulanowicz, R. 1997. *Ecology: The Ascendent Perspective*. New York: Columbia University Press.

Ulanowicz, R., and B. Hannon. 1987. Life and the production of entropy. *Proceedings of the Royal Society of London* 3232: 181–92.

van de Vijver, G. 1998. Evolutionary systems and the four causes: A real Aristotelian story? In *Evolutionary Systems: Biological and Epistemological Perspectives on Selection and Self-Organization*, ed. G. van de Vijver, et al. Dordrecht: Kluwer.

van de Vijver, G., S. Salthe, and M. Delpos, eds. 1998. *Evolutionary Systems: Biological and Epistemological Perspectives on Selection and Self-Organization*. Dordrecht: Kluwer.

van Fraassen, B. 1980. *The Scientific Image*. Oxford: Oxford University Press.

van Gelder, T. 1990. Compositionality: A connectionist variation on a classical theme. *Cognitive Science* 14: 355–84.

van Gelder, T. 1992. Connectionism and dynamical explanation. In *Proceedings of the 13th Annual Conference of the Cognitive Science Society*, Chicago.

van Gulick, R. 1995. Who's in charge here? And who's doing all the work? In *Mental Causation*, ed. J. Heil and A. Mele. Oxford: Oxford University Press.

Waldrop, M. 1992. *Complexity: The Emerging Science at the Edge of Order and Chaos*. New York: Simon and Schuster.

Weber, B., D. Depew, and J. Smith, eds. 1988. *Entropy, Information and Evolution*. Cambridge, MA: MIT Press.

Wilson, G. 1989. *The Intentionality of Human Action*. Stanford, CA: Stanford University Press.

Wimsatt, W. 1976. Reductionism, levels of organization, and the mind-body problem. In *Consciousness and the Brain*, ed. G. Globus, G. Maxwell, and I. Savodnik. New York: Plenum.

Winter, S. 1989. The cognitive dimension of the *Agon* between legal power and narrative meaning. *Michigan Law Review* 87: 2225–79.

Winter, S. 1990. Indeterminacy and incommensurability in constitutional law. *California Law Review* 78: 1441–1551.

Woodfield, A. 1976. *Teleology*. Cambridge: Cambridge University Press.

Wright, L. 1976. *Teleological Explanations*. Berkeley and Los Angeles: University of California Press.

Yates, F. E., ed. 1987. *Self-Organizing Systems: The Emergence of Order*. New York: Plenum.

Zeeman, C. 1977. *Catastrophe Theory: Selected Papers 1972–1977*. Reading, MA: Addison-Wesley.

Zeleny, M., ed. 1980. *Autopoiesis, Dissipative Structures, and Spontaneous Social Orders*. Boulder, CO: Westview.

Index